WELTKULTUREN
MUSEUM

GREEN SKY, BLUE GRASS

Colour Coding Worlds

Edited by
Matthias Claudius Hofmann

KERBER CULTURE

CONTENT

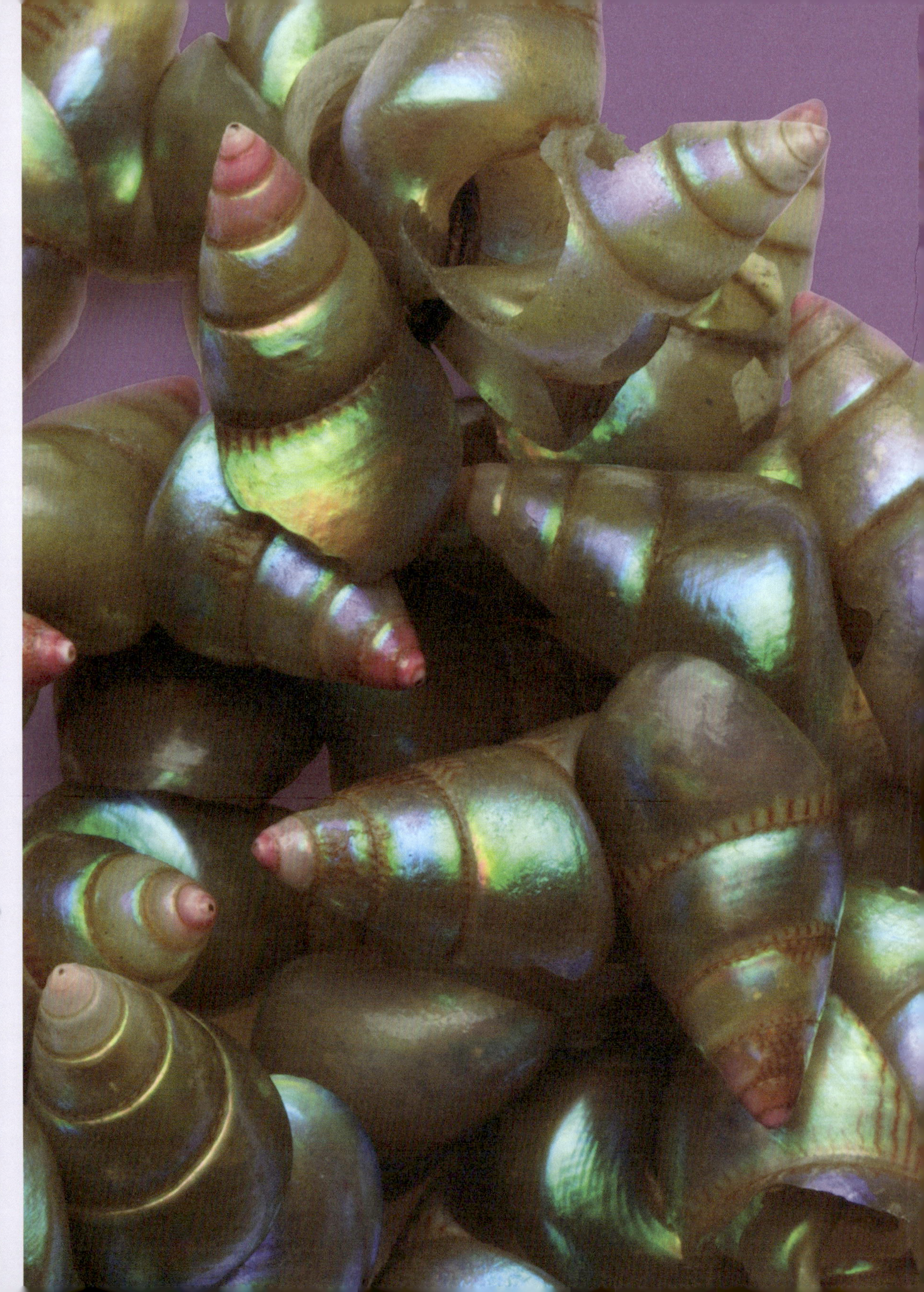

“The dark nature of colour …”

The small bracelet made from sea snails captivates with its iridescent sheen in the colours of the rainbow. Samoan Islands, Polynesia. Donation from the Gramlich family, 1933.

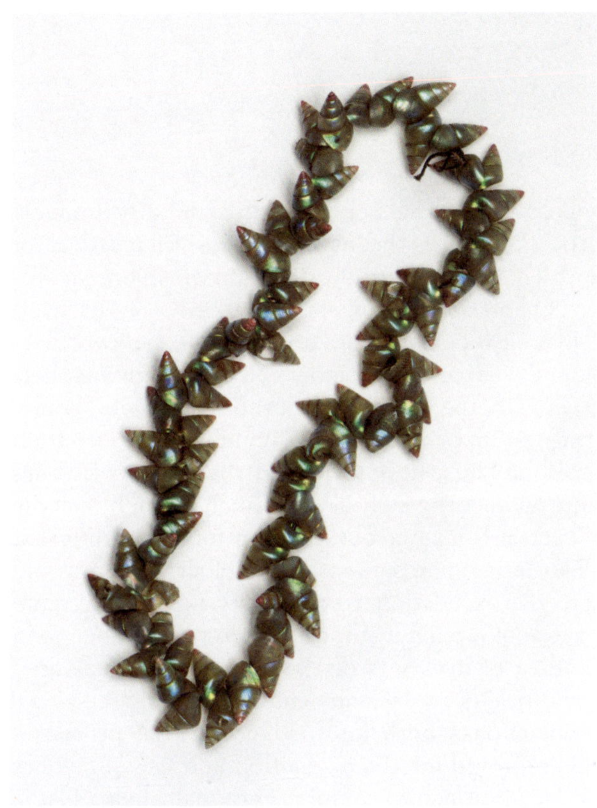

FOREWORD

The painter Philipp Otto Runge, an important representative of Early Romanticism, wrote to his eldest brother: "Colour is the last art that is still mystical for us, and must remain so, and which, in a wonderfully divinatory fashion, we only understand in the flowers" (to Johann Daniel Runge, 7. 11. 1802).

In order to explain the diversity of colours as a unified system of contrasts and transitions Runge developed a three-dimensional colour system in spherical form, which he discussed with Goethe, the author of the 'Theory of Colours'. In Runge's work studies on the system of colours went hand in hand with their Christian, mystical interpretation. Thus, he interpreted the primary colours yellow, red and blue as an expression of the Holy Trinity. Such a simultaneity of religious interpretation and research into colours can be found, in different cultural manifestations, in all societies. The perception of colours triggers emotions, and thus they are used to give expression to spirituality. In order to create ritual objects and sacred images coloured substances are required. The manufacture of colourants, the binding of dyestuffs or the processing of coloured materials has to be learned and practiced. In many cultures, there are special areas of knowledge, which encompass both knowledge of ritual processes and rules, as well as the skills required for the extraction and use of colours. However, in contrast, the holistic approach to colours is gradually being lost in Western industrial societies. Research into light, matter and colour is reserved for physics, the production of paints takes place in chemical factories and the professional use of colours is the province of the creative occupations. At the same time, in the age of the digital camera and smartphone, coloured pictures are being ceaselessly produced, without the necessity of acquiring special knowledge or skills. However, none of this means that colours appear any less mystical to us. During the course of the increasing secularization of society their religious interpretation only appears to have slipped into the background. However, through popular esoteric movements and healing methods, the symbolic meaning of colours and their effect on the human psyche have found their way back into our everyday lives.

The title originally chosen for this exhibition was 'Farbgewaltig' (English: powerfully colourful). This word evokes the idea of large, colour-intensive images and their sensuously overpowering effect. However, during the selection of the artefacts from the museum's own collections, it was the small things that gave occasion for amazement and reflection. Red shells, coloured glass beads or iridescent feathers were like tesserae, which, on their own, appeared unimposing, but put together, piece by piece, produced a multi-coloured whole. The special aura of many objects was generated by the colour of their material, although it was not the application of paint but the object itself that determined the colour. Consequently, in many cultures it is not the colours but the different materials that are crucial for the manufacture and design of ritual objects, tokens of dignity or status symbols. When developing the exhibition content we repeatedly encountered ways of viewing colour completely different to common, European-influenced approaches. Ultimately, in light of the project content, it appeared more accurate to point out in the title that the sky does not always have to be blue and grass does not always have to be green. The world of colours is too diverse and colourful to treat it in a comprehensive, encyclopaedic fashion in one exhibition and its accompanying publication. Instead, we set out to inspire reflection and lateral thinking through the use of examples.

I would like to thank the entire museum team for the realisation of the project, in particular Matthias Claudius Hofmann for the development of the theme and the conception of the exhibition and accompanying publication, as well as Vanessa von Gliszczynski and Oliver Hahn who made a decisive contribution to the content, curation and organisation of the exhibition and the editing of the publication. Special thanks goes to our co-curators, without whom it would not have been possible to realise certain content and exhibition units: The cooperation with Arno Holl was indispensable for us. He made a fundamental contribution to all issues, and in addition, with his knowledge of the cultures of the Amazon region, contributed valuable expert knowledge. Roger Erb took on the far from easy task of presenting the physics of colour to non-physicists in an understandable fashion. Tomi Bartole generously made the results of his field research amongst the Avim in Papua New Guinea available to us. The section of the exhibition under his curatorship establishes a connection to a group of painters who, without his contribution and mediation, we would not have been able to enter into dialog with. Finally, I would like to thank all the authors for their contributions, U9 visuelle Allianz for their design of the exhibition and publication, as well as Wolfgang Günzel, who faced a number of special challenges with the photographic work.

Eva Ch. Raabe, Director

ながめするみどりのそらもかき曇りつれづれまさる春雨ぞふる

Nagame suru / midori no sora mo / kakikumori / tsurezure masaru / harusame zo furu

Even the green sky

Which I behold in reverie

Becomes overcast with clouds

And adding to the weariness

A spring shower

Fujiwara no Shunzei (1114–1204)

木漏れ日の光を受けて落ち葉敷く小道の真中草青みたり

Komorebi no / hikari wo ukete / ochiba shiku / komichi no manaka / kusa ao-mitari

Breaking sunlight

Its rays catching

Fallen leaves

There, in the middle of the path

I behold the young blue grass

Emperor Emeritus Akihito (*1933, r.: 1989–2019)[1]

GREEN SKY, BLUE GRASS

Introduction

Matthias Claudius Hofmann

What is green? What is blue?

Within Japanese poetry the sky is sometimes described as green *(midori)*, grass in contrast as blue *(ao)*. A colour attribution which is very unusual and bewildering for speakers of European languages. Physically, colours are sense impressions mediated by the eye and the brain which are generated by the spectral components of white sunlight. In accordance with the wave character of light, the colours correspond to the different wavelengths. This distance between one wave peak and the next determines the colour impression that we perceive, and in the visible range extends from 700 to 400 nanometres, from deep red to blue-violet. Green belongs to the medium wave spectral colours, blue to the short wave. In this respect, the colour impressions which we call green and blue in English are, precisely speaking, medium wave and short wave light. The colour of objects is a result of their diverse, respective reflection properties, i.e. the scattering and absorption of light. Things appear to us, for example, as green or blue when they reflect the medium wave or short wave light (and swallow the other light waves).

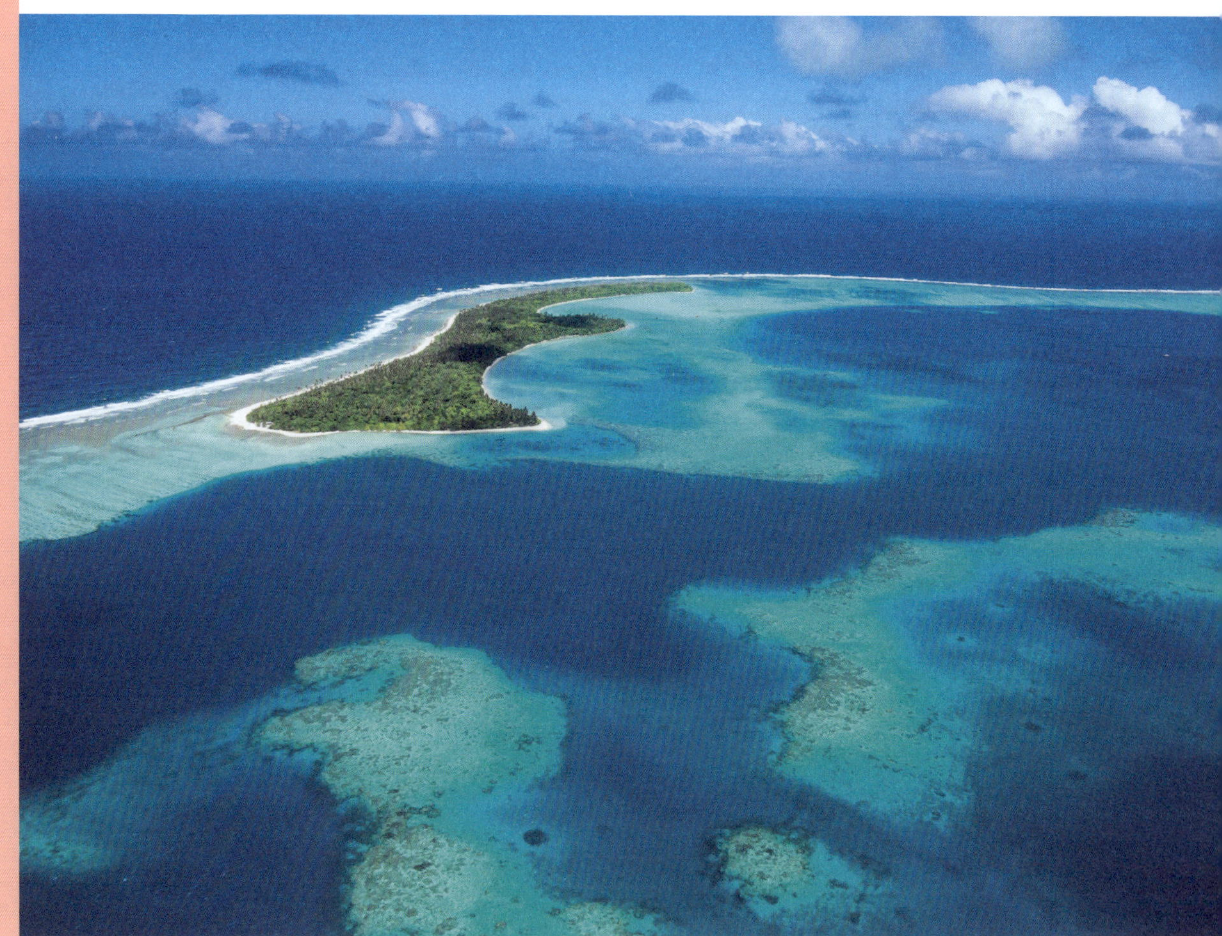

Fig. 1 The colours of the Pacific. Arial photographs of the Polynesian Wallis and Futuna Islands. Photo: picture alliance, Westend61, Michael Runkel, 2020.

The wavelength of light determines the colour impression which we receive from our world. However our world is far more than just light; and colour is far more than a purely scientific phenomenon. It has no influence on how we name these colour impressions, how many categories we divide them into (and to what end), i.e. systematize them, and what meaning we ascribe to these colours. These can all be very different, depending on the language and culture. For example in Russian there are the colour words *zeljonyj, goluboj* and *sinij* for green and blue. The latter two distinguish between light and dark blue, what we call colour shades in English, and are independent colour names just like the 'green' *zeljonyj.* In classical pre-colonial Nahuatl, the old Aztec language, the green-blue spectrum indicated by the umbrella term *xiuhuitl* was even divided into a total of thirteen shades.[2]

Thus colours are not always equivalent, and the meaning of the Japanese colour word *ao* is not identical with the English colour word blue, just as *midori* does not have the same meaning as green. For a long time Japanese – as was the case with many other languages and cultures – did not make a clear distinction between green and blue. Originally the colour word *ao,* which is now primarily used to denote blue, covered the entire green-blue spectrum and referred, amongst other things, to the young shoots of plants and fresh foliage. Similarly *midori,* which, however, was used in medieval Japanese literature to describe the colour of the deep sea and the sky (cf. Conlan 2005: 94–109 et passim). The ascription, which of the two colour words represented which colour impression, changed over the course of time. A clearer division between the terms *midori* and *ao* as green and blue probably first emerged under Western influence after the Meiji era at the beginning of the 20th century. Nevertheless, even today, some plants are still described as *ao* (in the sense of young and fresh) in modern Japanese language use (Conlan 2005: 415, 406). However, young Japanese people tend to use the English loan words *buruu* und *guriin* to describe the corresponding colour impressions. Today, 'green sky' and 'blue grass' are now only found in Japanese proverbs and poetry.

We are used to understanding colour as an abstract, immaterial, purely visual sense impression which we can assign to different things. However, colours are far from being insubstantial, and colour names are not just abstract descriptive terms. Instead, our colour words are derived from the things which provide us with these colour impressions. In the Polynesian languages the colour names for green and blue are directly related to observations and things from nature. The ethnologist Augustin Krämer summarised this for Samoan colour perception as follows: [...] "the long waved colours, are indeed always distinguished with certainty, but not to the same degree the short waved blue and green, which are frequently confused. And here I find it to be characteristically typical that the latter colours have no specific names as do the former but that their designations are formed only in relationship to the objects of blue or green shades, f.i. lanulau'ava 'kava leaf colour' [*lanu* = colour, *lau'ava* the leaf of the narcotic pepper kava, *Piper methysticum,* an important cultivated plant], or a fish, usiusi [the parrot fish *Pseudoscarus Forskali,* a popular edible fish], representing green, while lanumoana 'open sea colour' means blue [*moana* = ocean]. But it also happens frequently that green is stated for blue"[3] (Krämer 1995: 351).

In the colour vocabulary of the Polynesian inhabitants of the Island of Bellona in the Solomon Archipelago the green-blue spectrum is summarised under the colour word *'ungi* for black. The word *sinusinu* describes shiny black, blueish and green colour impressions – generally as poetic or ritual formulations (e.g. the backs of wales and dolphins, a freshly inked tattoo, a clear sky and a calm sea). In contrast the term *'usi'usi,* as used in Samoan to describe the greenish-blue parrot fish, is also used for the colour of leaves and the sky (Kuschel and Monberg 1974: 227f.). A direct translation of the Bellonese colour terms *sinusinu* and *'usi'usi* into colour words of the English language does not appear possible here, so that the sky on Bellona can just as easily be 'green' and the grass 'blue'.

Such metaphorical colour expressions can also be found in German. In their *Deutsches Wörterbuch* (German Dictionary) Jacob and Wilhelm Grimm traced the etymological roots of the adjective 'grün' (green), showing that it was initially applied to young plant growth in the sense of "sprouting", whereby it was quickly associated with the colour green. Thus green in its most general use was synonymous with the "colour of plants in sap". In contrast, 'blau' (blue) is derived from the Old High German for to bloom, shine and twinkle (DWB 1854–1961).

Fig. 2 The 'kava leaf colour'. The narcotic pepper kava *(Piper methysticum)* is an important cultivated plant in Polynesia and in Samoan a point of reference for green or pale blue. Photo: Gerda Kröber-Wolf, 1997.

However colours, i.e. colour words, do not just order the natural world that surrounds us. Colours also serve us in ordering our social world, highlighting hierarchies, differences in status and social affiliations and communicating them to the outside world in visible form. For example, in Japan at the beginning of the 7th century, according to imperial decree the colour of clothing had to reflect the social status of the wearer. An *ao* coloured, i.e. 'blue' robe, indicated that the wearer was a member of a privileged class of nobility. Finally, at the bottom end of the multilevel social hierarchy, one was forced to cloth oneself in *midori* green, and thus display one's low social status (Conlan 2005: 106).

Although, in terms of physiology, all people see the same, colours are not perceived the same everywhere. As shown by the examples for green and blue, the colour words used to indicate them are often ordered according to very different criteria in different languages and cultures. Furthermore, colours can be connected to a diversity of social and cosmological ideas. Colour and cultural concepts of colour help us to orientate ourselves in the world, to wrestle meaning from it and organize our lives together. Exploring the meanings of the various colour worlds involves seeing cultural connections in a new light, thus opening ourselves up to other world views.

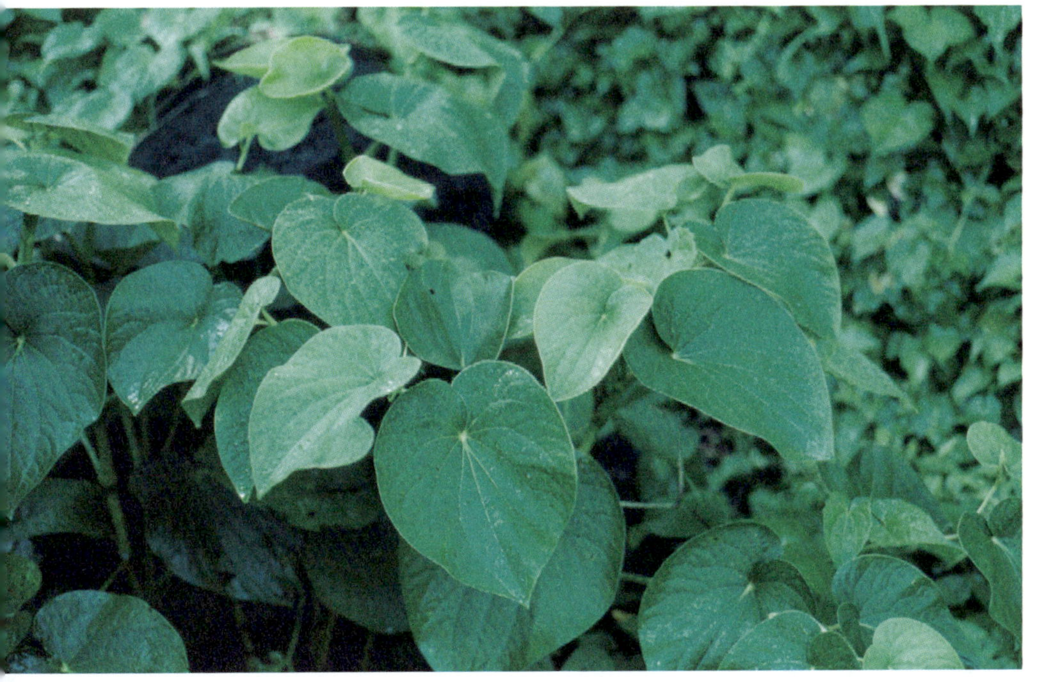

Light, matter, language

Even though this publication primarily addresses the cultural aspects of colour and colour perception, it is still important to examine their scientific foundations. Consequently, the book begins with the essay from the physicist Roger Erb. Colours are more than light, colour mixing and interference. However, they are the necessary preconditions for the cultural phenomenon of colour.

As already sketched, linguistic classification plays a central role in our engagement with colours. The study *Basic Color Terms. Their Universality and Evolution* from Brent Berlin and Paul Kay (1969) proved especially influential within linguistics and the social sciences, stimulating a multitude of ethnological research projects. The heart of their theory is formed by the 'basic color terms', which they define as abstract colour concepts which indicate the pure colour impressions which are not, or no longer, materially bound – in distinction to the Samoan colour word *usiusi,* which refers to the parrot fish.

Berlin and Kay interviewed speakers of different languages, presenting them with colour cards and recording the terms they used for them. The reference model employed for the survey was the Munsell Colour Order System, which was developed by the American painter and art teacher Albert Henry Munsell (1858–1918) between 1898 and 1905. Within this system he ordered the colours in a three-dimensional colour space according to precise coordinates based on hue, saturation and lightness. The Munsell scale[4] with its 329 colour cards employed by Berlin and Kay thus became a basic instrument of the cultural-scientific research into colour.

Extrapolating from the collected data, Berlin and Kay concluded that a language contains a maximum of eleven abstract colour terms which occur in a seven-stage series in predictable combinations. If a language has two basic color terms, then these are always black and white. In the case of three colour terms they are joined by red. These are followed by green and yellow and only at stage five are they followed by blue. Then comes brown, and at stage seven purple, pink, orange and grey. They assumed the universal validity of this model of stages of cultural evolution which enabled societies and their languages to be classified according to their number of basic color terms.[5]

However Berlin and Kay's approach falls short in many cases and fails to consider all colour classification systems. For example, decisive criteria employed in the colour classification system of the Philippine Hanunóo are lightness and darkness, as well as dampness and dryness (Conklin 1986). In contrast, the aforementioned inhabitants of Bellona divide their colour space into three colour areas. Things are red or not red, black or not black and white or not white. A large number of further colour words are subsumed under this. If one follows Berlin and Kay, then the Bellonese only have three basic color terms, although they possess an extremely sophisticated system of colour notation, with

Fig. 3 Green or blue? In Polynesia the parrot fish is a point of reference for the colour impressions of the green-blue spectrum. Photo: Philippe Bourjon.

Fig. 4 Munsell projection of the Bellonese colour term *'usi'usi* according to Kuschel and Monberg (1974: 35).

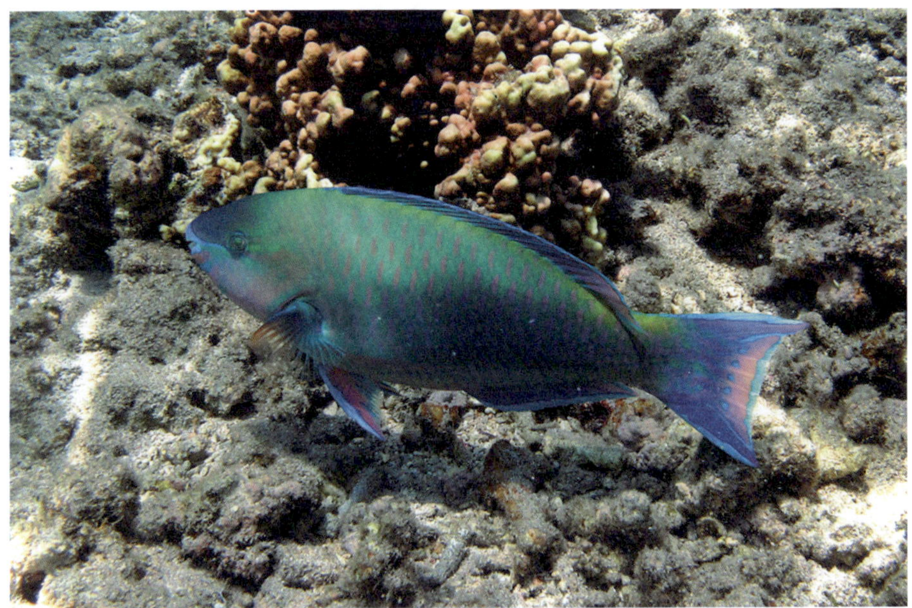

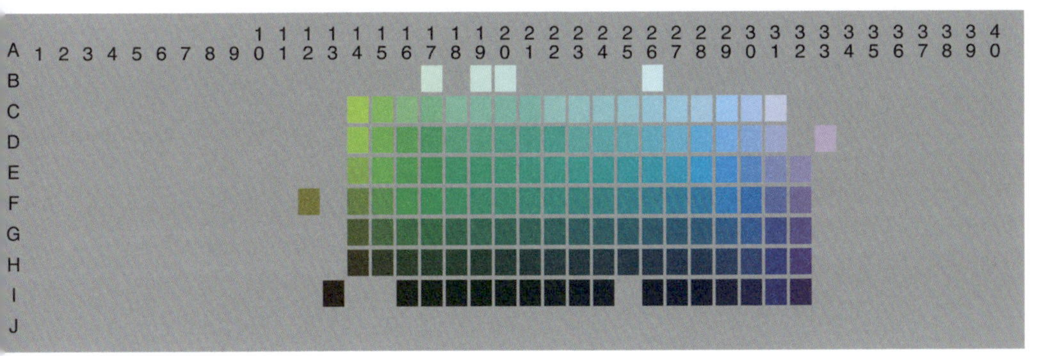

countless object and context-related colour words, which goes far beyond the Western system and is thus far more discriminating. Kuschel and Monberg also initially worked with the Munsell colour cards and the methodology of Berlin and Kay (fig. 4). However, in conclusion to their study they posed the justified question of whether this was sufficient to adequately capture a culture's colour system (Kuschel and Monberg 1972: 241). Whether a colour word indicates an abstract colour impression, and how many such basic colour terms a language displays, is potentially of only limited importance for our understanding of colour as a social phenomenon. Put plainly, this means that the speakers of a language no longer know the etymological derivation, i.e. the original meaning of a colour word. However, it is precisely the origin of a word and its material and symbolic associations that enable us to gain an insight into a society's cultural colour cosmos and its world of ideas.

Furthermore, the fact that with the Munsell scale Berlin and Kay declare a supposedly objective colour system to be the sole valid reference model for the recording of colour terms and determining what colour is – which the ethnologist Diana Young described as "the dominant means to control colour in the twentieth century" and the Munsell scale itself as a mere "cultural artefact" (2018: 3f.) – is also the subject of the essay from the philosopher Olaf L. Müller. On the basis of the colour dispute between Goethe and Newton, Müller exposes the cultural construction of the supposedly objective Western colour system, which is used to 'measure' the non-Western colour worlds.

In contrast, the linguist Eystein Dahl takes Berlin and Kay's theory as the starting point for his considerations on the origin and development of colour words in the Indo-Germanic languages. According to the author, these could form a fruitful point of departure for the study of the history of colour concepts, however, without raising any claims to their universal validity.

Materiality

The Munsell scale is not just an ethnocentric tool for exploring colour terms. It also masks the relationship between colour, the environment and materiality. For Diane Young, for example, it is precisely "the material stuff of colour" that is at the focus of her research interest, and states "that colour is a crucial but little analysed part of understanding how material things can constitute social relations" (Young 2013: 173). Ornaments from feathers or beads, dyestuffs and painted ceremonial accoutrements – the quality of coloured objects goes beyond their mere visual impression, is displayed in their different material characteristics and cultural connections. Thus in her essay Eva Ch. Raabe explains how the small red beads made from the Spondylus shell connect the people on the Trobriand Islands via a ceremonial system of exchange and how 'Trobriand red' has had a lasting influence on their cultural identity and world view. On the other hand, Gustaaf Verswijwer shows how some indigenous groups in the Amazon region deliberately manipulate the feather colours on living birds using the praxis of tapirage, employing the feather ornamentation thus produced, with its great cosmological and social meaning, to highlight their own group identity. The article from Arno Holl focuses on the Annatto bush *(Bixa orellana),* a plant whose seed capsules serve as a red dyestuff. He places this cultivated plant at the centre of a global network extending from indigenous body painting in the Amazon region with its social and ritual function as a protection from illness and evil spirits, to its industrial usage as a food dye, the colouring for red lipstick and its employment in medical research.

World views

Colour is more than light, more than a colour concept and more than its material properties. In his essay on colour symbolism in the Polynesian cosmogony, Matthias Claudius Hofmann shows the connection established between mythology, material culture and ritual praxis using the colours black, red and white as a cultural processing of elementary experiences.

However, colours don't always mean one and the same thing. They can place the cosmos in a context. However, sometimes they don't mean anything at all. As the Tibetologist Eric Huntington has shown using the example of colours in Buddhism, the meaning assigned to a colour is always context-specific and dependent on neighbouring sense functions and correlations. Thus the colours of the puppets in the Javanese shadow play indicate both their character traits as well as their emotional state, which can change from scene to scene along with the colour. At the same time the colours in the shadow play enable the characters to be situated within the Javanese cosmology, as Vanessa von Gliszczynski explains in her contribution.

Finally, using the example of the Abelam from New Guinea, Brigitta Hauser-Schäublin describes an indigenous colour system, whose praxis, as a central element of rituals, generates images which are connected to a world of experience beyond the everyday, and whose immanent logic can neither be explained nor understood using European colour theories.

Change

In general, colour concepts are not static. Instead they are continually subject to new influences which result in changes to both the colour palette and the dyestuff. Colours can reflect social change. However, new, unfamiliar colours and new colour materials can also initiate cultural change.

In a dialogue with René Fuerst, Chantal Courtois points out that, over a long period, glass beads were extremely popular in the Amazon region as trading goods and that they influenced both the material culture and the indigenous colour system thanks both to their material properties and their colour. In her contribution Frauke Gathof addresses the question of the 'authenticity' of African masks in the art trade. In the process the colour and the painting, i.e. their conscious removal, emerge as central criteria for what is considered a 'genuine' mask.

In conclusion, Tomi Bartole shows, using the example of the paintings from the village of Avim in Papua New Guinea, that despite decades of missionisation and cultural change, the aesthetic concepts and mythical motifs of the pre-Christian era have been preserved and find bold visual expression in the paintings of the Avim. Although acrylic paint and paper have replaced the natural colours and Sago plam sheaths, spirits and myths live on in the paintings.

Green sky, blue grass

This catalogue, in accompaniment to the exhibition of the same name, attempts to provide insights, suggestions and impulses on the theme of colour as a cultural phenomenon, and encourage us to look at our colour worlds with new eyes. The German writer Gotthold Ephraim Lessing (1729–1781), in a quote attributed to him, once lamented: "Ah, these eternally green trees, why can't they be blue for once". They can by all means. It is only a question of where. And sometimes the sky is even green.

1 We are especially grateful to Niels H. Bader for the research into the Japanese poems, as well as their translation from the Japanese original. The second text is a New Year's poem from the Japanese Emperor Emeritus Akhito (www.kunaicho.go.jp/e-culture/utakai.html). In 2010, it opened the ceremonial New Year's gathering at the Royal Court, during which poems of the Tennō are traditionally recited.

2 For the colour terms in Russian cf. Corbett and Morgan 1988; on Nahuatl cf. Ferrer 2000: 202–205.

3 A list of colour words in George Pratt's 'Grammar and Dictionary of the Samoan Language' (Pratt 1911: 102) confirms this assessment. The 'green' 'kava leaf colour' from Krämer is translated here as 'pale blue', the 'high sea colour' with 'sky blue'. In contrast, the colour word for dark blue, which we would tend to associate with the deep ocean, is given as *vaiuli* – 'black water'.

4 For a depiction of the colour scale according to Henry Munsell see p. 47, fig. 4 (top) in the article from Olaf L. Müller in this volume.

5 For a depiction of this model of stages from Brent Berlin and Paul Kay see p. 53, fig. 1 in the article from Eystein Dahl in this volume.

References:

— **Berlin, Brent and Paul Kay. 1969:** *Basic Color Terms. Their Universality and Evolution.* Berkeley: University of California.

— **Conklin, Harold C. 1986:** 'Hanunóo Color Categories'. In: *Journal of Anthropological Research* 42 (3). 441–446.

— **Conlan, Francis. 2005:** *Searching for the Semantic Boundaries of the Japanese Colour Term 'ao'.* Edith Cowan University, Western Australia: Ph. D. Thesis. https://ro.ecu.edu.au/theses/58 (01.09.2020)

— **Corbett, Greville and Gerry Morgan. 1988:** 'Colour Terms in Russian. Reflections of Typological Constraints in a Single Language'. In: *Journal of Linguistics* 24. 31–64.

— **DWB: Deutsches Wörterbuch by Jacob and Wilhelm Grimm. 1854–1961:** 'Erstbearbeitung. Digitalisierte Version im Digitalen Wörterbuch der deutschen Sprache'. https://www.dwds.de/d/wb-1dwb (09.11.2020). [Entry: Grün; Blau].

— **Ferrer, Eulalio Rodríguez. 2000:** 'El Color entre los Pueblos Nahuas'. In: *Estudios de cultura Náhuatl* 31. 203–219.

— **Krämer, Augustin. 1995:** *The Samoa Islands. An Outline of a Monograph with Particular Consideration of German Samoa, Vol. 2: Material Culture.* Translated by Theodore Verhaaren. Auckland: Polynesian Press.

— **Kuschel, Rolf and Torben Monberg. 1974:** 'We Don't Talk Much About Colour Here'. A Study of Colour Semantics on Bellona Island'. In: *Man* 9: 213–242.

— **Pratt, George. 1911:** *Grammar and Dictionary of the Samoan Language.* 4th edition. Apia, Western Samoa: Malua Printing Press.

— **Young, Diana. 2013:** 'The Colours of Things'. In: Tilley, Christ et al. (eds.): *Handbook of Material Culture.* London: Sage. 173–185.

— **Young, Diana. 2018:** 'Introduction'. In: Young, Diana (ed.): *Rematerializing Colour. From Concept to Substance.* Canon Pyon: Sean Kingston. 1–21.

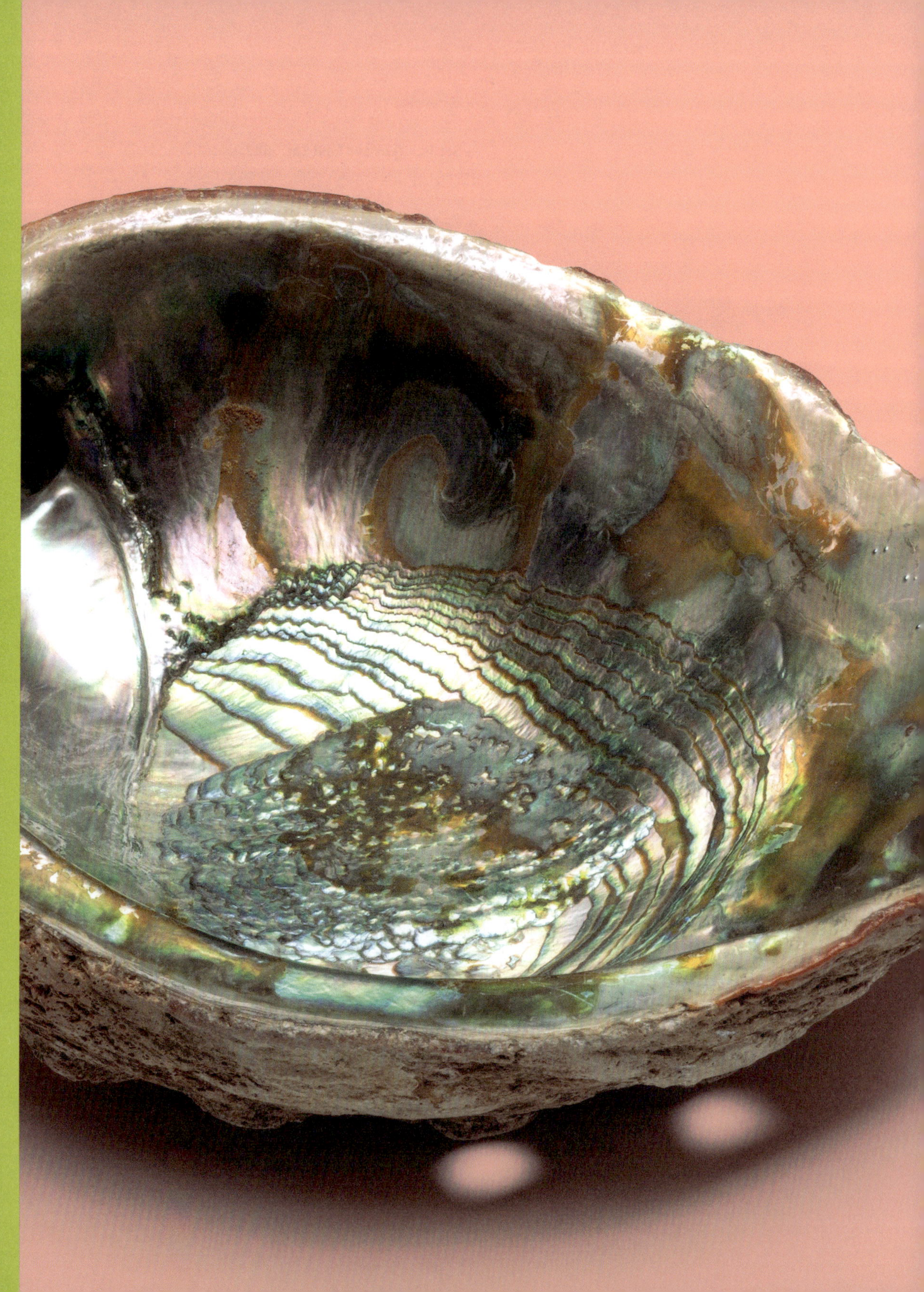

LIGHT, MATTER AND LANGUAGE

The interference seen in this shell is produced by the layering of microscopically small, transparent platelets on its interior. Part of the incidental white light is reflected and part of it passes through. Thus the shell's mother of pearl displays a multi-layered colour palette. Depending on the angle it is possible to see gold-yellow, greenish, silvery or violet nuances.

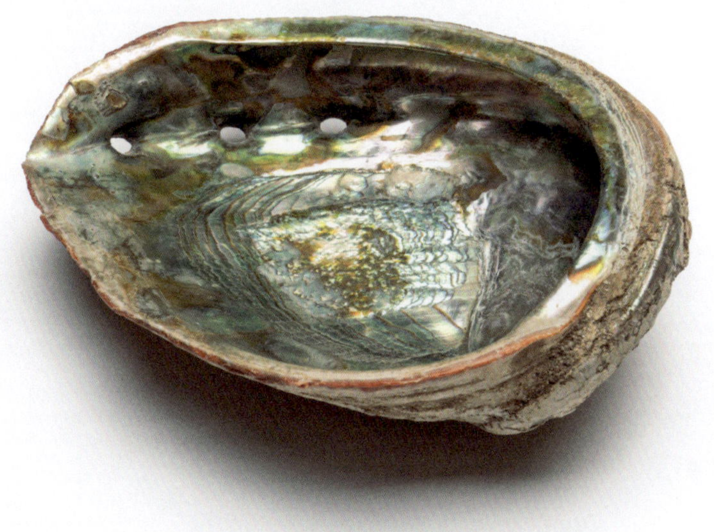

COLOUR AND COLOUR PERCEPTION

Roger Erb

Colour is everywhere

Colour has a very special significance for our experience of the world: We associate 'colourfulness' with the variety of our impressions, in contrast 'colourless' is synonymous with monotony. We associate the colour green with nature, we sense blue as calming, and red, in contrast, signals that our attention is required. The precondition for this is that all people perceive and interpret colour in a similar way – although cultural determinants do influence our perception, as this exhibition catalogue shows. This perceptual correspondence is not a natural given as the property 'colour' is not just supplied by the light or the coloured objects, but is assigned in the eye during perception. Naturally we are familiar with this on a daily basis when we speak of the colour of the light or an object.

In order to see one needs light and eyes

The world around us is filled with objects, and we can perceive them with our sense organs. We can see them with our eyes, but for this we need light. There are bodies which themselves emit light, such as the sun, the flame of a candle or a light bulb. However, the majority of objects are visible to us not because they are themselves luminous, but because they reflect the light. If light from a light source strikes the table in front of me, the sea in the distance or the moon in the night sky, then it is scattered – that means re-emitted without direction.

If the light scattered in this way enters the eye, the ocular lens forms an image of the object which is captured on the retina on the rear of the eyeball like a screen. The surface of the retina is covered with light-sensitive receptors which convert the pattern of light striking it into nerve impulses, which are finally processed by the brain.

There are two types of light-sensitive receptors on the retina: The rods register every part of the visible light; they also work in twilight, however they do not distinguish between the different colours of the incident light ('At night all cats are grey'). In contrast the cones – of which there are three types – can distinguish between the different colours of the light signal. However, they are only involved in the visual process at greater luminosity. On the one side, the activation of these different sensory cells is caused by the colour distribution, i.e. the spectral distribution of the light. This colour stimulus is a physical property of the light emitted by the light source or the light scattered by an object. On the other side, the spectral sensitivity of the cones themselves influences how we perceive colour. The three types of cones respond differently to the colour stimulus and pass on the sensation as a neural signal. This neural signal is the colour stimulus specification. As there are three types of cone, whose response can be expressed by a numerical value, a specific colour stimulus specification is described by three numerical values. Ultimately, colour perception results from the processing in the retina and the brain and is dependent on observation conditions as well as complex perception effects.

We perceive our surroundings as colourful both as a result of the light's colour stimulus as well as the processing in the cones, and only thus is it meaningful to speak of 'colour'. Consequently, the same colour stimulus in a differently constructed eye, for example in insects, but also amongst mammals, leads to a completely different perception. And conversely, our perception of the same colour impression can be caused by different colour stimuli.

The spectrum of light

Large parts of optics, the theory of light, function without recourse to a description of colour: Light propagates in a straight line, is reflected by mirrors and other smooth surfaces and randomly scattered by rough surfaces. If light encounters a transparent object it is refracted at the point of transition, i.e. is deflected slightly from its original direction of propagation. In its general formulation, refraction occurs at the boundary surface when light shines through (transmission) two transparent mediums, for example when light, passing through air, meets a water or glass surface. This deflection of the white light of the sun or a lamp generates the corresponding colour spectrum (fig. 1). This is especially distinct in the case of a triangular prism, a glass body with a triangular base.

Sir Isaac Newton (1642–1726), one of the most important scientists in the field of mathematics and physics, recorded that the white light of the sun (and that of the majority of artificial light sources) is composed of many coloured lights, i.e. can be broken down into them. In an experiment known as *experimentum crucis* he demonstrated that a glass prism generates the colour spectrum of white light, however the prism does not lend the light its chromaticity, it merely makes it visible.

This approach focuses on the path of the light through the prism. However, one can adopt an alternative approach, as did Johann Wolfgang von Goethe (1749–1832), taking the view through the prism as the starting point of one's considerations. If one looks through a prism at the crossbar of a window, or another area with a bold light-dark contrast, the image is shifted sideways. The dark area remains largely dark and the light area largely light – however at the edges between the light and dark areas coloured borders appear.[1]

In the natural world we experience the spectrum of sunlight in rainbows. It extends from violet and blue, through green and yellow, to red. It contains all the colours, with the exception of crimson (magenta). In contrast, what is not clear is how many colours with their own names can be distinguished within the spectrum, and where exactly the borders between these colours are. Light bulbs also deliver a very similar spectrum, while some other light sources only deliver a partial spectrum, even when they transmit white light, for example energy-saving lamps. However, there are also light sources which only emit light of one colour: The red light of a red light-emitting diode, for example, cannot be broken down any further by a prism.

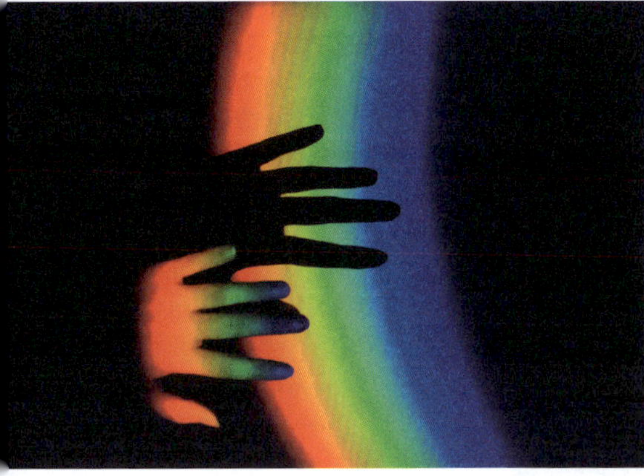

Fig. 1 White light can be broken down into its colour spectrum and captured on a screen.

Wave model

Colour (more precisely: colour stimulus) is connected to a physical property of light, namely its wavelength. It is not easy to formulate what light actually is. Consequently, different models are employed in order to describe optical phenomena. One of these models is the light ray, which is used to explain reflection and refraction. However, it cannot be used to explain the chromaticity of light. Here the wave model is of use, which conceives the propagation of light as analogous to the propagation of water waves – only that there is nothing material that is in motion here such as the surface of the water. In this model the light can also be allocated a wavelength, which in the case of the water wave is the distance between two wave crests. If one throws a stone into water the wavelength of the resulting wave is several centimetres long. The wavelength of the waves at the coast is typically a number of meters long. In contrast, light waves are very short: Their wavelength is in the range of a fraction of a micrometre, which is less than a thousandth of a millimetre. Here the wavelength is connected to the colour: blue light has a short wavelength, red light a long wavelength. All the colours of the spectrum lie between the ranges mentioned. Ultraviolet light has an even shorter wavelength, infrared a longer wavelength. We are unable to see either of them with our eyes, thus they are not part of the visible spectrum (for us). In contrast, bees perceive part of the ultraviolet light, while the camera of a smartphone is also sensitive to infrared light.

Additive colour mixing

The white light of the sun can be broken down into its spectral colours. If one re-combines the spectrum (which can be done with a converging lens), then the elements are mixed to form white light again. One can also project the light from two coloured lamps so they overlap, and again the eye is no longer able to see the original colours. Instead, a new sense impression is generated, a mixed colour. In fact, one can mix all the colours of the light spectrum using three suitable coloured lights, namely the primary colours red, blue and green (fig. 2).

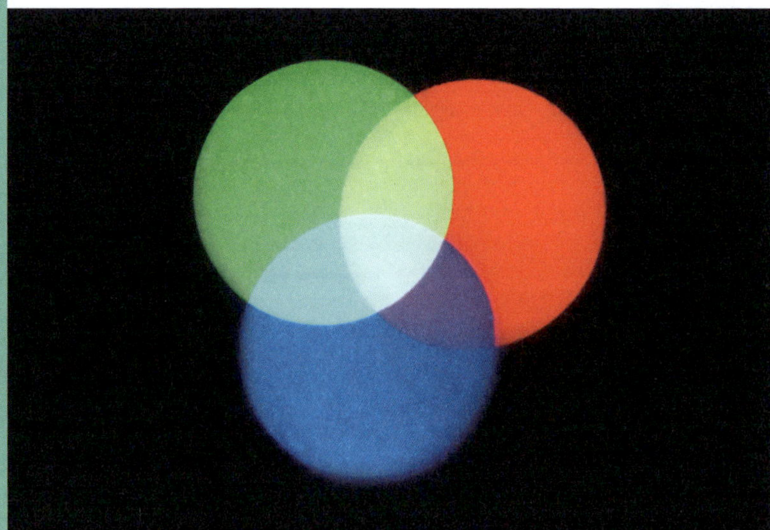

Fig. 2 All the colours of the spectrum can be mixed using the three coloured lights red, blue and green. Thus red and green, for example, produce the colour yellow.

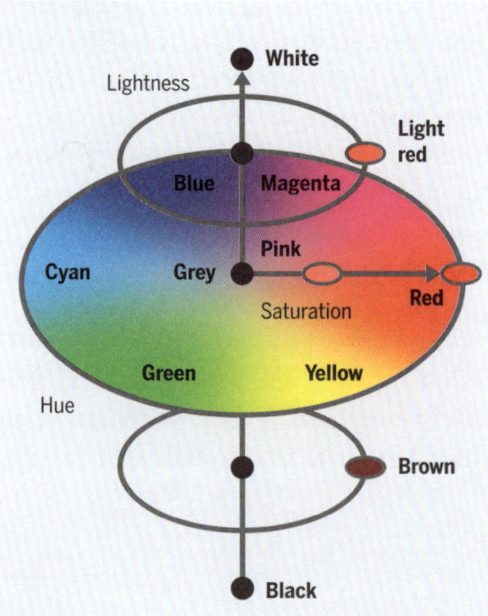

Fig. 3 The arrangement of colours in a three-dimensional space.

This mixing of light colours is called additive colour mixing: red and green produce yellow; blue and red produce magenta (light purple); green and blue produce cyan (turquois). Yellow and cyan are already contained in the spectrum of white light as colour components, but not magenta, which is a new addition in the form of a mixed colour (in contrast, violet refers, somewhat diffusely, to either the non-visible range of the shortest-waved blue, or a mixture of blue and red with a high proportion of blue). In particular, the mixture of the three primary colours produces white again, just as the mixture of all the components of sunlight does.

Other colours are produced when two or three primary colours with different luminosities are mixed: When, for example, the proportion of red in the lighting is greater than the green, then the mixed colour appears orange instead of yellow.

The primary and mixed colours can be depicted on a circle (fig. 3). All the colours of the spectrum, from red to blue, are arranged around its circumference. Between red and blue there is the additional colour magenta. Opposite colours are described as complementary colours (example: magenta and green are complementary colours). The position of the colour on the circle indicates the hue.

Colours positioned closer to the centre have a lower saturation. They possess a greater proportion of white. For example, unsaturated red is pink, which is generated when a blue and a green component is mixed with the red. Finally, the middle of the circle is occupied by achromatic white (or grey).[2]

In order to provide a complete description a third dimension, the lightness (or the lightness value) is required, thus the arrangement of colours becomes three dimensional. Decreasing lightness results in the veiled colours, and thus red becomes brown, while increasing lightness produces a light red. Both this light red and the brown have the same hue and the same saturation as red – in contrast to pink (different saturation) or for example magenta (different hue). The central axis displays the range of achromatic grey values from black to white.

In this colour model a colour is described by three coordinates: hue, saturation and lightness. This is no accident, instead it results from the fact that we perceive colours with three different types of cones, which also code the information using three values (red, green, blue).

The colours reproduced by a monitor are also mixed in a very similar fashion. This is composed of a very large number of light points (pixels), each of which is in one of the three primary colours. The points are so close to each other that they can no longer be perceived separately, thus generating the impression of the respective mixed colour.

Colour stimulation and the retina

Thomas Young (1773–1829) and Hermann von Helmholtz (1821–1894) developed the three-colour theory of colour perception from experience gained with additive colour mixing, concluding that there must be three different receptors with overlapping spectral sensitivity curves. The cones do not see exactly one spectrally distinct colour, instead they are each sensitive to a certain spectral range. These ranges each possess a maximum sensitivity. One of the cones responds to light in the short wave range (S, maximum sensitivity at violet blue), one in the long wave range (L, maximum at yellow) and one in the medium range (M, maximum at green). The sensitivity curves are quite broad so that in the case of the L cones red light can still be perceived.

However, this insight still does not explain why the mixture of red and green does not produce a greenish red, but yellow. Ewald Hering's (1834–1918) opponent colours theory can be used to explain this. All colour perceptions are traced back to the relative proportion of four primary colours: blue, yellow, green and red.

These four primary colours are arranged into two opposing pairs blue – yellow and green – red (in addition there is the opposing pair of the achromatic perceptions black – white). This explains why one doesn't perceive a yellowish blue or a greenish red, as here opposing impressions face one another, however one does perceive a reddish-yellow.

Both theories have their own significance. Thus the three-colour theory according to Young and Helmholtz describes the events on the retina, while the further processing can be understood in the manner explained by Hering. Today there are explanations that combine both approaches.

Chromaticity

A body that is not itself luminous, but is lit up instead, scatters the light. As already explained above, this means that it directs light to our eyes in an undirected fashion, not directed like a mirror. A white body scatters the light irrespective of its spectral composition. Colourless substances also appear white when they have scattering centres: Water is colourless and transparent as the majority of the light is transmitted (allowed to pass through). Snow and bath foam are composed of colourless water, however they appear opaque white as the light is scattered on the snow crystals and air-filled bubbles. If snow is illuminated with coloured light it takes on the colour of the light.

A grey body scatters a smaller proportion of the light compared to a white body. The portion of light that is not scattered is absorbed at the surface and heats the body. Accordingly, a perfectly black body must absorb all the incident light, however, in actual fact, bodies with the best realisation of a black surface still scatter a small part of the light.

A coloured body absorbs light dependent on the colour of the light (selective absorption). The explanation is to be found in the microscopic structure of the surface: The atoms or molecules absorb the light, re-emitting certain wavelengths and not others, which are absorbed instead. A red body, for example, is very good at scattering red light and absorbs the light of other wavelengths, especially that of the complementary colour or the other primary colours. As a result, a tomato appears red in red and white light, but dark to black in green light.

Subtractive colour mixing

A colour filter provides a graphic demonstration of how coloured bodies effect light. An ideal yellow filter only allows the transmission of yellow light, that is light within a narrow wavelength range. There are such narrowband colour filters, which reflect the light of all other wavelengths, and thus appear in the complementary colour. However, the majority of colour filters are simply coloured, transparent plastic or glass plates. Such a yellow filter only absorbs light of the complementary colour, blue. All other light, yellow, but also red and green light, is both transmitted and scattered. The filter is both yellow when looked at or through. In contrast, a simple cyan coloured filter absorbs red light, blue and green light is allowed through.

Both the simple yellow and the simple cyan filter allow green light to pass through – if one places the two filters in sequence, then only green light can pass through the two filters. As successive spectral components are removed from the original white light this is known as subtractive colour mixing. In contrast to additive colour mixing, where coloured lights are added, it is the transmitted and scattered components of light that are observed.

The mixing of paints is also carried out in this fashion. The greatest diversity of mixed colours, starting from just a few starting colours, is obtained by using the complementary colours of the primary colours, namely yellow, magenta and cyan: when mixed, yellow and magenta produce red, yellow and cyan produce green, magenta and cyan produce blue. That is why these colours are used in a colour printer.

In a simple filter the colouring component, atoms and molecules which absorb specific spectral components of the light, are evenly distributed throughout its volume. In a liquid dyestuff this colouring component is dissolved in a liquid, this is the case with e.g. chlorophyll. Leaves from plants contain this dyestuff. It absorbs red and blue light, which are then used for photosynthesis.

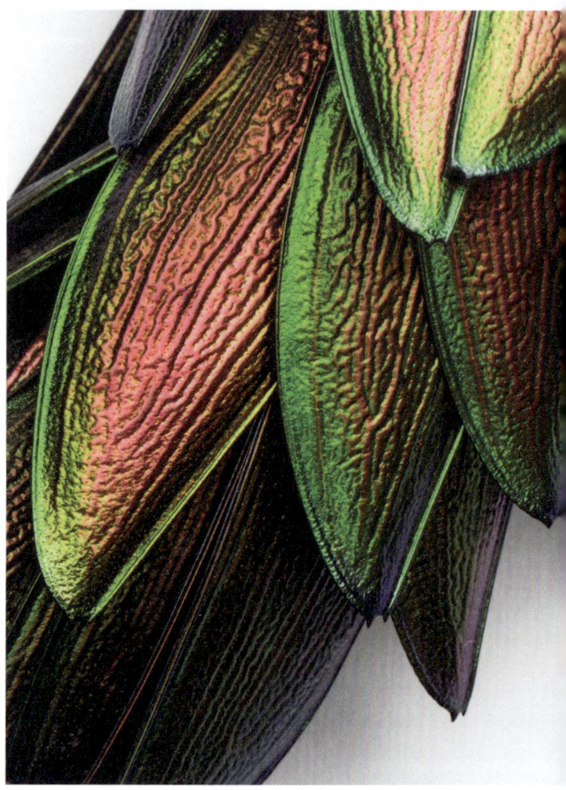

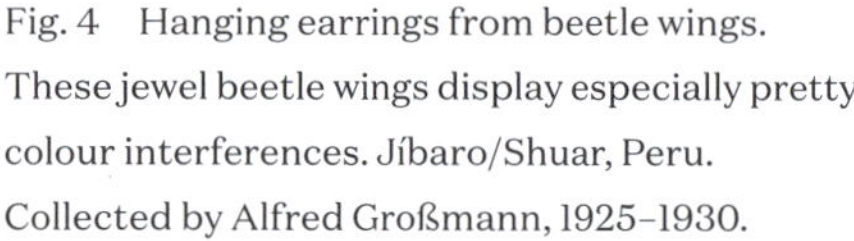

Fig. 4 Hanging earrings from beetle wings. These jewel beetle wings display especially pretty colour interferences. Jíbaro/Shuar, Peru. Collected by Alfred Großmann, 1925–1930.

In contrast, paints often contain insoluble colouring particles, pigments, in a colourless carrier substance. The light is scattered by the pigment particles, but also penetrates them, which overall results in selective absorption. Especially shiny paints are varnishes, whose smooth surfaces additionally reflect the light. In contrast, watercolours from the paint box reflect very little light. They are relatively transparent and allow the light to pass through to the paper, where it is scattered and passes through the paint once again. Watercolours operate in a fashion similar to colour filters.

The colour of hair is also produced by an embedded pigment, melanin. This can be yellowish or reddish, through to brown and black. With increasing age the ability of the hair cells to produce melanin diminishes. The light is then merely scattered by embedded (colourless) air bubbles and therefore appears increasingly grey or white.

Colours produced by interference

Soap solution is clear – in contrast soap bubbles are coloured! The reason for this chromaticity is not a dyestuff, but the multiple reflection of the light. In contrast to coloured substances, this colour phenomenon is not fixed. It changes with changes in the object, or in some cases with the viewing angle too. The soap film shimmers or is iridescent.

Transparent materials such as glass allow light to pass through, but also reflect it to a small degree: When it is twilight outside and the lights are on inside, one can now see one's reflection in the same pane of glass which one looked through during the day. If you look very closely you will actually be able to see two reflections of every light source in a single pane of glass. This is because part of the incident light is reflected on the front of the pane and part on the rear (in the case of multiple glazing there are additional reflections).

In the case of especially thin layers, i.e. a small distance between the front and rear sides, one observes a special phenomenon resulting from the superposition of the reflected white light, interference: Due to light's wave characteristics an amplification as well as a cancellation of the light of certain colours can occur when light travels along a variety of paths from the source to the viewing point. As the wavelength (and thus the colour) of the light plays a role here, the soap bubble displays different colours at different points, which is also dependent on the viewing angle.

Natural chromaticity produced by reflection and interference

The inside of the shells of many species of molluscs is composed of mother of pearl (see figure, p. 24). Mother of pearl has an iridescent sheen, which is also produced by interference. The material of the shell is calcium carbonate, composed of microscopically small, transparent platelets. These are aligned lengthwise across the surface to form a layer; numerous such layers are arranged one on top of the other. Part of the incidental white light passes through, and part of it is reflected by these layers. The light reflected by the numerous layers is superimposed for the viewer. This results in interference and thus colour phenomena similar to that observed with the soap film.

Many jewel beetles possess shiny, coloured, metallic wing covers (fig. 4). The sheen provides greater protection from the solar radiation. The different colours of these jewel beetles, depending on the viewing angle, is due to the layered structure of the wing covers composed of transparent material, which results in the light reflected by the different layers interfering with each other.

Natural chromaticity produced by scattering and interference

A CD or a DVD also displays the colour spectrum of the reflected white light. In this case this is not due to the reflection from a number of parallel layers but a regular surface structure. This is composed of microscopically small depressions whose sequence determines the coding of the music. The light is scattered by these depressions. Due to the regularity of the structure it is referred to as a reflection grating. As the depressions are arranged at regular intervals, the light scattered by the neighbouring depressions also has the same path length difference which results in interference. Thus at certain angles the light of certain wavelengths is amplified.

The feathers of some birds also have a coloured shimmer. We are most familiar with this effect from the neck feathers of the male mallard duck. They are actually black, however they contain a regular arrangement of melanin platelets which scatter the light resulting in interference. It is only due to this that the feathers appear green or blue (cf. plate 12).

Conclusion: With open eyes

Our world would be almost completely dark if our planet wasn't illuminated by the sun. Its white light is composed of a spectrum of coloured lights. From a physical perspective they differ from each other with respect to their wavelength. Objects absorb part of this light in their volume or at their surface, thus changing the spectrum of the transmitted and scattered light. However, the colour impression is first generated in the eye of the observer.

Plants and animals have adapted to the sunlight which reaches us at the surface of the earth. Plant leaves are green because the other part of the light spectrum is absorbed for photosynthesis. The eyes of humans and animals only perceive part of the total light emitted by the sun.

Due to the different needs of humans and animals the world appears to them in different colours. Evolution has made use of the possibilities of colour perception. For example, bees and the colour of flowers have passed through a co-evolution, developing together. The hover fly imitates the colour and brightness signals of the wasp with its yellow-black markings in order to imitate its defensive powers – which only functions because predators can see this colouring. The magnificence of the coloured plumage of some birds is only of use if potential female partners can see it and are impressed by it.

The shimmer of soap bubbles, the bright red of the tomato, shiny plumage – sometimes they serve a purpose, sometimes they are merely the result of a whim of nature. In each case our eyes open up to the beauty of our colourful world.[3] While the scientific basis for the perception of colours is everywhere the same, cultural interpretations are sometimes markedly different. This catalogue provides a series of insights into the diversity of colour, its meanings and perception. Keep your eyes open!

1 You can see a reconstruction of this experiment in the exhibition. You will find further information on Goethe and Newton in the article from Olaf L. Müller in this volume.

2 White, black and grey are described as achromatic as they do not privilege any colour but just different degrees of the brightness of white light, i.e. bodies illuminated with it.

3 If you want to continue exploring the fascinating world of light and colours, you can do this with the app 'Color Uncovered': https://www.exploratorium.edu/explore/apps/color-uncovered.

References:

- **Abendroth, William. 1898:** *Sir Isaac Newtons Optik.* Leipzig: Engelmann.
- **Falk, David S; Dieter R. Brill and David G. Stork. 1990:** *Ein Blick ins Licht.* Basel: Springer.
- **Goethe, Johann Wolfgang. 1810:** *Zur Farbenlehre. Entwurf einer Farbenlehre.* Tübingen: Cotta.
- **Welsch, Norbert and Claus Christian Liebmann. 2006:** *Farben. Natur, Technik, Kunst.* Munich: Elsevier.
- **Zawischa, Dietrich. O. J.:** *Vielstrahlinterferenz, Schiller- und Strukturfarben* https://www.itp.uni-hannover.de/fileadmin/arbeitsgruppen/zawischa/static_html/vielstrahl.html (18.09.2020).

LET A HUNDRED SPECTRA SHINE

A Note of Protest Against Eurocentrism in the Linguistics of Colour

Olaf L. Müller

Gladstone's astonishment

Former British prime minister William Gladstone (1809–1898) was a learned man. During a spell away from politics, he wrote three volumes on the Homeric age, posing a provocative question: could the ancient Greeks see colours the way we do?

Gladstone answered the question in the negative. His answer was not based on minor differences in colour perception, which are widespread (even in the absence of colour blindness). Rather, Gladstone claimed that the ancient Greeks were surprisingly insensitive in their perception of colours (Gladstone 1858: 457–499). Could Homer and his contemporaries, he suspected, not even recognise the glorious blue of their sky? Gladstone remarked that "Homer had before him the most perfect example of blue. Yet he never once described the sky. His sky is starry, or broad, or great, or iron, or copper; but it is never blue" (Gladstone 1858: 483). Assuming that these observations are correct, it is far from clear what follows from them. Does it mean that much if a great singer doesn't mention the everyday colour of the sky?

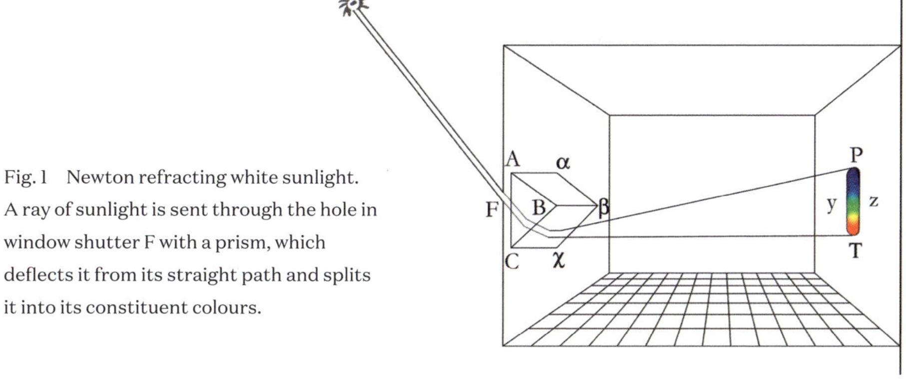

Fig. 1 Newton refracting white sunlight. A ray of sunlight is sent through the hole in window shutter F with a prism, which deflects it from its straight path and splits it into its constituent colours.

Gladstone came up with two further observations in favour of his provocative claim. Firstly, Homer used astonishingly little colour vocabulary in the *Iliad* and the *Odyssey,* and secondly, when he did use it, it was often inapposite. The first observation is irrelevant; few great works of poetry contain olfactory vocabulary, and yet nobody would assume that poets are insensitive in their perception of smells.

Gladstone's second observation is trickier; he complained about Homer's unsophisticated description of the rainbow. Instead of neatly reciting its seven colours, Homer merely described the rainbow as "dark". And – *horribile dictu* – on occasion the poet lumped together three of the seven colours, making no difference between light blue, indigo and violet. True enough, this isn't the most accurate description. But how many colours does the rainbow have? Is it seven? Anyone familiar with the history of colour research will recognise the Newtonian background of Gladstone's approach. Indeed, he criticised the fact that "Homer's perceptions of the prismatic colours [...], which depend on the decomposition of light by refraction [...], were, as a general rule, vague and indeterminate" (Gladstone 1858: 483). In other words: how unfortunate that Homer wasn't a Newtonian ...

A visit to Newton's darkroom

As is well known, Isaac Newton (1643–1727) sent a thin ray of sunlight through a prism into the darkness of his *camera obscura* and discovered that the light fanned out into the colours of the rainbow (fig. 1). This was published in 1672; within three decades, Newton's spectrum had become an icon of science (fig. 2, left). He deduced from this and further experiments that white sunlight is not homogenous; according to Newton, it consists of multicoloured rays of light that are refracted to a greater or lesser degree on their way through a prism (Newton 1672).

Strictly speaking – Newton claimed – there are infinitely many kinds of light of different colours; in his colour wheel (fig. 3, top left) he reduced this variety to the seven colours that Gladstone would later so sorely miss in Homer's work. Yet Newton viewed these seven colours as a pragmatic convention, nothing more; conventional differences do not imply differences in colour perception.

Moreover, Newton himself often only spoke of three spectral colours, conforming with the leading artists of the day, who had adopted a three-colour system (Shapiro 1994). Should Gladstone by the same logic hold that the colour perception of these artists was unsophisticated? And is it not often true that we see only three colours in a rainbow?

While Gladstone was writing his work on ancient history, he changed allegiance from the Tories to the Whigs. Amusingly, historians of science regard it as a blunder to practise what in the trade is known as 'Whig history': to relate the history of past achievements solely from the perspective of the winners and to dismiss any diverging theories. That is precisely what Gladstone did with his claim about the defective vision of Homer and his contemporaries: he criticised the Greeks for their non-Newtonian conception of colour. The critique is ill-founded, since there is more than one way of systemising colour.

Gladstone could well have known this, and he probably suspected it – for he had read Johann Wolfgang Goethe's *Theory of Colours* (Gladstone 1858: 489, 493). In these three volumes (Goethe 1808, 1810), Gladstone came across an idea which seemed to support his criticism of Homer. According to this idea, which Goethe (1749–1832) traced back to ancient times and embraced for himself, colours spring from the contrast between light and darkness (rather than resulting from the Newtonian elements of white light). With this in mind, Gladstone suggested that the Ancient Greeks did not apply their words for colour in the sense of Newton's multicoloured spectrum, but merely used them for referring to distinctions between light and dark. It speaks in Gladstone's favour that he noted an alternative to Newton's theory; it speaks against him that he did not consider the alternative thoroughly enough – as if a contrast between light and darkness could only result in a monochrome world of black, white and grey. But that is not what Goethe's theory states.

Fig. 2 Newton's und Goethe's spectra compared.
Left: Newton sent a ray of light in a dark setting through a prism and captured the known spectrum.
Right: Goethe exchanged the roles of light and darkness at the prism and captured a spectrum of the same size. Each colour in one spectrum corresponds to its complementary colour in the other.

Fig. 3 Colour wheels.
Top left: Goethe's six-part colour wheel.
Top right: Newton's colour wheel comprising seven colours.
Bottom left: Viennese colour wheel with colour gradations.
Bottom right: Viennese colour wheel with spectral colours of red/turquoise contrasts.

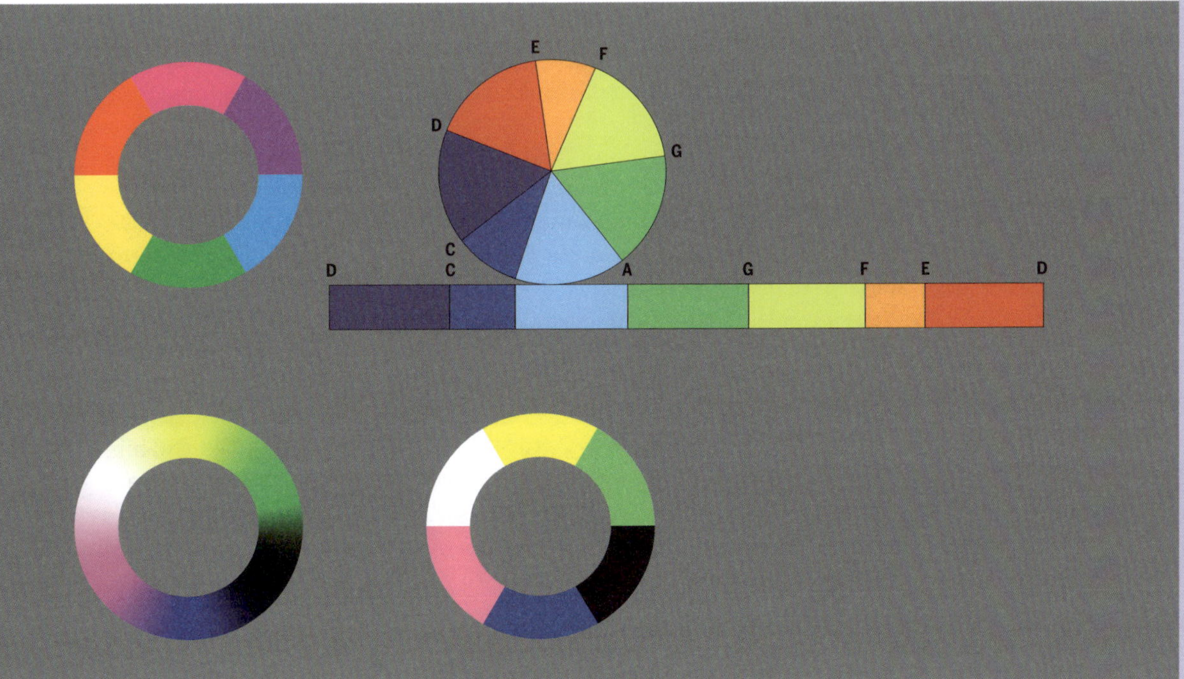

Colour theory in Weimar

As Goethe sought to show in his anti-Newtonian *Theory of Colour (Zur Farbenlehre),* colours are not contained in white light, but created by the interplay between light and darkness. In order to prove that these opposing poles are equally important factors for the emergence of colours, he varied Newton's experiments, systematically exchanging the roles of light and darkness. Whereas Newton sent a sharply defined ray of light through a prism in a dark setting (fig. 1), Goethe turned the tables and sent a sharply defined shadow through the very same prism – but in a bright setting (Goethe 1808: § 215, § 331).

If the shadow on the prism has the same diameter as Newton's aperture, and if all other dimensions of the experiment remain the same, the result is striking: the inverted set-up produces a new spectrum (fig. 2, right). This spectrum is just as colourful and beautiful as Newton's.

You may wonder whether all this is irrelevant, since neither Goethe's *Theory of Colour* nor his spectrum have become established in the science of colour. But why should that matter? If you avoid a historiography of winners – such as a Gladstonian 'Whig history' – you have to admit that both spectra are equivalent. Clearly, there is no justification for using only a Newtonian categorisation in order to gauge the perceptions and sayings of other countries and eras. Why not choose the colours of Goethe's spectrum, and then accuse Newton of e.g. overlooking the glorious crimson shade which Goethe called *Purpur* and which shines in the very centre of his spectrum (fig. 2, right)? Was Newton unable to perceive it? Preposterous idea! So there must be some fault in Gladstone's logic.

In judging the colour habits of distant times and peoples it is important to bear in mind the many ways in which colours can be, and in fact are, conceptualised, systemised and combined. Could we perhaps learn something from these distant times and peoples?

Let me note that Goethe didn't hold that his spectrum should be the sole basis for colour theory – which would merely repeat what he considered the worst mistake of Newtonianism. It wouldn't mean progress to posit shadows rather than light as the main and only factor in optics; according to Goethe, both options are equally one-sided (Müller 2016).

What was Goethe's aim, then? As indicated above, he sought to uphold the opposition of light and darkness, thus conforming to ancient ideas about colour (Goethe 1808: § 696–§ 703; Müller 2017). According to these, yellow (as a bright colour) would be one of the two primary colours, with blue (as a shadowy colour) being the other. Mixing these two primary colours would create green. Enhancing them, or intensifying them, or deepening or purifying them, would produce orange and violet, respectively[1]. And mixing these two colours, in turn, would lead to Goethe's *Purpur,* shown at the top of his colour wheel (fig. 3, top left).

I will refrain from comparing Goethe's system with Newton's, as it is but one of many conceivable alternatives. Instead, let us return to Ancient Greece. Gladstone accused Homer of describing the rainbow and its mythical representative Iris with only two colour terms (instead of seven): a single term for blue and one for saffron or gold. He called it "a most inadequate treatment of the colours of the rainbow" (Gladstone 1858: 485).

If he had taken the ancient idea of a yellow/blue extension of the basic light/dark contrast seriously, he might have arrived at a different verdict. It would have become clear to him that it is permissible to highlight a greater or fewer number of colours of the rainbow as a way of representing the rest. Newton sometimes highlighted seven, at other times three or five, while Homer, just like Goethe, mentioned two – even though he was well aware, according to Gladstone, that Iris is a multi-coloured messenger of the gods. To sum up, conventional simplifications are one thing; perceptions are another.

Field linguistics with 320 colour samples

When investigating alien customs, eras and peoples it is easy to presuppose too much that is common practice at home. This seems to have been Gladstone's mistake. Of course, an investigation completely free of preconceptions is illusory. Nonetheless, researchers can and should make every effort to bear in mind the pre-existing filters of their culture.

I would like to illustrate this by considering an influential linguistic research tradition that emerged half a century ago from North America. It started with a groundbreaking study by American anthropologist Brent Berlin (born in 1936) and his linguist colleague Paul Kay (born in 1934). Berlin and Kay argued that the linguistic classification of colours was by no means based on arbitrary conventions, as was widely held at the time. Rather – as they sought to show – the same "basic color terms" crop up in every language (Berlin and Kay 1969).

According to Berlin and Kay, every language has up to eleven basic words for colours, which represent surprisingly similar areas of colour across all cultures. Interestingly, these colours are arranged in a hierarchy: the two 'colours' black and white have their own word in every language; red has a specific word in almost every language; if a language has at least five different colour terms, there are always terms for black, white, red, yellow and green; only languages with six or more colour terms have their own word for blue; the next colour in this hierarchy is brown, etc.

These claims started a vast research programme. Its details would go beyond the scope of this essay; criticism of the fascinating results is not what matters here. But we do have to take a critical look at the methods. Both in the initial study and in those that followed, the subjects were linguistically evaluated using the same chart of colour samples (fig. 4, top); this comprised a total of 320 colour chips taken from and categorised according to the criteria of the Munsell system, which happens to be widespread in America. Now, this is indeed one of our most comprehensive colour systems, but take note: it is one of *our* colour systems, moulded by the European tradition of Newtonianism.

This should make us wary. Why were subjects from other cultures confronted with these 320 colours sorted in a Newtonian manner?[2] Why was the possibility ignored that different criteria elsewhere exist for sorting colours? Or perhaps none at all? (Gladstone sends his regards; as mentioned above, he believed that his ancient sources were lacking a system).

And why weren't other colours chosen? The first, and smallest, version of Munsell's system comprised ten times as many colour samples. Which of these colours are important enough to feature in linguistic field research? What if 320 different Munsell colours (such as in fig. 4, bottom) had been employed? My selection is based on Goethe's spectrum (fig. 2, right) – just as Berlin and Kay were guided by Newton's spectrum (fig. 2, left). I am by no means saying that the results of the field research would have been different if the ethnologists had been sent out with different colour samples, whether pre-sorted in a Western manner or not. But it makes me uneasy that little heed seems to have been paid to such alternatives.

Let a hundred flowers bloom and a hundred spectra shine

With Goethe's assistance, I have introduced a single alternative to the North American field linguists' colour tableau. So have I simply replaced an Anglophone paradigm with a German one – one from Weimar? And are we not all sitting in the same Western boat?

That may well be; but it doesn't mean that we ought to leave everything as it is. Instead we should try harder to imagine what is possible. Here we can learn a lot from the arts. The Viennese artist and colour researcher Ingo Nussbaumer (born in 1956) kept an eye open for alternatives to the traditional spectra – and struck gold (Nussbaumer 2008: 132, 160, 200–204 et passim; Müller 2020).

Recall that conventional spectra (fig. 2) result from a narrow white ray in dark surroundings à la Newton (fig. 5, column 0 bottom) – or a narrow black ray in a bright setting à la Goethe (fig. 5, column 1 bottom). Instead, Nussbaumer uses geometrically identical but colourful contrasts; he prismatises, say, a green ray in a crimson setting (fig. 5, column 2 bottom), or a crimson ray in a green setting (fig. 5, column 3 bottom).

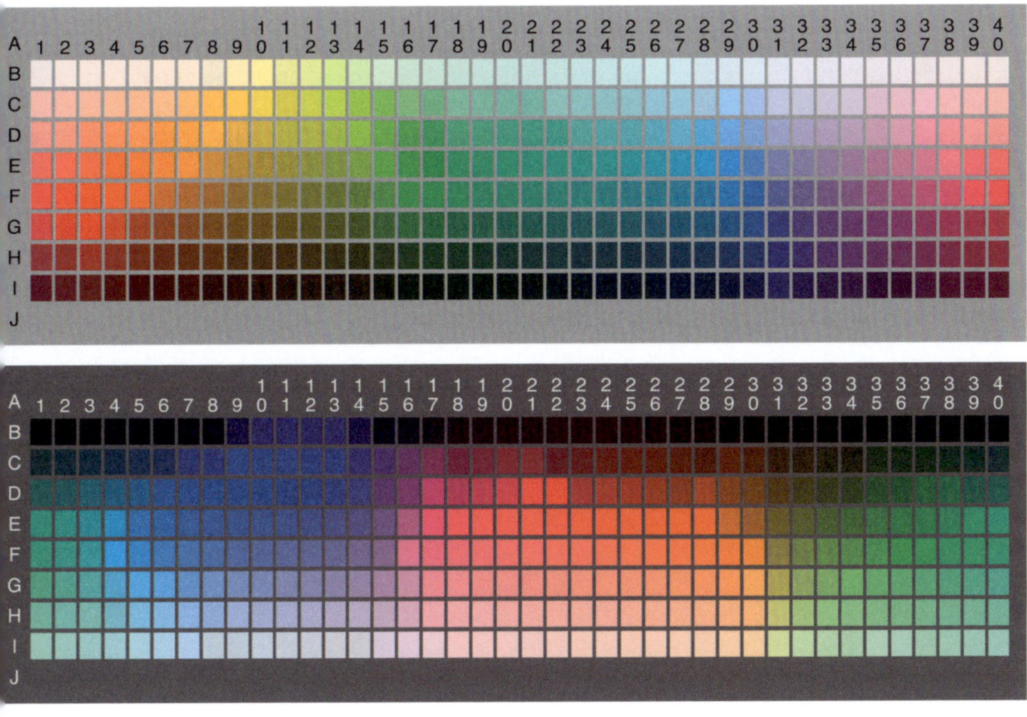

Fig. 4 Colour tableaux for field linguists.
Top: The colours which have been used for decades of linguistic field research.
Bottom: What would have happened if the Anglophone research on basic colour terms in the world's languages had been conducted with this selection, which I created by inverting the original tableau?

The breathtaking results of these experiments are depicted in the upper sections of fig. 5. In each of the eight cases a specific spectrum emerges: in every single case it is just as beautiful and colourful as Newton's spectrum (column 0), but each spectrum features a different sequence of colours. In the new spectra, the unusual roles of black and white are conspicuous (columns 2–7); black and white can feature as spectral colours, too, which is not the way it is supposed to be in the Newtonian tradition. With a green ray in crimson surroundings (column 2 bottom), the colours red, yellow, white, turquoise, blue stand out from the background (top). The thin yellow zone is hard to detect in the photo, but if you come across the experiment yourself one day, its yellow will make an impression, I promise.

Now consider the colour wheel that is formed on the basis of one of the new spectra (fig. 3, bottom right). Prejudice against black and white aside – isn't it just as harmonious as the traditional wheel that we know and love? Or are you concerned that its colours cannot be arranged into a continuum, in contrast to the Newtonian model? Then take a closer look; of course the new wheel can be depicted as a continuous sequence (fig. 3, bottom left).

With Goethe's spectrum, and even more so with Nussbaumer's spectra, we have left behind the solid ground of established Western science; for ethnological purposes this is but a minor liberation: even the unorthodox experiments were conducted by Europeans in a Western manner. So let us broaden our horizons. If we want to see the colourful world with fresh eyes, we have to learn as much as we can about the colours of the most distant cultures – without first squeezing them into our own colour schemes. This exhibition takes a good step in the right direction, but we ought to go further. Where are the field linguists from other cultures? Wouldn't it be the time to invite them?[3]

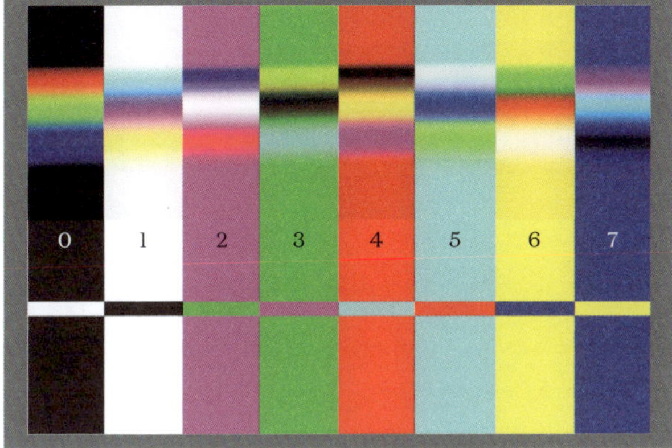

Fig. 5 Eight spectra with their contrast outputs. Sending or observing one of the eight contrasts (bottom) through a prism generates the spectrum depicted above it (top): on the left are Newton's and Goethe's spectra (columns 0 and 1), next to their six siblings, detected and photographed by Ingo Nussbaumer.

References:

— **Berlin, Brent and Paul Kay. 1969:** *Basic Color Terms: Their Universality and Evolution.* Berkeley: University of California Press.

— **Gladstone, William Evert. 1858:** *Studies on Homer and the Homeric Age.* Volume III. Oxford: Oxford University Press.

— **Goethe, Johann Wolfgang. 1808:** *Zur Farbenlehre: Entwurf einer Farbenlehre.* Tübingen: Cotta.

— **Goethe, Johann Wolfgang. 1810:** *Zur Farbenlehre: Enthüllung der Theorie Newtons. Materialien zur Geschichte der Farbenlehre.* Tübingen: Cotta.

— **Müller, Olaf. 2016:** 'Prismatic Equivalence – A New Case of Underdetermination. Goethe vs. Newton on the Prism Experiments'. In: *British Journal for the History of Philosophy 24.* 322–346.

— **Müller, Olaf. 2017:** 'Goethe contra Newton on colours, light, and the philosophy of science'. In: Silva, Marcos (ed.): *How Colours Matter to Philosophy.* Cham: Springer. 73–95.f

— **Müller, Olaf. 2020:** 'A Brief History of Polarity in Physics'. In: Lindemann, Wilhelm and Theo Smeets (eds.): *Thinking Jewellery 11 Two.* Stuttgart: Arnoldsche Art Publishers. 9–39.

— **Newton, Isaac. 1672:** 'A letter of Mr. Isaac Newton, professor of the mathematics in the university of Cambridge; containing his new theory about light and colors'. In: *Philosophical Transactions 6 (80).* 3075–3087.

— **Nussbaumer, Ingo. 2008:** *Zur Farbenlehre. Entdeckung der unordentlichen Spektren.* Vienna: Edition Splitter.

— **Shapiro, Alan. 1994:** 'Artists' colors and Newton's colors'. In: *Isis* 85 (4). 600–630.

1 English lacks a term conveying the exact meaning of Goethe's expression "steigern", which lies somewhere in between the four verbs given above.

2 To be more accurate, the Newtonian ordering of the Munsell colours was presented to the subjects in only one of their two tasks.

3 I tested the arguments of this essay in an online seminar *Farbe und Objektivität* (Colour and Objectivity), held at the virtual Humboldt University in the summer semester of 2020. I would like to thank the participants of the seminar as well as Kerstin Behnke, Laura Goronzy, Terry Regier and Bernhard Kraker v. Schwarzenfeld for valuable comments. Many thanks to Nicola Morris and Emanuel Viebahn for the English translation.

WHITE STARS AND GOLDEN SUN

The Creation and Development of Colour Terms in the Indo-European Cultural Sphere

Eystein Dahl

People in modern western culture have a wealth of colour terms at their disposal, enabling them to differentiate between the colours in their lifeworld in great detail. It would thus be easy to conclude that this is the natural state of affairs, as it were, and that people all around the world and in all epochs have expressed their perceptions of colour under more or less similar linguistic conditions. The groundbreaking work conducted fifty years ago by Berlin and Kay (1969) established that this was not, in fact, the case, identifying seven systems of colour terms which could be interpreted to a certain extent as different chronological stages of development. Fig. 1 is a graphic representation of these systems and how they relate to each other chronologically.

At this point, it is important to emphasise that words meaning 'white' and 'black', which are situated at the first stage, probably encompass a far broader palette of colour perception than their equivalents in modern English, for example, due to the absence of other colour terms. For this reason it is possibly more appropriate to consider the two terms at Stage I as being 'light/warm' and 'dark/cold', although in each case their meanings become more precise or more limited in proportion to the gradually increasing complexity of the system of contrastive colour terms. This model creates a strong diachronic hypothesis with clearly defined diachronic stages of development, which appear in the order depicted. However, this leads us to ask whether the hypothesis can really claim universal validity – a problem to which we will return later in this essay.

Red, black, white

Data from the Indo-European languages indicate that some colour terms are diachronically extremely stable – in the sense that they are attested in many language branches – while others tend to be replaced over the course of time. One example of the former case is the widespread word ‘red’, which appears in Proto-Germanic as **rauda-*[1] (cf. Gothic *rauþs,* Old Norse *rauđr,* Old High German *rōt* etc.), in Greek as *eryth-rós,* in Old Indic as *róh-ita-,* in Old Irish as *rūad,* in Lithuanian as *raũdas,* in Russian as *rúdyj* and in Latin seemingly somewhat anomalously as *ruber* or *rufus* (but compare this with the extremely rare term *russus* < **rud-s-,* which is the root of Italian ‘rosso’), bearing evidence of an Indo-European root **$h_1$rud^h*.[2] Interestingly, by comparison the ostensibly archaic terms for ‘black’ and ‘white’ are less stable. According to Mallory and Adams (2006: 331–334), two potential Proto-Indo-European words for ‘black’ and five for ‘white’ can be identified. On the one hand, in Indic, Iranian, Baltic and Slavic we find a word **k^wr̥snós* ‘black’ (Old Prussian *kirsnan,* Old Church Slavonic *črŭnŭ,* Old Indic *kr̥sná-*), although the corresponding term in Lithuanian, *kéršas,* which Mallory and Adams (2006: 332) interpret as referring to a shiny black colour, actually means ‘black and white, piebald’. On the other hand, there are several branches which exhibit reflexes of the root term **mel-n-,* such as the Latvian *melns* and the Greek *mélās,* which both mean ‘black’. However, this root has

Stage I	II	III	IV	V	VI	VII
[white / black]	→ [red]	↗ [green] → [yellow] ↘ ↘ [yellow] → [green] ↗		[blue] →	[brown] →	[purple / pink / orange / gray]

Fig. 1 The developmental stages of colour terms according to Brent Berlin und Paul Kay’s *Basic Color Terms* (1969).

different meanings in other languages, such as the Latin *mulleus* 'reddish', the Lithuanian *mélynas* 'blue', and the Old Indic *maliná* 'dirty, grey, black'. Moreover, there might also be the Lithuanian word *mul̃vas* 'yellow, red, dyed with clay' and the Welsh *melyn* 'yellow'.[3] The diverse potential meanings for the latter word can be interpreted in various ways. One option would be that the word originally described the colour black, perhaps even a matt black (cf. Mallory and Adams 2006: 331), and that the other meanings are secondary. One direct advantage of this assumption is that it allows us to reconstruct a proto-linguistic lexical distinction between shiny and matt black, of the kind that we know exists in several Indo-European languages. On the other hand, it might be assumed that the meaning of 'dirty' attested in Old Indic is primary, and that words such as 'black', 'grey', 'clay coloured', 'yellow' etc. could easily have derived from this.[4] Although it is ultimately difficult to determine which of these two possibilities is the more likely, both examples mentioned above illustrate that words meaning 'black' are diachronically unstable.

With regard to colour terms that mean 'white', the following analogue features can be observed. In this semantic field, the Indo-European root *h_2*erĝ*- 'white' is the most widespread, with reflexes in Hittite (*harkis* 'white'), Old Indic (*árjuna*- 'white, pale'),[5] Tocharian[6] (B *ārkwi* 'white') and Greek (*argḗs* 'white'), as well as with the meaning 'silvery, silver', which is found, for example, in the Old Irish *argat,* Latin *argentum,* Armenian *arcatʻ,* Avestan *ərəzatəm,* Greek *árguros* and Tocharian (B) *ñkante.*[7] Although both documented meanings are attested in three Indo-European linguistic families (Indo-Iranian, Greek, Tocharian), it is doubtful whether silver being labelled 'white (metal)' is of Indo-European origin. It is probably, as with similar labels for bronze and copper as 'red metal' and for gold as 'yellow metal' a secondary development in an individual language (cf. Mallory and Adams 2006: 241–242). Other roots which are attested as meaning 'white' in several individual languages are *h_2elb^h, **k̂woit/*k̂wit* and *b^h*elH.* The root *h_2elb^h- appears as a colour term in Latin (*albus* 'white') in Greek (*alp*^{h}*ós* 'pale white leprosy'), in Hittite as *alpā*- ('cloud'), and in Germanic and Slavic meaning 'swan' (cf. Old High German *albiz* and Old Church Slavonic *lebedĭ).* The root **k̂woit/*k̂wit* is attested in Baltic, Slavic and Indo-Iranian; we can, for instance, compare the Lithuanian *švitrùs* 'white', the Old Church Slavonic *světŭ* 'light', Avestan *spaēta*- 'white', and Old Indic *śvetá*- 'white, pale'. Moreover, the root *b^h*elH*- in Celtic (Welsh *bal* 'white'), Baltic (Lithuanian *bãlas* 'white', *bálti* 'becoming white'), Slavic (Old Church Slavonic *bělŭ* 'white') and Greek (*p*^{h}*alós* 'white') is documented as a colour term, while in Latin the root appears as *flāvus* 'blond' and in Old Indic as *b*^{h}*ālam* 'shimmer, brow'. As can be seen from the data above, reconstructing the Indo-European colour terms for 'black' and 'white' is complicated by the fact that the comparative evidence is somewhat inconsistent. Shields (1979) was of the opinion that the original words for 'black' and 'white' had been lost because, under his analysis, the basic vocabulary of a language tends to be replaced by new words over time. In a later work (Shields 1996), he pointed out that this line of argument cannot account for just these two specific colour terms having been replaced, while others remain diachronically stable. He posited a more imaginative hypothesis, namely that rather than the original colour terms becoming lost they had been reinterpreted as the names of deities. Assuming that the original terms described the concepts of 'light/warm' and 'dark/cold', they were probably frequently used to describe the two aspects of the sky: the light daytime sky and the dark sky at night. Thus, along the lines of Shields (1996), we can presume that the original word for 'light/warm' is cognate with the word **dyew-* 'day, sky(god)', which has developed via the meaning of 'the light-white sky'.[8]

Gold, yellow, green

On the other hand, several Indo-European languages display reflexes of a root **ĝʰel-*, which is ultimately also the origin of the German word *gelb* (yellow). In reference material, the meaning 'yellow' is most widespread but the fact that related words designate 'green', such as the Greek *khlōrós,* Lithuanian *žālias* and Old Church Slavic *zelenъ,* indicates that the root **ĝʰel-* refers to a colour shade within the yellow-green spectrum, thereby allowing us to reconstruct a meaning of 'yellow, yellow-green, green'. Moreover, it is interesting that in several languages this root forms the basis for words that mean 'gold' or 'golden'. However, as mentioned above, this is probably dependent on secondary developments in individual languages. In this respect, an example like the Old Indic sū́raś *cakrám̐ hiraṇ yáyam* 'the golden wheel of the sun' (Rigveda VI: 53.3) is interesting, because the link between the meanings of 'yellow' and 'golden' still seems entirely transparent. According to Mallory and Adams (2006: 333), reflexes in Slavic (Serbo-Croatian *modar* 'blue'), Anatolian (Hittite *āntara-* 'blue') and Tocharian (B *motartse* 'green') allow us to reconstruct an adjective **modʰro-* for 'blue' or 'green-blue'. If the model developed by Berlin and Kay is used as a basis, the more probable assumption would be that this root originally meant something approximating 'green-blue', i.e. it described a broader colour spectrum in Indo-European than its equivalents in individual languages, which are broadly speaking semantically more specific.

So far, this essay has largely addressed the reconstructed meanings of Indo-European colour terms, which generally, it seems, had a wider application than their representatives in modern European languages. To take one example, the words in Germanic that stem from **ĝʰel-* consistently mean 'yellow' rather than 'green', which is a consequence of introducing **grōni-* as a special colour word to describe the specifically green aspect of the yellow-green colour spectrum. This raises the question of where the new word, which seems to represent a pan-Germanic innovation (cf. Bjorvand and Lindeman 2019: 431), actually comes from. The generally accepted view is that **grōni-* for 'green' is a derivation of the Germanic verb **groa-* meaning 'germinate, sprout, grow', that the word originally meant something like 'sprouting' and the meaning 'green' metonymically emerged from the colour of young, sprouting plants. The Latin verb *vireō,* meaning 'to be green', which comes from the Indo-European root **u̯ei̯s-* and designates 'sprout, flourish' (cf. LIV^2: 671), forms a semantic parallel to this. These examples give the impression that, at least in our Indo-European context, one has to move into the region of individual languages or individual language families in order to identify the etymological origin of the colour terms in Stage IV (cf. fig. 1), as defined by Berlin and Kay (1969).

Brown and grey

In several languages, adjectives can be turned into nouns by changing the accent, as for example in Old Indic, which features minimal pairs such as *kr̥ṣṇá-* 'black' and *kŕ̥ṣṇá-* '(black) antelope', a process of derivation which is also found in Greek; we can, for instance, compare *dolikhós* 'long' and *dólikhos* 'long racecourse'. This derivation can thus be viewed as a Proto-Indo-European process. One comparatively widespread root, namely **bʰreu̯-,* is interesting in this respect, appearing in Germanic in the form **brūno-*[9] and in Old Indic in the form *babhrú-*[10] as an adjective meaning 'brown'. In other cases, however, forms of this root are used as animal names, such as the English *beaver* / German *Biber* (cf. Old English *beofar,* Old High German *bibar*)[11] and *Bär* for 'bear' (cf. Old High German *bēr,* Old Norse *bjǫrn*), two words which are very different in terms of their age. For while the word **bʰebʰru-* 'beaver' is attested in Baltic (cf. Old Prussian *bebrus*), Indo-Iranian (cf. Young Avestan *bawra-*) and Italic (cf. Latin *fiber*) and thus represents an ancient designation for an animal, the word **beran-* 'bear' only appears in Germanic, where it has replaced the corresponding Indo-European animal name **h₂ŕ̥̥tḱos* 'bear' (cf. Hittite *hartaggas,* Greek *árktos,* Latin *ursus,* Old Irish art etc.). Interestingly, both words are interpreted as 'the brown one', i.e. the brown colour designation seems to be the primary factor here. In the case of the Germanic **beran-* for 'bear', this assumption is not a problem because, considering what we know about taboos, it is easy to imagine that the inherited word was avoided in favour of a paraphrased term such as 'the brown one'.[12] Interpreting the word for beaver as 'the brown one' is rather more noteworthy, at least within the typological framework devised by Berlin and Kay (1969), as colour terms meaning 'brown' only appear at a fairly late point in development, during Stage VI. With the Germanic and Latin words for 'green' we have seen that colour terms can, in some cases, result from metonymy, and so it is conceivable that this also occurred with the word for beaver. One is, however, forced to ask oneself how realistic it is to assume that a semantic transfer from *beaver* to 'brown' took place in multiple languages independently. There is a similar problem with the word *hare* (German: *Hase*), which is similarly an ancient animal name, like the Indo-Iranian parallel *śasá-* and other related stem forms with the same meaning, such as the Old Prussian *sasins* and the Cymric *ceinach*. All of these point to an Indo-European root, namely **k̂as-*.[13] Other associated words are the Old Norse *hǫss* and Latin *cānus,* both 'grey', as well as the Paelignian *casnar* 'old man' and Latin *cascus* 'old'. In this case too, we can anticipate two alternatives: either that the meaning 'hare' is primary for the root **k̂asó-* and the meanings 'grey' and 'old' resulted from metonymy; or, on the other hand, that the meaning of 'grey' is older. Here too, the latter assumption is unlikely from a typological perspective, as colour terms meaning 'grey' only appear in the final developmental stage of Berlin and Kay's model; however, the philological data do seem to support the argument. A further option is that the diachronic model illustrated in fig. 1 is not the sole developmental path in this semantic field, but rather that the Indo-European data reflect an alternative path where terms for 'brown' and 'grey' appeared earlier on.

Shiny and matt

As we have seen above, some researchers believe that Proto-Indo-European already distinguished between matt black and shiny black. Interestingly, Latin has two pairs of colour terms that mean 'black' and 'white', namely *āter/niger* 'black' and *albus/candidus* 'white'. All the main dictionaries state that *āter* is a matt black while *niger* designates a shiny black, and *albus* means 'matt white' but *candidus* 'shiny white'. We can, for example, compare phrases such as *oculis nigris* 'with black eyes' (Plautus, Captivi: 647), *pix atra* 'black pitch' (Plautus, Captivi: 597), *equis albis* 'with white steeds' (Cicero, De Natura Deorum: 2.6) or *splendens stella candida* 'shining white star' (Plautus, Rudens: 3).[14] The different meanings of the word pairs can, to some extent, be explained by their etymology. To take one example, as mentioned above *albus* belongs to the Indo-European root **$h_2$elb^h-*, which is attested in other languages with meanings such as 'cloud', 'swan' and 'pale white leprosy', terms which are very clearly consistent with their Latin meaning of 'matt white'. On the other hand, the adjective *candidus* and the associated verb *candeo* have a totally different origin because they are derived from a root **(s)kend-*[15] 'gleam' (cf. LIV2), which supplies a clear semantic rationale for the colour nuance denoted by the adjective.

The origin of *niger* remains unclear, although the word is possibly associated with the root **neg$^{u̯}$-* 'becoming dark, twilight', as is also the case for the word *night* (Latin *nox,* Gothic *nahts* etc.) (cf. Wodtko et al. 2008: 504ff.), which would presuppose a highly plausible development in meaning from ‘dark’ to ‘black’. Finally, the word *āter* seems to stem from an Indo-European word $^{*}h_2eh_1tro$-, which originally designated a hearth, whereby a development in meaning is estimated to have taken place in Latin, along the lines of *‘hearth’ > * ‘rust’ > * ‘rust coloured’ > ‘matt black’.[16] These data clearly show that the semantic field of what are supposedly the most primitive colour designations is engaged in an ongoing process of renewal and is thus diachronically somewhat unstable; indeed, out of all these Latin colour terms only *niger* still has descendants with the same meaning in the Romance languages. While it can be assumed that the semantic difference between matt and shiny black has become obsolete over the course of time, because only one colour term has survived, we can equally speculate that a similar development has taken place in the region of colour terms referencing white, although *candidus* has been retained as an adjective with a somewhat different meaning. In Romance language, the originally Germanic loanword **blank* ‘shiny, radiant, glossy’ subsequently replaced the successors of *candidus* as expressions of ‘white’.

The aforementioned considerations create the impression that the individual Indo-European language branches feature diverging systems of colour terms despite some lexical correspondence or overlapping, thereby making it virtually impossible to reconstruct a unified system for the proto-language. We have seen that several colour terms, such as the word for red, the Indo-European $^{*}h_1rud^h$-, have proven themselves to be extremely stable, while others tend to be replaced. Moreover, it has become clear that several formally reconstructable colour terms exhibit divergent meanings in the individual languages. In our context that is particularly interesting if different colours are involved, such as with the root **mel-n-*, which can mean not only ‘black’ but also ‘red/reddish’, ‘blue’, ‘grey’ and ‘yellow’. On the other hand, there is the adjective $^{*}mod^hro$-, which presumably meant ‘green-blue’, and which has semantic parallels in several languages such as Latin *caeruleus*[17] ‘dark blue, dark green’ and Old Irish *glas,* which covers the spectrum ‘green-blue-grey’ and apparently belongs to the Indo-European root $^{*}g^helh_2$- ‘yellow-green’ as described above. It should be noted that in this latter case the inclusion of ‘blue’ in the spectrum of meaning is apparently secondary; this can probably be explained by the existence of the word buide ‘yellow’, which is in turn related to the Latin *badius* ‘brown, chestnut coloured’, indicating an original adjective $^{*}bod^hios$ ‘yellow-brown’.[18] These examples illustrate how colour terms with partially overlapping meanings diachronically adapt to each other in the same individual language system, and consequently etymologically related colour terms can display meanings that diverge from each other.

In the model developed by Berlin and Kay, colour concepts such as ‘pink’, ‘violet’ and ‘orange’ belong to Stage VII (cf. fig. 1). For this reason, it is not particularly noteworthy that the designations for these colours in individual languages are clearly either secondary or loanwords. In Old Indic, for example, we find words such as *dhūmala* 'smoke-coloured, violet', *pāṭala* 'pale red, pink'[19], and *kuṅkumākta* 'dyed with saffron, orange'[20], although only *d^hūmala* is etymologically Indo-European as the word is derived from the Old Indic *d^hūma* 'smoke, fumes'; this, in turn, is related to the Latin *fūmus,* Old Prussian *dumis,* Old Church Slavonic *dymъ,* all meaning 'smoke, fumes', as well as Old High German *toum* 'steam' and Greek *t^hūmós* 'spirit, courage, anger', which has obviously developed a secondary meaning.[21] Corresponding colour terms in Latin are *purpureus* 'violet' and *lūteus* 'orange', which are derived from the Greek loanword *purpura* 'purple, violet' and from the plant name *lūtum 'reseda luteola'* respectively.

This essay has, I hope, shown that the model developed by Berlin and Kay provides a fruitful starting point for a diachronic study of colour terms, even though it does not tally in every philological detail. The data from Indo-European languages discussed above give the impression that the trajectory of how certain colour terms developed semantically is frequently idiosyncratic, or at least not always predictable, and that these kinds of words seldom exhibit a significant degree of diachronic stability.

1 Forms starting with an asterisk (*) should be read as reconstructed.

2 At this point it should be noted that word-internal Indo-European $^*d^h$ normally becomes Latin *d,* but after *u, r* and before *r, l* it becomes *b.* The form *rufus* illustrates the Sabellic development from $^*d^h$ to **f* in word-internal sound.

3 It should be noted that the etymology of the Welsh word *melyn* is disputed. An alternative hypothesis is that the word belongs to the same family as Indo-European **mel-* 'honey'.

4 Moreover, compare the Germanic adjective **svarta-* 'black', which is etymologically related to Latin *sordes* 'dirty' etc. In this case, too, the direction of the semantic development is unclear.

5 The Old Indic *arjuna* is still found in the Mahābhārata epic as the name of the third Pandava brother, Arjuna. In Javanese shadow puppet theatre he is depicted in certain situations with a white face. On this and on Krisna ('the black one'), see the essay by Vanessa von Gliszczynski in this volume.

6 Tocharian is an Indo-European language branch with two known languages: 'Tocharian A' and 'Tocharian B'. Only examples from Tocharian B are considered here, and these are labelled as such with a 'B'.

7 In terms of the initial sound, the Tocharian *ñ-* probably developed into the subsequent *n* instead of the more expected **r* by means of assimilation.

8 The corresponding word for 'dark-cold' is more difficult to reconstruct. Shields (1996) agrees with Haudry (1988) that this fact can be explained by taboos, whereby naming the word was avoided due to its associations with the night, such as death, suffering and other evil forces.

9 This word form reflects an expansion $^*b^hru$*-H-no-*, where the long **ū* comes from **uH.* Moreover, the initial sound **b* in the Germanic from the Indo-European $^*b^h$ is to be expected, and is consistent with sound law (the First Germanic Sound Shift, also known as Grimm's Law).

10 This word reflects a reduplicated form $^*b^heb^hru$*-,* where the initial sound *b* in Old Indic can be explained by aspiration dissimilation (Grassmann's Law).

11 The Germanic words for 'beaver' came from the reduplicated form $^*b^heb^hru$*-.*

12 Compare the Old Church Slavonic word for 'bear' *medvědĭ* 'honey eater', which is also an example of taboo-based lexical innovation.

13 It should be noted here that there are two variants of the word for 'hare' in the Germanic: compare the German *Hase* with the English *hare.* The first form can be traced back to **hásan,* and the second to **hazán* from the earlier **hasán.*

14 In connection with this, the phrase *albis dentibus* 'with (pale) white teeth' (Plautus, Epidicus: 429) is interesting, because our notion of teeth is that they are gleaming white. The use of *albus* in this context may either be connected with the two terms for 'white' getting mixed up in Latin, or they could indicate that white teeth were indeed pale. It was possibly connected to inadequate dental hygiene, an idea supported by the fact that dentures were known about in the ancient world and were apparently fairly widespread.

15 This root is reconstructed with what is known as an s-mobile, i.e. a seemingly optional or functionally unclear initial s- sound.

16 It should be noted that in Avestan, the parallel word *ātarš* means 'fire', which probably similarly reflects a secondary semantic development because the Indo-European word for fire, *ágnis,* is retained in the closely related Old Indic, but is not attested in Iranian.

17 This colour adjective is derived from the word for sky *caelum,* with a secondary dissimilation of the first l (**caeluleus* > *caeruleus*).

18 The reconstruction of the adjective suggested is pursued by de Vaan (2008: 68). An alternative reconstruction would be **badʰios,* cf. de Vaan loc. cit. for counter-arguments to the latter possibility.

19 According to Mayrhofer (1996: 116–117) the colour word *pāṭala* has no clear etymology.

20 The word is a transparent composite formed from *kuṅkuma* 'saffron' and *akta* 'dyed'. According to Mayrhofer (2001: 95), *kuṅkuma* is an old *Kulturwort* which is associated with Akkadian *kurkanû,* Hebrew *karkōm,* Greek *krókos* etc.

21 The proto-linguistic form is usually reconstructed as **dʰuh₂mó-* (cf. Mayrhofer 1992: 795–796).

References:

– **Berlin, Brent und Paul Kay. 1969:** *Basic Color Terms: Their Universality and Evolution.* Berkeley: University of California Press.

– **Bjorvand, Harald and Fredrik Otto Lindeman. 2019:** *Våre Arveord: Etymologisk Ordbok.* Oslo: Novus Forlag.

– **Cicero, Marcus Tullius. 1917:** *De natura deorum.* Edited by Otto Plasberg. Leipzig: Teubner.

– **Haudry, Jean. 1988:** 'The Cosmic Religion of the Indo-Europeans'. In: Jazayery, Mohammad Ali and Werner Winter (eds.): *Languages and Cultures: Studies in Honor of Edgar C. Polomé.* Berlin: De Gruyter. 225–233.

– **LIV² (2001):** *Lexikon der indogermanischen Verben: Die Wurzeln und ihre Primärstammbildungen.* Edited by Helmut Rix et al. Wiesbaden: Reichert.

– **Mallory, James and Douglas Q. Adams. 2006:** *The Oxford Introduction to Proto-Indo-European and the Proto-Indo-European World.* Oxford: Oxford University Press.

– **Mayrhofer, Manfred. 1992:** *Etymologisches Wörterbuch des Altindoarischen.* Three volumes. Heidelberg: Winter.

– **Plautus, Titus Maccius. 1904:** *Comoediae.* Two volumes. Edited by Wallace Martin Lindsay. Oxford: Clarendon Press.

– **Rigveda. 1877:** *Die Hymnen des Ṛigveda.* Edited by Theodor Aufrecht. Bonn: Marcus.

– **Shields, Kenneth. 1979:** 'Indo-European Basic Colour Terms'. In: *Canadian Journal of Linguistics/ Revue Canadienne de Linguistique* 24 (2). 142–146.

– **Shields, Kenneth. 1996:** 'Typological Inconsistencies in the Indo-European Color Lexicon: A Cosmic Connection?' In: *Indogermanische Forschungen* 101. 94–98.

– **Vaan, Michiel de. 2008:** *Etymological Dictionary of Latin and the other Italic Languages.* Leiden: Brill.

– **Wodtko, Dagmar; Irslinger, Britta and Carolin Schneider. 2008:** *Nomina im indogermanischen Lexikon.* Heidelberg: Winter.

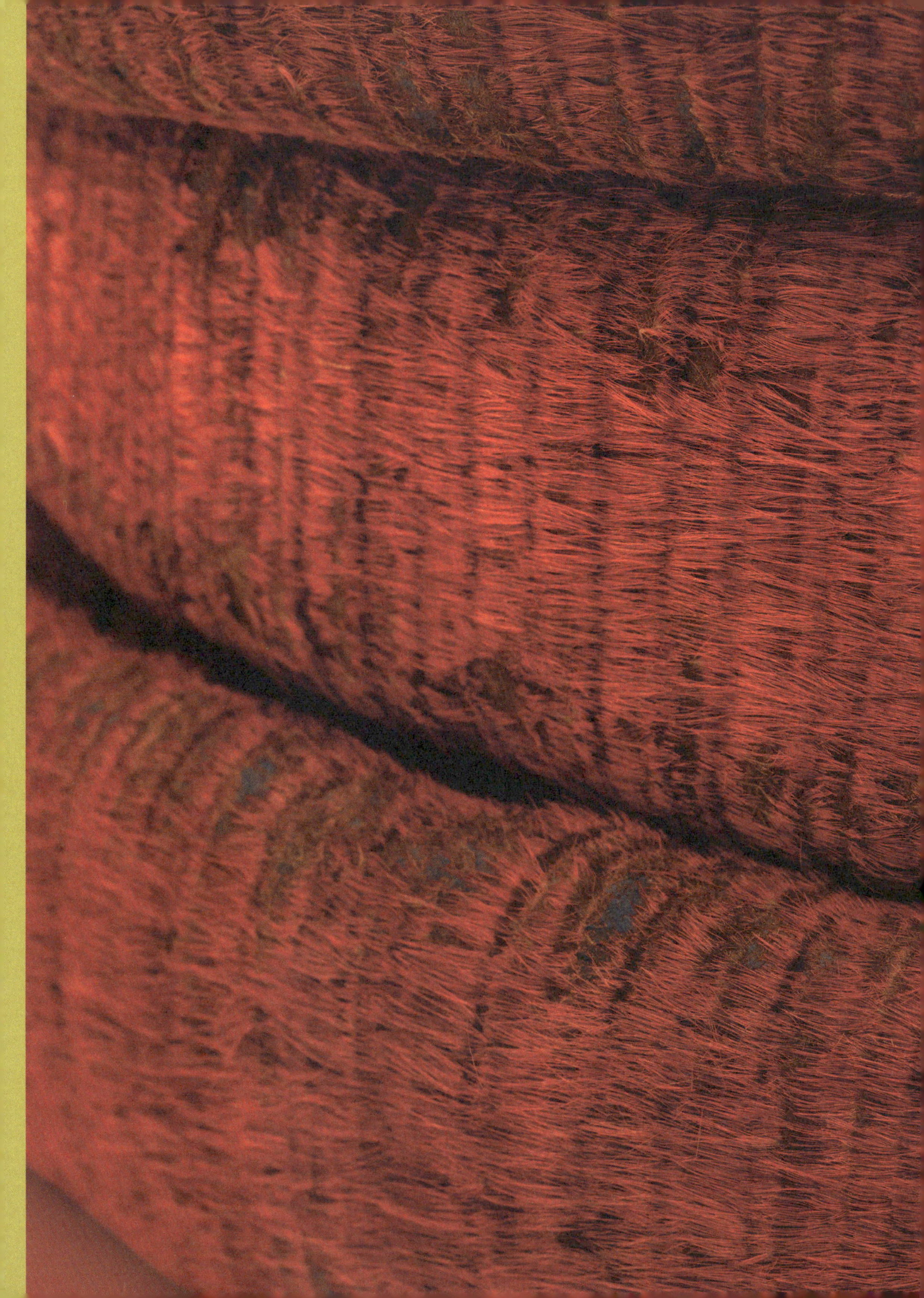

MATERI-
ALITY

The intensive red of the feather money *(mangahau)* from the Melanesian Santa Cruz Islands is produced by the artful arrangement of up to 60,000 small cinnabar red feathers of the honeyeater *(Myzomela Cardinalis).* If the red fades over time, then the feather money roll also loses its value. Feathers, bark, barkcloth, snail shells, Job's tears seeds. Collected by Volker Schneider, 1980s.

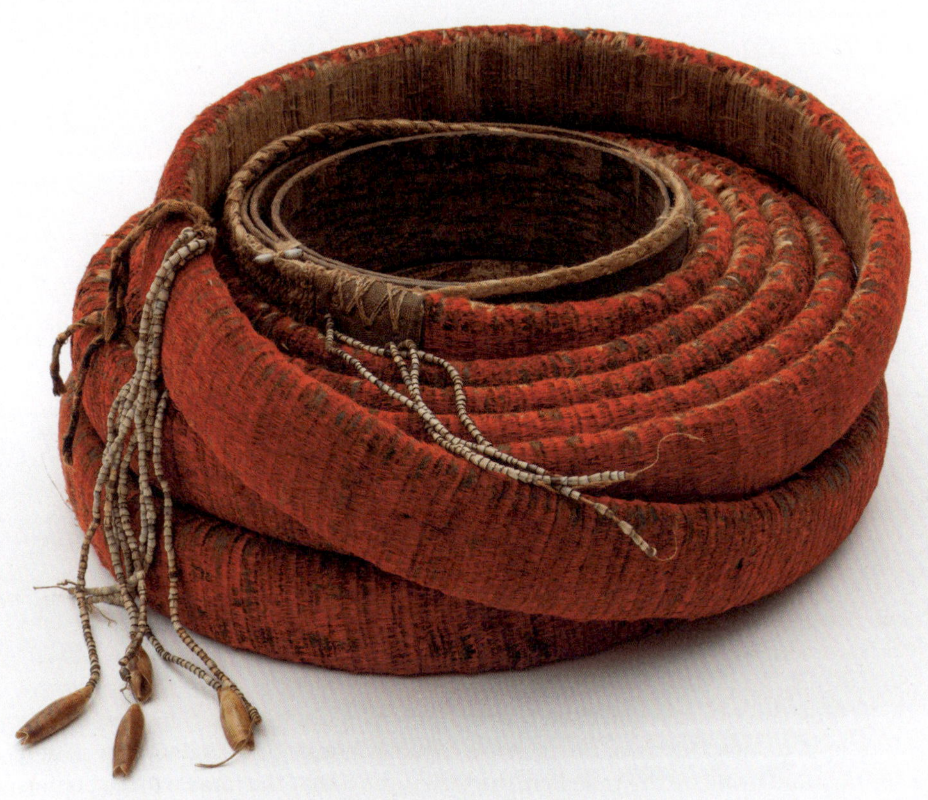

TROBRIAND RED

Values and Colours in the Massim Region, Papua New Guinea

Eva Ch. Raabe

Before a man dives for *Spondylus* shells, he asks the woman he is closest to – wife, daughter, or mother – to establish a close bond with their best female friend. Both women visit each other, exchange gifts and work together in the garden. "So the men go diving. They take their baskets. They knock off the shells. All shells look the same. When they break them open, and inside they find all are white-lipped ones, the rims, 'oh no, it is a casual friendship, not a deep one'. But if they dive and bring up the red shell, then they know that the female force behind them, the friendship, is a rich and embracing one" – as described by the poet and author John Kasaipwalowa from the Trobriand Islands (Malnic 1998: 123f.).

The Spondylus shell, with its red inside edge, is one of the most important materials for the production of precious items in New Guinea's coastal and island regions, where it plays a central role, especially on the islands of the Massim region at the south-eastern tip of Papua New Guinea. The inhabitants of the Trobriand, Amphlett and D'Entrecasteaux Islands, as well as the inhabitants of Misima in the Louisiade Archipelago and Muyuw (Woodlark) and Gawa participate in the *kula* trade.[1] In this system of exchange necklaces made from the red Spondylus or from red Chama shells, and bangle bracelets made from the shell of the Conus snail, circulate in opposite directions. In a circuit of fixed trade partnerships bracelets are always exchanged for necklaces, or vice versa, necklaces for bracelets, but never necklaces for necklaces or bracelets for bracelets. Alongside this, on the islands of the Calvados Chain and the Louisiade Archipelago further south in the Massim region, there are other exchange systems of a rather monetary character, within which discs and pieces of red shell also play an important role (cf. Armstrong 1928; Leach and Leach 1983: 23; Liep 1983: 507). Consequently, the red shell is a highly prized raw material used for the manufacture of a product whose material value is largely determined by being red.

Colours and values

The *soulava* and *bagi*[2] necklaces employed in the *kula* trade consist of very small rows of discs made from red shells. At both ends these strings are extended with rows of banana pods and larger discs made from red shell. The ends of the necklaces are decorated with pendants made from glass beads, pieces of shell and seed pods. At one end there is an Ovula shell, and at the other, a half-moon shaped disc of mother of pearl respectively. However, it is the middle string composed of the red shell discs that gives the necklace its actual value. Many discs of the same colour are required for its manufacture, and in turn many Chama or Spondylus shells are required for their production. However, in both species it is often just a narrow inner border that is actually coloured red, while all other parts are white or yellowish in colour. Completely white specimens without any red at all are quite common. Furthermore, all the shells appear the same when closed – the inner colouration cannot be seen from the outside. As expressed in the initial quote, fishing for red shells requires a certain amount of luck, which one attempts to influence positively through female loyalty. The red of the Spondylus thus also becomes a symbol for a functioning community, which is very much dependent on the solidarity of the women. The necklace itself is assigned to the female sphere. Its material value is determined by the size, uniformity and colour of the shell discs, and very much by the age and the history of the respective necklace. As every temporary owner in the *kula* circle of exchange files and polishes the necklace they have received, its individual shine and smoothness is a sign that it has been passed on many times and has reached a great age. Both the Chama and Spondylus species display a great variety of red tones, ranging from yellow and orange, to pink, purple-red and red-brown (cf. Lindner 1975: 102, 222). In combination with their surface haptics, these colour differences are decisive for the valuation of the string of shells. Based on her field research on the most southerly Trobriand Island, Vakuta, Campbell (1983) described the ranking system of the *kula* necklaces: The colour salmon pink was clearly rated the highest. Very thin, finely ground strings in this red tone are positioned very high in the ranking. In second and third place are the salmon pink strings with rough surfaces. This is followed by those necklaces whose shell discs are of very varied quality. One says, 'its face is different', as they display an uneven surface with colour variations (Campbell 1983: 241). The last place but one is occupied by thicker, less well ground necklaces of a very dark, muddy-looking red, followed by even coarser, thicker necklaces in brown-red. Due to their dark red colouration these last two categories of shell string are also referred to as black (Campbell 1983: 242).

As the occurrence of subspecies of Spondylus varies from island group to island group, the origin of the material also determines the colour and constitutes a further criterion in the quality rating. Thus, for example, in the waters around Muyuw there are only white Spondylus with a hint of pink. The *bagi* necklaces manufactured there can be highly valued due to their size and fine polish. However, they remain outside the ranking system as they can never rise to the highest category due to their pale colour. In contrast, on the island of Dobu in the D'Entrecasteaux Archipelago, the necklaces from Yela (Rossel Island), an island in the Louisiade Archipelago, are assigned the highest value due to their pale red colour (Kuehling 1998: 123).

The basic colour of the *kula* bracelet *(mwali)* is white. They are cut from the shell of the cone shaped white Conus snail, and the edges are studded with white Ovula shells. The value of such a bracelet is determined by its width and age. As more Ovula can be fitted onto a wide bracelet, their number is an important criterion for the bracelet's position within a ranking system. However, its colour also plays an important role: Similar to ivory, the colour of the Conus shell yellows with increasing age, with red-brown stripes appearing in the material. A yellowish, red-veined surface is therefore a sign that the bracelet has been in circulation for a long time, and has already written history, so to speak. Bracelets that have circulated in the *kula* ring for some time can, with increasing colouration, rise to a higher rank and increase in value. The relationship between the sexes also plays a role when fishing for Conus shells: Before heading out the fishermen must practice sexual abstinence. Absolute loyalty is expected of the female family members in order to ward off misfortune. Wives must be faithful to their husbands, daughters and nieces must show the necessary respect to their fathers and uncles. For young men diving for Conus shells for the first time this undertaking is equivalent to an initiation ritual (Malnic 1998: 122f.). Consequently, the bracelet is assigned to the male sphere. Well-known necklaces or bracelets, which have already been in circulation for a long time, are often given individual names. If a famous, valuable bracelet is exchanged for a necklace of equal status, they are called a married couple and the transaction is seen as a marriage ceremony (Campbell 1983: 245; cf. also Kuehling 1998: 125; Raabe 2001: 127f.) (fig. 1).

Fig. 1 *Kula* jewellery: bracelet and necklace, Trobriand Islands, South-East New Guinea. Collected by Volker Schneider. Purchased in 1987.

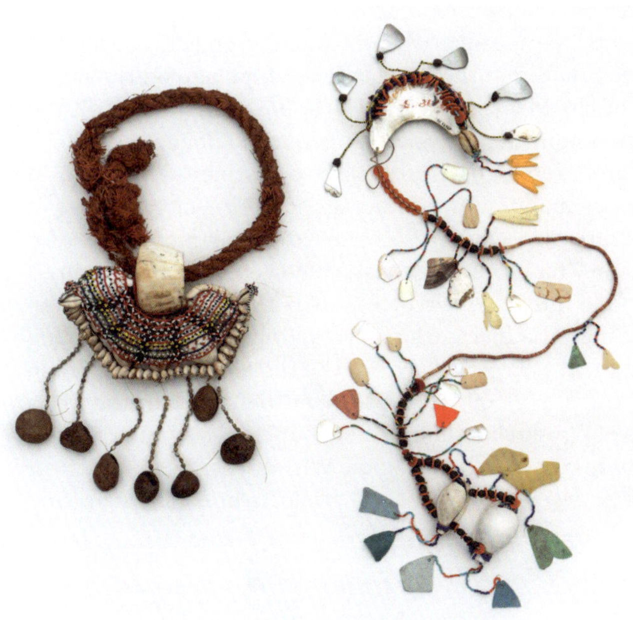

While the *kula* ring is about winning prestige and standing through spectacular exchanges, other gift exchange systems in the region tend to have a more monetary character. Their standards of value primarily come into play during the ceremonial exchange of gifts within the island communities on the occasion of birthday and marriage celebrations or funerals. Battaglia (1983a: 452ff. and 1983b: 289ff.) names two fundamental standards of value for Sabarl, an island of the Calvados Chain: Necklaces and flat, smoothly ground axe blades made from black-green igneous rock. The *bak* necklaces are primarily exchanged on Yela in the Louisiade Archipelago, where there is a greater incidence of red-edged Spondylus. Like the *kula* necklaces, they are subject to a value system in which light yellow-orange is ranked higher than dark red (Battaglia 1983a: 454). In funeral ceremonies, the shafted axes represent the bodies of the deceased. Their blades stand for ritual fatherhood and are seen as masculine, although the red wood of their shafts are associated with maternal blood. The necklaces express the feminine. They are composed of strings of red shell discs and a pendant of white shell referred to as the head, whereby they display both of the colours of human procreation: the maternal red and the white of the paternal blood (Battaglia 1983b: 298ff.). A further category of precious objects are the flat, mushroom-shaped lime spatulas[3] made from tortoise shell or wood. They serve as holders for the red string of shells, of which one or two are attached to the ends respectively so that the small red discs stand upright. The number of red shell discs thus determines the value of this 'money holder' (fig. 2). Held upright they are seen as a person, with the ornamental stick representing the head, i.e. face, the side extensions the arms, and the red shell discs fixed on the top, the hair. When inverted, the form of the spatula is interpreted as a boat with a mast, and the red discs are referred to as islands. The triangular holes carved into the middle represent a 'person who guides' (Battaglia 1990: 128).

The necklaces, axes and lime spatulas used as precious objects can also be found on the island of Yela, situated in the Louisiade Archipelago on the outermost south-eastern edge of the Massim region. Here, in distinction to all the other islands of the region, a non-Austronesian language is spoken (Liep 2009: 29ff.), and the system of gift exchange also displays a distinctive feature: In addition to the *bagi* necklaces manufactured for export, a further two types of shell money, *kö* und *ndap,* are also employed. Each *kö* consists of a row of c. ten polished discs made from Chama shells, whose value is primarily measured according to size and surface finish. Nevertheless, it is the colour that determines the design of the string: The discs, which are mainly whitish on the one side and reddish on the other, are threaded so that the red side is always facing the same direction (Liep 1983: 512, 2009: 191ff.). Ranked higher than the *kö* is the *ndap,* individual pieces of Spondylus shell, either round or triangular, whose value is determined by their age, not their colour. Within the pieces of lower rank distinctions are made between colours, namely violet, white, brown or wine

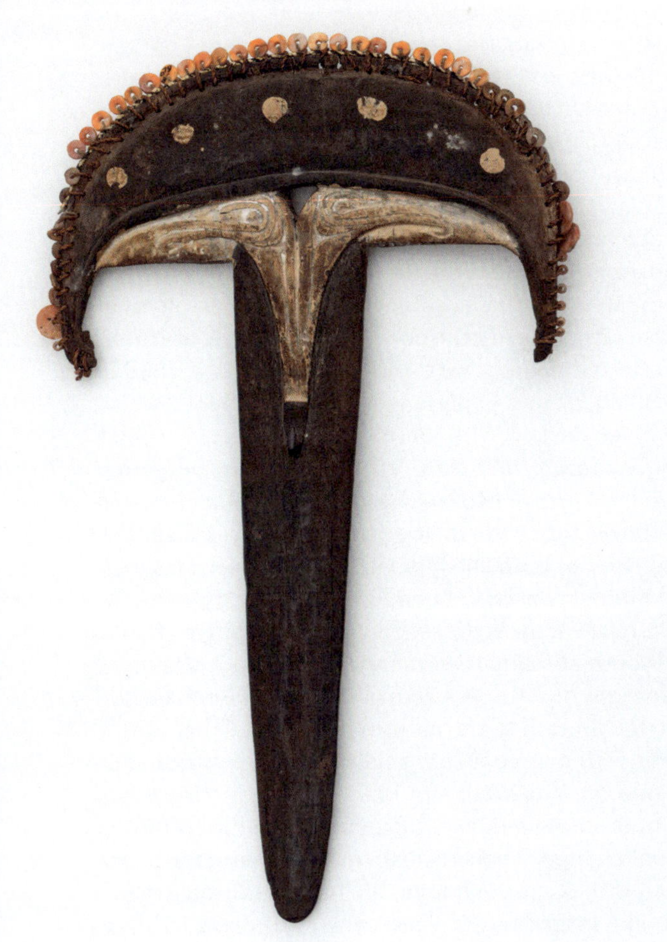

Fig. 2 Lime spatula with red shell discs, southern Massim region, South-East New Guinea. Purchased from the Galerie Lemaire in 1989.

red, however the categories of the *ndap,* which are ranked higher due to their patina and age, are not defined according to uniform colours. The pieces of especially high rank are predominately yellow or red, are named individually and as individual pieces are known under their proper names (Liep 2009: 168ff., cf. Armstrong 1928).

The colours of people

The personification of the precious objects, the equating of age-related darkening with a fulfilled life rich in history, and the frequent correlation of red with femininity and the female sphere of life is striking. That a colour symbolism also resonates within social contexts is especially clear in the case of the Trobriand Islands, where the artistic and symbolic meaning of the colours in the *kula* has been systematically examined (Campbell 1983 and 2002).

Here, similar to the European context, white stands for all that is new and pure, red stands for vitality and eroticism and black for mourning. Determined by growing up and ageing, the human individual is subject to continuous physical and mental change, which is also paralleled by the changes in their social status. The Trobrianders associate different colours with each stage in life. A child is born with pale skin: still unsullied by any experiences it is considered white. When it grows up its skin becomes darker: with increasing life experience and sexual activity it becomes more mature and thus 'redder'. Unmarried young girls wear short fibre skirts dyed red in order to emphasise their sexual power of attraction and signal their readiness for erotic relationships. However, after the wedding, marital fidelity is expected of both the husband and wife. Accordingly, the everyday attire of married women consists of undyed, knee-length skirts. At the end of her period of mourning a widow is dressed in a newly made red fibre skirt as a sign of her regained youth and ability to marry. Prior to this she must wear black body paint for up to eight months as a sign of her grief. However, it is not just spouses that make a contribution to the mourning period. Other family members also black themselves with charcoal. It is said that with increasing infirmity the skin of ageing people becomes dull and black, thus equating black with illness and death. Colours are not seen as a permanent condition but as stages in a process of continual change. Their transformative character is not just displayed by being equated with stages in human life but also through their connection to day and night. The bright day is white, the dark night is black, however the transitionary times, dawn and dusk, are red. Accordingly, white can become red; red can become black, but black can also become red and red white. All colours can transition into each other or fuse with each other. Accordingly, the meaning attributed to them is not always unequivocal. If they are used in social life to indicate human characteristics they are often connected with ambivalent feelings. White does not just mean purity, it also stands for something harmless, as it is located in the light, is not hidden and can therefore be clearly recognised. Black can stand for wickedness. Witches and wizards are not just said to have black skin, but also blackened insides as a result of the baneful effects of their magic knowledge. On the other side, old people who already have dull, black skin are not considered bad. They are not as attractive outwardly, however they possess great spiritual maturity and comprehensive knowledge.

On the one side, people with a light complexion are considered to have less erotic charisma than people with dark skin, referred to as red skin. On the other side, precisely because of this, they are considered to be more faithful and reliable life partners (Campbell 1983 and 2002: 118ff.; Raabe 1998: 17ff.).

The meaning of colours with reference to people and the ambivalence in the allocation of positive and negative characteristics are also carried over into the classification system of the *kula* trade. In any event, red is the colour that makes the pieces valuable and lends them their high rank. However, the red of the necklace is interpreted differently compared to that of the bracelet, which is thought of as masculine. A newly manufactured Conus bracelet which is employed in exchange for the first time is still white – in other words, still too young to possess sufficient maturity and experience. If, when circulating continuously in the *kula* ring, it should display the brown red grain of the ageing material, then its value increases. One says that it is now black; like a person it becomes darker with age and gains in knowledge and power. In contrast, in the case of the necklace, which is seen as feminine, a dark, brownish red is called black in a negative sense. It is a sign of dwindling attractiveness, of illness and infirmity, as suffered by an old person. In contrast, light red, which assigns a necklace a higher rank, is an expression of the special power of youth, which is manifested in lived sexuality and an erotic power of attraction. The red of the bracelets and the red of the necklaces are mutually attractive, thus complementing each other, just as the different qualities of old age and youth do in human societies (Campbell 2002: 121ff.).

Red in abstraction

In the Oceania Collection in Frankfurt there are only a few shell necklaces from the Massim region, collected at the beginning of the 20th century. In one specimen originating from Yela the discs of shell are strung together like a collar necklace. The form of the row does not correspond to the shell money *kö* as described by Armstrong (1928) and Liep (2009). Nevertheless, the individual elements have the same circular form drilled in their centres as the *kö* discs and like them are made of Chama shells. Furthermore, as in the case of the *kö,* they are aligned so that the light red surface is always pointing in the same direction (fig. 3). In the case of two older strings of shells from the Trobriand Islands, the small discs of Spondylus shell are threaded, i.e. tied onto the string individually and at great distances from one another. Their colour effect appears restrained, however the value of every single red particle is clearly emphasised. In contrast, the shell strings of the *kula* necklaces are composed of many individual, closely threaded discs, whose red combines to form a concentrated mass. If one takes a look at the *kula* jewellery in the collection, especially that originating from the 1980s, the red colour appears to almost jump out at one. The necklaces and

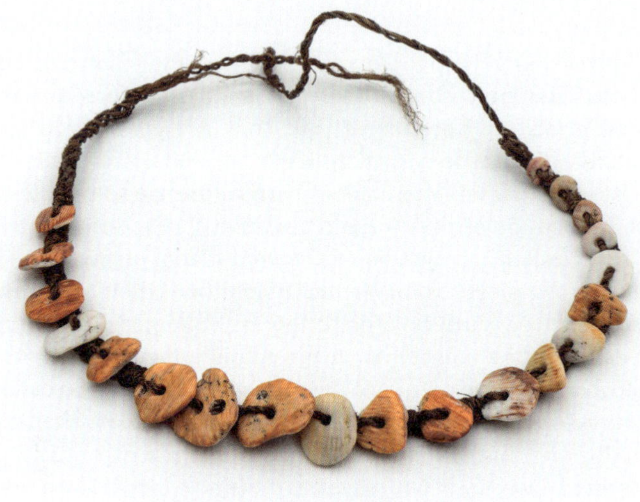

Fig. 3 Necklace, shell money, Yela (Rossel Island), South-East New Guinea. Collector unknown, prior to 1912.

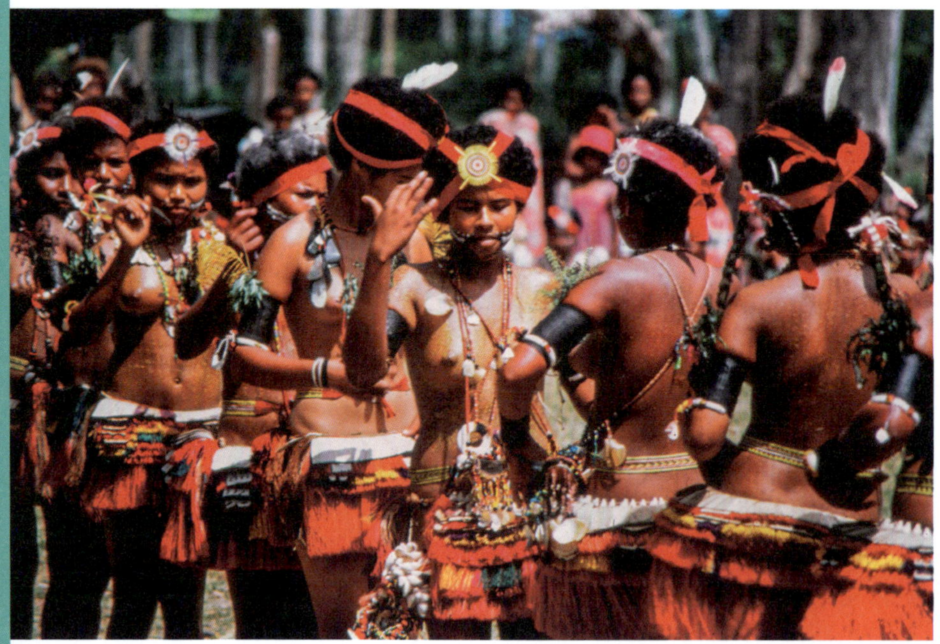

Fig. 4 Young girls in the red skirts of the unmarried women, adorned with kula necklaces. Photo: Volker Schneider, 1986.

bracelets are decorated with additional ornamental elements composed of strings with red glass beads and bright red plastic pendants. While the core of the necklaces is still composed of Spondylus discs, they are often extended with additional red discs cut from plastic buckets or rubber water hoses (cf. Kuehling 1998: 121 and Battaglia 1983a: 454) (fig. 1). The use of a multitude of red plastic decorative elements makes the necklaces appear even 'redder'.

The colour photographs taken on the Trobriand Islands in the 1980s show young people in fibre skirts or loincloths, adorned with red headbands, who are wearing the colourful *kula* jewellery, thus using the festivities as an occasion to display the wealth and prestige of their fathers and uncles. Many of these pictures are virtually dominated by the colour red. Red in all its shades is always present in the ritual context and at ceremonies: A bold red is used to paint objects laden with power, such as the gabled fronts of the chiefs' yam storehouses or the splashboards of the boats used for the *kula* expeditions. The dyed skirts made from banana fibres, important objects of value in the ritual exchange of gifts among women, are of a bright red-orange, like the short skirts of the young, unmarried women. On the other hand, salmon pink is the colour of the *kula* necklaces. When all this comes together during festivities, the intensified red reaches a climax and leaves a lasting impression (fig. 4).

Thus it is clearly no coincidence that it was precisely the artists from the Trobriand Islands who elevated the colour red to their own stylistic device within Papua New Guinea's contemporary art scene. Since his studies at the *National Arts School of Papua New Guinea,* the painter Samuel Laguna has made an intensive study of the *kula* traditions of his native country. To this day, he repeatedly chooses necklaces and bracelets as the motif of his acrylic paintings, which are generally characterised by powerful, warm red tones. His depiction of an abstracted *kula* bracelet, entirely bathed in red and orange tones, possesses a special radiance: The painting appears as if its surface is radiating heat. The colours lend the depicted object a special aura, making it appear as if it is charged with energy. For Samuel Luguna, *kula* is a special part of his cultural identity.[4] In order to show this he uses a dominating red: the precious and desirable Trobriand red (cf. Raabe 2003 and 2011: 139f.) (fig. 5).

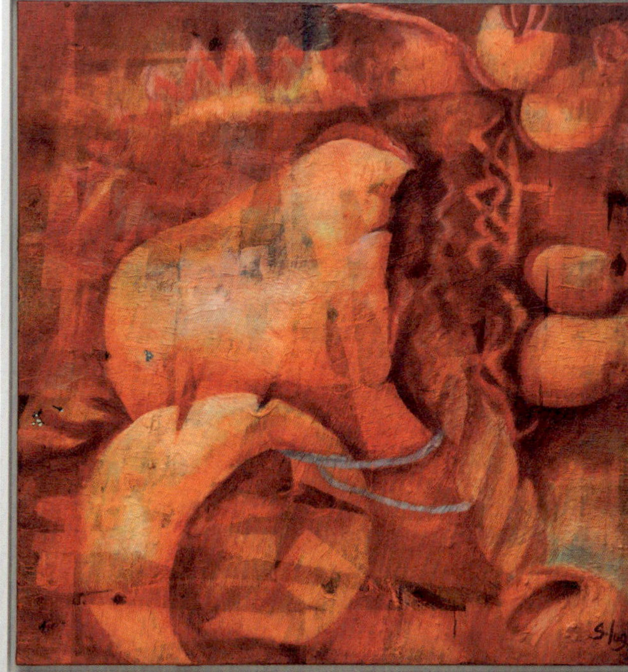

Fig. 5 Samuel Luguna: *Mwali Abstraction,* 1998. Signed and dated 1999. Mixed media (tissue paper, silicone powder, marble dust, glue, acrylic) on canvas, 120 × 120 cm.

1 This circular exchange system is described in detail e.g. by Malinowski 1922; Leach and Leach 1983; Kuehling 1998; a detailed description of the art forms in *kula* and the associated colour symbolism is provided by Campbell 2002.

2 This description is provided above all by Malinowski (1922), according to Campbell (1983: 247) it has now been replaced in many cases with the term *vaiguva.* In the southern *kula* region the necklaces are known as *bagi* or *bak* (cf. Kuehling 1998; Battaglia 1990: 128ff.; Liep 1990: 204).

3 Lime spatulas are normally used for scooping lime, which is chewed together with pieces of the Betel nut.

4 Personal interview with the artist (1999) conducted by the author, Raabe Documentation, Weltkulturen Museum, Frankfurt am Main.

References:

– **Armstrong, Wallace E. 1928:** *Rossel Island. An Ethnological Study.* Cambridge: Cambridge University Press.

– **Battaglia, Debbora B. 1983a:** 'Syndroms of Ceremonial Exchange in the Eastern Calvados. The View from Sabarl Island'. In: Leach, Jerry W. and Edmund Leach (eds.): *The Kula. New Perspectives on Massim Exchange.* Cambridge: Cambridge University Press. 445–465.

– **Battaglia, Debbora B. 1983b:** 'Projecting Personhood in Melanesia. The Dialectics of Artefact Symbolism on Sabarl Island'. In: *Man. Journal of the Royal Anthropological Institute* 18 (2). 289–304.

– **Battaglia, Debbora B. 1990:** *On the Bones of the Serpent. Person, Memory and Mortality in Sabarl Island Society.* Chicago: The University of Chicago Press.

– **Campbell, Shirley F. 1983:** 'Attaining Rank. A Classification of Shell Valuables'. In: Leach, Jerry W. and Edmund Leach (eds.): *The Kula. New Perspectives on Massim Exchange.* Cambridge: Cambridge University Press. 229–248.

– **Campbell, Shirley F. 2002:** *The Art of Kula.* Oxford: Berg.

– **Kuehling, Susanne. 1998:** *The Name of the Gift. Ethics of Exchange on Dobu Island.* Australian National University, Canberra: Ph.D. Thesis.

– **Leach, Jerry W. 1983:** 'Introduction'. In: Leach, Jerry W. and Edmund Leach (eds.): *The Kula. New Perspectives on Massim Exchange.* Cambridge: Cambridge University Press.

– **Liep, John. 2009:** *A Papuan Plutocracy. Ranked Exchange on Rossel Island.* Aarhus: Aarhus University Press.

– **Liep, John. 1983:** 'Ranked Exchange in Yela (Rossel Island)'. In: Leach, Jerry W. and Edmund Leach (eds.): *The Kula. New Perspectives on Massim Exchange.* Cambridge: Cambridge University Press. 503–525.

– **Lindner, Gert. 1975:** *Muscheln und Schnecken der Weltmeere. Aussehen, Vorkommen, Systematik.* München: BVL Verlagsgesellschaft.

– **Malinowski, Bronislaw. 1922:** *Argonauts of the Western Pacific. An Account of Native Enterprise and Adventure in the Archipelagoes of Melanesian New Guinea.* New York: Dutton.

– **Malnic, Jutta. 1998:** *Kula. Myth and Magic in the Trobriand Islands.* Wahroonga: Cowrie Books.

– **Raabe, Eva Ch. 2011:** 'Individualism and Tradition, Curating Contemporary Art from Papua New Guinea'. In: Stevenson, Karen (ed.): *Pacific Island Artists. Navigating the Global Art World.* Oakland: Masalai Press. 137–148.

– **Raabe, Eva Ch. 2003:** 'Gefühltes Rot. Ein zeitgenössisches Gemälde von den Trobriand Inseln'. In: *www.journal-ethnologie.de*. Schwerpunktthema Ethnologie und Kunst.

– **Raabe, Eva Ch. 2001:** 'Verbindung'. In: Suhrbier, Mona and Eva Raabe (eds.): *Menschen und ihre Gegenstände.* Roter Faden zur Ausstellung 22. Frankfurt am Main: Museum der Weltkulturen. 119–131.

– **Raabe, Eva Ch. 1998:** *Im Auge des Betrachters. Kunst und Sehen in Papua Neuguinea.* Galerie 37. Kunst im Museum für Völkerkunde 3. Frankfurt am Main: Museum für Völkerkunde.

TAPIRAGE

The Art of Changing the Colour of Feathers on Living Birds in the Amazon Basin

Gustaaf Verswijver

Soon after meeting the Tupinambá and other Amerindian groups along the Brazilian coast, the European colonisers were astonished to observe that the indigenous peoples were adept in changing the colour of feathers on living birds. This technique became known as 'tapirage', a term derived from the Creole word *tapi,* meaning 'red' (Berthier 2016: 40). Alfred Métraux (1928) was the first anthropologist to study this phenomenon as applied throughout South America. His research provided evidence that the artificial decolouration of feathers on living birds was achieved by using various animal substances: frog blood; the milky secretion from the skin of a small frog, or toad; the fat of *pirarara* fish. In other areas, the natives used vegetable substances, such as unguents of dyes like annatto *(Bixa orellana).*[1] The active substances causing the colour change are often applied to the wounds following the plucking of the feathers. In some cases, however, they are mixed in with the bird's diet. Therefore, two basic techniques are in use: cutaneous and oral. This illustrates that tapirage has many aspects and forms, but the result is fairly similar in all cases. It is used mainly on parrots and macaws, which then no longer produce their natural green or blue feathers, but rather yellowish-orange ones, at times with red spots that look as if they had been painted on by hand (cf. plate 15).

In his analysis of tapirage, Métraux (1928: 182) published a map locating 27 Amerindian populations who were known to have used this technique. Three regions stand out: the northern Amazon, between the Guianas and today's Venezuela; the Brazilian coast; and the border region between today's Brazil, Bolivia and Paraguay. Métraux takes the view that tapirage seems to have had its centre of diffusion in today's French Guiana, mainly in the regions inhabited by Arawak-speaking groups, or those subject to their influence (Métraux 1928: 190). If Métraux's map was updated today, indicating the groups where tapirage is practised, the findings would be scanty since only a handful of tribes are known to still use this technique. This decline is partly attributable to the fact that many tribes no longer use feathers in their rituals or to express their identity. The following case studies will look at two groups that still practise tapirage. These cases illustrate not only two different techniques but also differences in the valorisation of the decoloured feathers.

Why feathers? Why tapirage?

But let us first have a look at the importance accorded to feathers by Amazonian indigenous peoples. In his work on Amazon feather art, Schoepf specifies that "to be 'genuinely human', the Indians have to decorate themselves with feathers, they have to become feathered beings – in other words, to be 'genuinely human', they need to use feathers to express themselves" (1985: 8). Amazon Indians chose birds because, being entirely covered in feathers, they lend themselves extremely well to the clear representation of diversity in their external appearance. Feathers can therefore be considered the best means of classification, and that is crucial for determining identity. The indigenous preference for feather ornaments is therefore an essential element of their cognitive system. This explains why the use of feathers is so widespread in the Amazon Basin. Indeed, if there is such a thing as a 'typically Amerindian' artistic and ideological expression, then it is surely feather art (Schoepf 1985: 8).

What is the reason for this predilection for feathers? Is it because of their unique polychromatic nature? This does indeed make them more useful than any other material for creating visually appealing ornaments. Or is it because they can be used to create both great uniformity and dramatic contrasts? This allows them to be an excellent agent for expressing personal, social or group identity. Feathers are thus ideal components for creating an ideal human being. A bird starts life as a macaw, parakeet or parrot: having the plumage of a macaw implies being a macaw, and also having the behaviour of a macaw. In contrast, a human being is not born as a Mehinaku, an Enawenê Nawê or a Kayapó. In the eyes of the Indians, cultural and social identity is not a given; it is not determined biologically and it is not inbred. A human being is born simply as a human

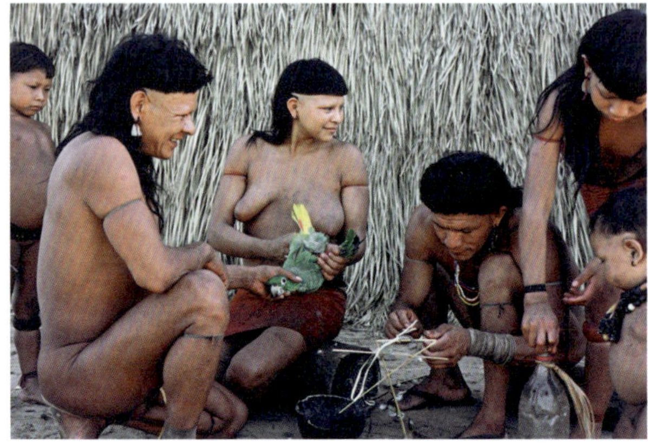

Fig. 1 Enawenê Nawê fixing a frog on a wooden frame, in order to withdraw the amphibian's secretion of milky fluid and then apply it to the small holes in the skin of the birds. Photo: Serge Guiraud, 2002, Courtesy of Jabiru productions.

being, and their real identity will only be determined later by a series of mechanisms specific to the society in question. Someone becomes a Kayapó by progressing through a succession of spiritual phases such as name-giving, learning the Kayapó language, initiation, membership of particular age grades, position in the system of relationships, and so on – and of course by using a haircut, body decoration or body painting to model their appearance.

It is in this concept of someone modelling their appearance that feather ornaments often play an eminent role, for the aim of wearing colourful attributes is not only to beautify but also to display elementary cultural ideas. To understand the essential reality of feathers, it is necessary to turn to the indigenous world of cosmology, ideology and myth. In other words, feathers are key elements in creating the ideal image that the indigenous groups possess, not only of themselves but also of their relationship to others, whether human or non-human. Tapirage, then, is often used to be different from the 'others', emphasising the identity of the group as a separate people.

The Enawenê Nawê

One group that still invests in tapirage today are the Enawenê Nawê, a small Arawak-speaking group that migrated from the north and eventually settled in the border region between today's Brazil and Bolivia in around 500 AD. In their villages, the Enawenê Nawê keep tame parrots and macaws, as well as eagles, plucking their feathers periodically. But only the parrots are subjected to tapirage. According to Mendes dos Santos (2006: 119–120), the Enawenê Nawê make a reddish liquid for this purpose, combining plant fibres with a transparent secretion from the skin of the poison dart frogs, which they keep carefully in glass bottles and feed regularly. The frog is fixed to a wooden cross and then its back is rubbed with a stick (fig. 1). The amphibian's natural reaction produces a secretion of milky fluid which is collected and mixed with other substances. This preparation is applied to the small holes left in the skin of the birds after their feathers are plucked. Thus, when the feathers grow back they are no longer green with a red spot in the centre, but golden yellow with a vermilion spot.

It is mainly during the major annual fishing rituals connected with the *yãkwa* ceremony that the Enawenê Nawê go in search of parrots in remote regions. They capture young birds from their nests, bring them back to the village and raise them with great care, weaning and nurturing them. The concept of nurture and weaning *(enawetene),* which applies both to breastfeeding infants and weaning parrots with cooked and sometimes masticated food, has the same root as the Enawenê's self-designation (Nahum-Claudel 2018: 191). The parrot has a special place in the mythology of the Enawenê Nawê as one of the sky gods. The special link between the birds and the spirit world is evoked when a tamed parrot is buried. The burial takes place in the hut, below the perch where the bird used to sleep at night. In this respect it parallels the funeral ceremony of the villagers, who are also buried beneath the place where their hammock used to hang. Only humans and parrots have the privilege of being buried inside the hut; other domestic animals are buried outside (Mendes dos Santos 2006). The Enawenê Nawê also believe that, as with humans, one of the components of the parrot's soul is destined for the celestial region of the universe, where the bird is reincarnated in its earthly form; there it will live with the gods of its former owner's clan. After the owner dies, in his capacity as a celestial divinity he will go and find his parrot in the celestial village, where he will be able to look after it and use it again. According to some of the Enawenê Nawê, parrots were 'made' by the celestial divinities and belong to them.

Like the other Amazon natives, the Enawenê Nawê use feathers in their ornaments not only for aesthetic reasons but also to express their identity. They make two types of head ornament. The golden yellow feathers that are the product of tapirage are used for only one specific type of headdress – the other is made from the feathers of two other types of bird reared in captivity: macaws and certain species of eagle. The ornaments made of golden yellow feathers are worn in all the main communal ritual dances (fig. 2). According to the Enawenê Nawê, the mythical hero Wadare is the origin of this crown. It is associated with the sun, which was created by humans. While discussing the ornaments made of golden yellow feathers in imitation of the sun, an Enawenê Nawê man said they wear these feathers "so that the sun does not forget that we are the ones who created him" (Mendes dos Santos 2006). Its colouring is a symbolic representation of the daily solar cycle, and the feathers in the centre of the headdress, whose nuclei are redder, symbolise the warmer midday sun (Rodrigues de Souza 2011: 43).

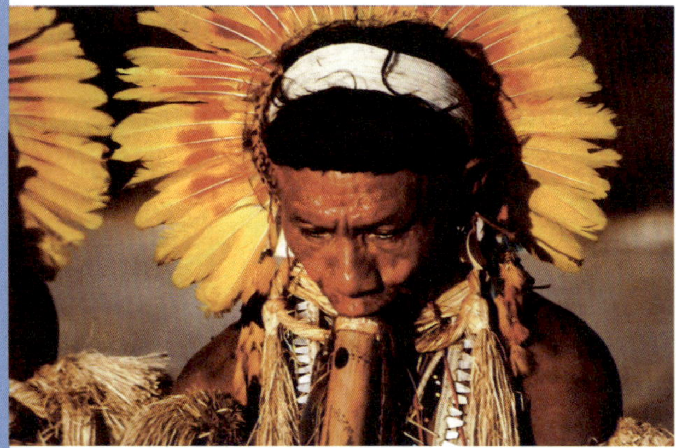

Fig. 2 Enawenê Nawê man dancing with the sun-diadem headdress, made with feathers that have been decoloured following the tapirage process. Photo: Louis Fernandez, 1992.

Fig. 3 After plucking the feathers on the chest and legs, the skin of the blue-and-yellow macaw is rubbed with a mixture of substance of herbs and liquid. Tapirapé. Photo: Gustaaf Verswijver, 2011.

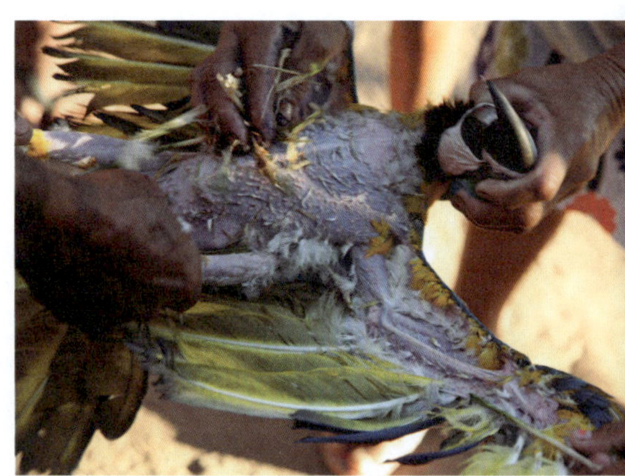

Since time immemorial, the Enawenê Nawê have bartered with their northern neighbours, the Rikbaktsa, who are renowned for their refined feather artwork. Before the first friendly contacts between the Enawenê Nawê and the Brazilians in 1974, the Rikbaktsa were their main source of consumer goods such as metal objects, which the latter could easily obtain because they were in regular contact with Brazilians. Yet the Enawenê Nawê were interested mainly in parrots and macaws. Interestingly, the decoloured feathers that the Enawenê Nawê obtain by tapirage are not exchanged with neighbouring tribes. This is partly due to the special link between the group and their parrots, and hence their plumage as well. Moreover, these precious yellow feathers are a vital component of the identity of the Enawenê Nawê as a separate people, and from that point of view it is logical that they should not trade the feathers that distinguish them from their neighbours: they do not want others to appropriate a fundamental element of their group identity.

Although the Enawenê Nawê still practise tapirage, relatively few visitors or researchers have witnessed or documented the actual application. For that matter, the same is true in the case of the Tapirapé, a Tupi-speaking group that lives near the middle course of the Araguaia River. In the 1930s, this group was studied by eminent anthropologists such as Herbert Baldus and Charles Wagley. Remarkably, the tapirage process was not mentioned in the main oeuvres of either scientist, although it was indeed practised – as it still is today. This illustrates that tapirage is not always immediately noticeable, partly because it is often carried out in the private sphere, and partly because the process itself is often over in an instant. I have witnessed the treatment of a blue-and-yellow macaw *(Ara ararauna)* among the Tapirapé; the inner side of the bird was quickly plucked after which the skin was rubbed with a previously prepared substance (fig. 3). The whole process took less than three minutes and, apart from the incessant shrieking of the macaw, passed by almost unnoticeably. If I had not been on the spot right then, it would have happened without me taking any notice of it.

The Xinguanos

The southern section of the Xingu Indigenous Park is home to eleven indigenous groups which, despite their linguistic diversity, hold many social and ideological features in common. Due to their cultural homogeneity, these different indigenous peoples are usually called Xinguanos. For several decades now, Xinguano groups have received particular attention from anthropologists, which means that the Upper Xingu Basin area is among the best studied in the Amazon region.

No researcher has ever mentioned the phenomenon of tapirage among the Xinguanos. However, as we have seen in the case of the Enawenê Nawê and the Tapirapé, the fact that it is not noticed doesn't mean it is not practised. And there is a further factor that helps us understand why this practice of tapirage is not always mentioned, even if it is applied. This has to do with the unobtrusiveness of the practice itself. There are certainly cases where tapirage is achieved by adapting the diet of pet birds. This process is undoubtedly much less conspicuous and can indeed go unnoticed.

This seems to be the case in the Xinguano area. While doing field research among the Mehinaku – one of the eleven Xinguano peoples – I was asked why I intended to conduct some brief research among the Enawenê Nawê, too. I referred to my interest in the tapirage techniques. Much to my surprise, my Mehinaku informants mentioned they also practise tapirage, and that they call it *uhipiutaj.* The linguist Angel Humberto Corbera Mori told me that the Mehinaku use the term *uhipiutaj* to refer to someone's skin changing to a whiter colour when they die. The effect of *uhipiutaj,* Mori added, is "very similar to the appearance of vitiligo". Since vitiligo is a condition that causes the patchy loss of skin colouring, whereby the skin loses its pigment cells, the parallel with the Mehinaku use of the term *uhipiutaj* for tapirage is manifest: the term reflects exactly what is involved in the tapirage process.

Among the Mehinaku, tapirage consists of persistently feeding river turtle eggs to the parrot or macaw throughout the entire dry season. The result is already visible by the end of the season: some of the newly emerging feathers are yellowish instead of the usual green for parrots (fig. 4).[2] During my stay in the Mehinaku village, a family owning two orange-winged Amazon parrots *(Amazona amazonica)* was feeding their pet birds with the aforementioned eggs, and some of the secondary remiges were consequently turning yellow.[3] The owner said that if he were to continue feeding river turtle eggs to these birds, their rectrices would also be affected. He also added that the effect was irreversible, so that after the altered feathers were removed, those that followed would retain the same yellowish colouring.

When inquiring as to why I had never heard of tapirage among the Mehinaku or their neighbours, the Mehinaku leader Yahati told me that "none of the researchers who worked among the Xinguanos noticed it because they all think the birds are just like that." In other words, the researchers simply didn't realise that the feathers of some pet birds had been altered. This can partially be ascribed to the lack of interest shown by many anthropologists in the material expressions of the cultures they study. As a result, such studies among the Xinguano groups are rare, and at times merely involve a presentation of the various objects manufactured, used or circulated by the Xinguano peoples (e.g. Baer 1960; Hartmann 1986a, 1986b). In other words, no real effort is made to try to understand "the social life of things" – to echo the expression used by Arjun Appadurai (1986) in his brilliant homonymous essay.

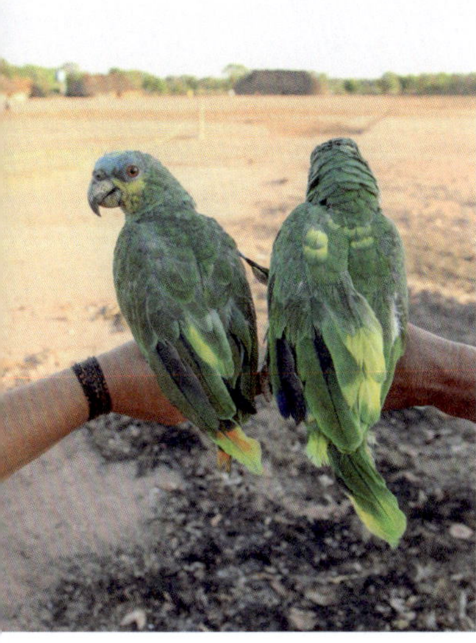

Fig. 4 Two parrots that have been put on a diet of turtle eggs. Following this tapirage technique, the colour of the wing feathers is already turning yellow. Photo: Gustaaf Verswijver, 2012.

According to the Mehinaku, tapirage is an ancient practice. And this may well be the case, especially if we consider that the Arawak-speaking peoples are said to be responsible for the spread of tapirage techniques in South America (Melatti 1972). The Mehinaku state that other Xinguano groups, such as the Kamaiurá, also apply this technique. I contacted Rafael de Menezes Bastos and Mark Münzel, both anthropologists who did extensive research among the Kamaiurá from the late 1960s onwards. Rafael Bastos informed me that he had never heard of tapirage among the Kamaiurá. Mark Münzel added that he had heard Dr Noel Nutels[4] mention tapirage, and that he himself "always thought tapirage was done by the Kamaiurá". Münzel's reaction shows that the Kamaiurá possibly do practise tapirage, but that no one ever paid any attention to it because no one really focused on the pet birds.

Except for the fact that no anthropologist has ever mentioned these practices in the Upper Xingu region, the question remains as to what the Mehinaku and other Xinguano groups do with the altered feathers. Why do these groups resort to tapirage? And this is where the Mehinaku are different from the other groups mentioned above. In their case, the altered feathers are only used in restricted circumstances. In fact, ornaments made with decoloured feathers are rarely worn during the final phases of major ceremonies when members of different Xinguano groups unite; their use is limited to intra-village ritual activities. Another restriction on the use of decoloured feathers among the Mehinaku is that only the owner of the treated bird can use its feathers.

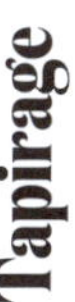

The Mehinaku use of tapirage stands out as noteworthy, because why resort to it if little value can be placed on the result? In other words, why would the Mehinaku waste such tasty river turtle eggs – a highly-prized food – on a pet bird if the aim is not to achieve something worthwhile? To understand this, we have to turn to a basic principle in Xinguano settings. Indeed, as Suhrbier (2010: 78) rightfully mentioned, during large Xinguano intergroup celebrations, the visual affirmation could be translated as "we are all the same". During these intergroup meetings and ceremonies, it is unequivocally the homogeneity of the participating communities which is emphasised rather than their otherness. This suggests that it is this very urge for homogeneity in the Upper Xingu river area which made the Xinguanos lose their interest in the practice of tapirage, i.e. it almost made tapirage redundant. Yet it is still practised. But then why do these groups still invest in manipulating a bird's plumage if the decoloured feathers obtained in this manner can essentially only be used during some local activities? The answer lies in the trading ceremonies that can be organised at both an intra- or intervillage level, and which are, just like the joint performance of major ceremonies, among the key elements of Xinguano homogeneity. As Yahati Mehinaku told me, "when *uhipiutaj* (tapirage) is done in this village, a Kuikuro, Kamaiurá, Kalapalo comes and sees this bird. That person will think 'I'm going to buy that bird from him.' Then he speaks to the owner, 'let's exchange'. So you will receive snail shells because for us snail shells are like money". Yahati's statement indicates that the real value of tapirage in Xinguano societies today lies in upgrading the value of the pet bird with respect to intergroup trading, more than the attention paid to the decoloured feathers per se.

This essay has shown not only that feathers are used to mark identity, but also that this aspect of tapirage adds an additional dimension to a group's wish to distinguish itself from the others. Tapirage is still actively practised in some corners of the Amazon basin, even if it is not always noticed by trained researchers or occasional visitors.

1 For more details about the use of annatto, see Arno Holl's article on the topic in this volume.

2 In the case of a blue-and-yellow macaw, the blue wing feathers also become yellowish.

3 Not to be confused with the *Amazona aestiva xanthopteryx,* which has yellow wing coverts on the bend of its wing. Remiges are the flight feathers of a bird's wings. The rectrices are the larger feathers in a bird's tail.

4 Dr Nutels was a physician who worked extensively in the Upper Xingu river area from 1948 onwards.

References:

– **Appadurai, Arjun. 1986:** *The Social Life of Things. Commodities in Cultural Perspective.* Cambridge: Cambridge University Press.

– **Baer, Gerhard. 1960:** *Beiträge zur Kenntnis des Xingu-Quellgebietes.* Basel: Philosophisch-Historische Fakultät.

– **Berthier, Serge. 2016:** 'Le Tapirage, l'Art de Personnaliser les Oiseaux'. In: *Pour la Science* 460. 40–46.

– **Hartmann, Günther. 1986a:** *Xingú. Unter Indianern in Zentral-Brasilien.* Berlin: Reimer.

– **Hartmann, Günther. 1986b:** *Keramik des Alto Xingú, Zentral-Brasilien.* Berlin: Museum für Völkerkunde.

– **Mendes dos Santos, Gilton. 2006:** *Da Cultura à Natureza. Um Estudo do Cosmos e da Ecologia dos Enawene-Nawe.* Universidade de São Paulo: Ph. D. Thesis.

– **Métraux, Alfred. 1928:** 'Une Découverte Biologique des Indiens de l'Amérique du Sud. La Décoloration Artificielle des Plumes sur les Oiseaux Vivants'. In: *Journal de la Société des Américanistes* 20. 181–192.

– **Nahum-Claudel, Chloe. 2018:** *Vital Diplomacy. The Ritual Everyday on a Dammed River in Amazonia.* New York: Berghahn Books.

– **Rodrigues de Souza, Edson. 2011:** *Sociocosmologia do Espaço Enawenê Nawê.* Universidade Federal da Bahia: Ph. D. Thesis.

– **Schoepf, Daniel. 1985:** *L'Art de la Plume. Indiens du Brésil.* Genève: Musée d'ethnographie.

– **Suhrbier, Mona. 2010:** 'Feather Headdress. Kamayura, Brazil, Upper Xingu River Reservation'. In: Sibeth, Achim (ed.): *Being Object, Being Art.* Frankfurt am Main: Weltkulturen Museum. 78–79.

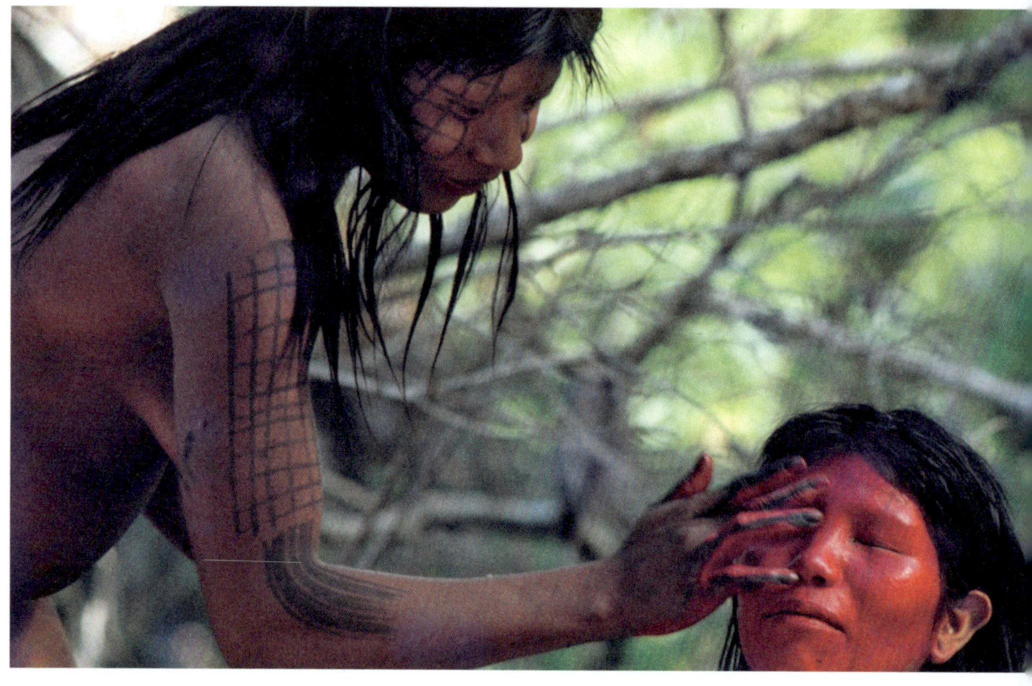

REDSKINS, CHEDDAR AND THE LIBIDO

Bixa orellana Conquers the World

Arno Holl

Fig. 1 In the forest. Tojti paints Wapu-res face with red 'annatto' paint. Kayapó Mekrãgnoti, Pará, Brazil. Photo: Gustaaf Verswijver, 1978

> Mouse was the first owner of urucu, which he made from blood. He caused himself to bleed profusely, collected the blood in a gourd, and covered his body with it, thus teaching the Yanomam the use of red body paint. Is urucu not red? First he rubbed his hands together with the blood before continuing with the rest of his body. From the blood he also made seeds, and that was how he caused the urucu shrubs to appear in the gardens. From the blood he created the urucu shrubs. He was the owner of urucu, which he made from his blood. When it dried and he was transformed into an animal his blood remained scarce. (Wilbert and Simoneau 1990: 209)[1]

This Yanomami myth tells of the origin of a special plant. Its wild form apparently originates from northern South America, from where, now domesticated, it spread to the south, and northwards as far as Mexico. Everywhere the three to five meter tall bush acquired great importance, was cultivated, gave birth to myths, and was attributed all kinds of properties (fig. 2). What is of interest here is that it was the red dyestuff contained in its seeds, which was primarily used for body painting, which made it so popular (fig. 1). This body painting was so widespread that it forms the origin of the term 'redskins'. Columbus's journal compares the actual skin colour of the indigenous peoples with that of the Canary Islanders, with no mention of a natural red colouring (Casas 2006: Chapter XL). The *Historia General de las Indias* by Francisco López de Gómara describes the source of the colours used by the inhabitants of Hispaniola:

> For war they paint themselves with jagua, which is the juice of a certain fruit, similar to the mimosa, but without the coronet, which makes them blacker than pitch coal, and with bija, which is also a tree fruit whose seeds stick like wax and produce a colour like cinnabar. (López de Gómara 1999: 48)

This sentence pays reference to the two most important sources of vegetable body paints in Central and South America, *genipapo/jagua (genipa americana)*, which to this day is known as *jagua* in Spanish and is used for black, and the small, sticky seeds, from which the colour red is extracted (fig. 3). The name given to this plant by the Caribbean islanders, which López de Gómara renders as 'bija', forms the first part of its botanical name, *Bixa orellana*. The second part refers to the conquistador Francisco de Orellana, who, together with his crew, was the first European to travel down the entire length of the Amazon. Beyond botany, there are a multitude of names: *Urucum* (also *urucu*), from the Tupi-Guarani language in Brazil, and the French derivation *roucou;* in Spanish *achiote,* from the Náhuatl *achiotl;* and the internationally used *annatto,* from a Venezuelan Carib language (Venugopalan et al. 2011: 9f.). 'Orlean bush' is a

Francisation of the name Orellana; in contrast, the English name 'lipstick tree' already points to its industrial usage.

The crew of the Portuguese ships who landed on the coast of today's Bahia (Brazil) in 1500, also commented on the body paint of the otherwise naked inhabitants. Their scribe, Pêro Vaz de Caminha, reported the following in a letter to the king:

> Some of them brought green fruit capsules, from trees, which resembled chestnuts in terms of colour, but were smaller. And they were full with small red grains, which, when one crushed them between one's fingers, produced a strong red colour which they painted themselves with. And the wetter they became, the redder they were. (1500)

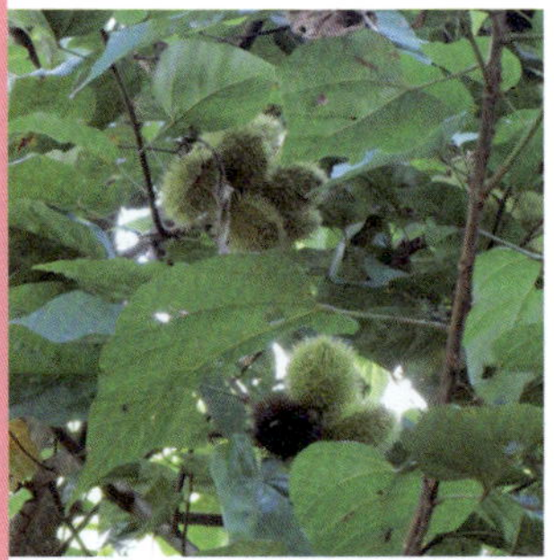

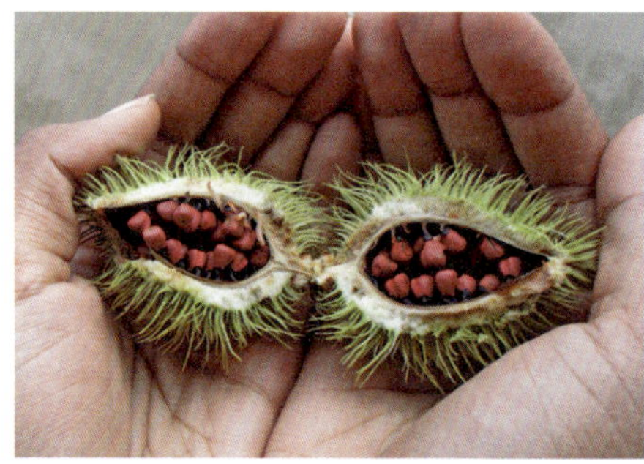

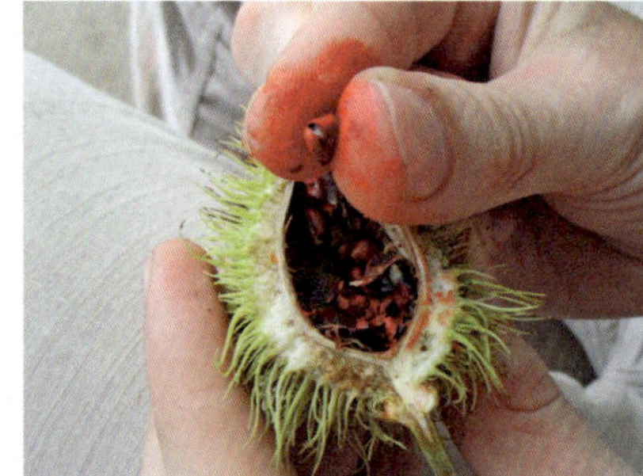

Fig. 2 *Urucum* bush with seed capsules in the plantation of the Kokama village Floresta (Amazonia, Brazil). Photo: Arno Holl, 2015.

Fig. 3 Opened seed capsule with red kernels. Photo: Arno Holl, 2015.

Fig. 4 The red dye is obtained from the shell of the kernels. Photo: Arno Holl, 2015.

The purpose of this repeated painting of one's body amongst the 'Indians' was a subject of speculation for a long time in Europe. The theses ranged from protection from the sun and insects, to pure beautification. Neither of them are wrong in themselves, however it wasn't until the 20th century that ethnographic work was undertaken that also made a closer examination of the social and ritual meaning of the painting.[2] The differences between individual groups and regions is great. However, what is striking is the dominance of the colours black, red, and to a lesser extent, white, as well as the availability of the materials used for the purpose: *genipapo* and charcoal (black), *urucum* (red) and white clay or chalk. The painting can indicate social status, i.e. membership of a clan or a village moiety, reflect momentary moods, enhance beauty and attraction, protect body and spirit and strengthen one's own ethnic identity. In this context, the body understanding widespread in indigenous Amazonia is especially important. Viveiros de Castro (1997: 99) contrasts it to the Western understanding as follows: While in European-North American naturalism, shaped by evolutionary theory, it is his soul that differentiates man from the animals, while the body with its functions and instincts is considered animalistic, the indigenous peoples of Amazonia see it the other way round. People, animals, plants, spirits are all considered, in equal measure, to be persons with souls, which are merely distinguished by their different bodies. In short, Naturalism means outwardly similar, internally different, Animism (or Amazonian perspectivism) means outwardly different and internally similar (Descola 2011: 190). Consequently, according to the indigenous understanding, every species sees itself as human as we are all animated by the same spirit. Thus, who is a person and who is an animal (or spirit) resides in the eye of the beholder, is a question of perspective.[3] What is important here is that 'body' also includes all forms of behaviour, emotions and capabilities which characterise a species. In addition, according to this understanding, no one is born a finished person, including in a physical sense. The human body is something that needs to be created. This is not one single act, but a lifelong, continual process. In the words of Viveiros de Castro, the indigenous body is not a fact but an action. The creation of a human body is the product of different interventions. These vary from group to group, so that consciousness of one's own humanity is strongly connected to the outward appearance of one's own group. Central elements here are body modifications such as the piercing of ear lobes and lips, the cut of the hair, the removal of body hair, ornaments and body painting. That this body, i.e. its humanity, has to be repeatedly confirmed or formed is due to its fragility. A change in spirit is always connected with a change in the body, which is why body modifications generally take place in transitional phases, thus giving outward expression to a person's development. Here Viveiros de Castro speaks of "performed character". In the same fashion that a body can become increasingly human through the adoption of outward features, a transformation into the non-human is also possible. Through the adoption of the behaviour and outward features of a certain animal it is possible to perform a metamorphosis. For a normal person this means the end of their humanity and thus their death. If his fellow men no longer recognise him as human, he no longer belongs to them. The essence of this cosmology is thus the question of how one sees and how one is seen. Religious specialists, frequently called 'shamans', a term which originates from the Tungusic, are normally the only people who can survive such a change of perspective and can reverse it. That means they are capable of entering into contact with other species, including the spirit world, on an equal footing. The non-shaman is only capable of this on very specific occasions: the rituals. Accordingly, participants in rituals are distinguished by especially elaborate ornaments, which is connected to specific animal species or spirits. On the one side, the painting of the body can protect it from the influence of other beings, and thus protect it from an undesired metamorphosis by emphasising its humanity. On the other side, body painting can serve as one of the aids for bringing about precisely such a transformation (Viveiros de Castro 1997: 102–109). This is especially the case in a ritual context, in combination with feathers, furs, claws and certain songs (cf. Brabec de Mori 2013).

Many body paintings are inspired by the appearance of animals, and are named accordingly. Others provide an insight into the mental or social condition of the wearer. However, it is not just the patterns that have meaning here, but also the colours employed. Of interest in this context is the consistently positive connotation of the red *urucum* paint (Nimuendajú 1946: 50f.; Brain 1979: 24), especially in its additional function as protection from illness and evil spirits (Schlerka 2010: 371f.). The predilection for the colour red amongst the indigenous peoples of South America was already noted by early travellers, for example Prince Maximilian of Wied-Neuwied: "Furthermore, they have a special liking for red woollen hats, knives and red handkerchiefs" (2001: 141), or Alexander von Humboldt: "The red body paint is simultaneously the only clothing of the Indians" (2001: 76). The ethnologist Curt Nimuendajú also let his own, more critical attitude towards the omnipresence of the colour red, in this case amongst the Timbira of north-eastern Brazil, show through:

> The Indian himself and everything he owns are more or less red with urucú. Whatever they take hold of turns red, as does anyone living among them [...] The Indians grow irritated if civilized people voice disparaging comments about the use of urucú; any person or article reeking with the pigment is a thing of beauty. [...] Especially when fresh the pigment emits a strong odor which civilized observers identifiy as 'stench', while it delights the Indian's nostrils no less than the red color pleases his eyes. (1946: 52)

On one occasion Nimuendajú met an acquaintance on the riverbank:

> He was carrying a gourd bowl with a handful of urucú seeds, which he mixed with water; then he drank the red liquid, declaring it would give him luck in the chase. He insisted in my taking a few drafts; eagerly overruling my objection that I had no intention of going after game, he informed me that that made no difference: urucú was good for *any* purpose, it was impossible to use enough of it. Whenever I obtained urucú for my collection, I was generally admonished to employ it extensely. (ibid., emphasis in the original)

In many groups, new-born babies, who are considered especially vulnerable as their humanity is not yet consolidated, are painted with *urucum*. The danger of objects can also be lessened by painting them red (Grupp n. d.:39). Amongst the Kayapó of central Brazil red paint means an intensification or vitalization. That is why those body parts, which extend into the environment and communicate with it, are coloured red with *urucum:* forearms, feet and shins, face, especially the eyes (Turner 2012: 493). In this manner the social aspects of the body, and thus the person as well, are strengthened.

The paint is manufactured by mixing the seeds with water or vegetable oil. Early travellers such as Humboldt (2009: 59) or Spix and Martius (1828: 697) also mention the use of animal fats. By this method the red dye is released from the seed casings (fig. 4). After straining or boiling off the water the mass is formed into a ball which can be stored for long periods. For the purpose of painting the hardened mass is moistened with fat or saliva and then applied to the body. In addition to its use for the painting of bodies and objects the addition of *urucum* to food, which colours it orange to red, is also popular. The *urucum* powder used for this is known in Brazil as *colorau.*

However, the plant is not just used for the manufacture of dye, it also has a medicinal significance. In the indigenous and folk medicine of Latin America it is used for the treatment of inflammations, bronchitis, sore throats (Barbosa et al. 2014: 2), liver complaints, venereal diseases, skin problems, snake bites, heartburn, fever, dysentery, diarrhoea, stomach, bladder and prostate afflictions, high blood pressure, high cholesterol, excess weight and renal insufficiency as well as an aphrodisiac (Barbosa et al. 2014: 2; Venugopalan et al. 2011: 17). Leaves, bark and roots are also used in this context. A number of these applications are thematised in a myth from the Runa of the Amazonian region of Ecuador, which can be read in more detail in Swanson (2009: 45–54). Two sisters experience a series of amorous misadventures together, before they meet a man called Machin. In an attempt to make sexual advances to them he invents/creates lice, fleas and various skin diseases in the hope that the sisters will ask him to treat them. Instead, the two girls learn how to free each other of the pests and cure themselves of the illnesses. After escaping from Machin they realise that, actively or passively, they have spoiled their chances with all men and that their human existence no longer has any future. Thus they decide to transform themselves into plants. The elder sister, Manduru, who frequently displayed more maturity and reason, says that her vulva is hairy, and for that reason she will transform herself into Manduru *(urucum),* whose seed pods are hairy. The younger sister Huituc, says that her vulva is hairless, and that is why she will transform herself into Huituc *(genipapo),* whose fruit is smooth and pear-like. The various men that they have met subsequently transform themselves into different species of animal and plant by painting themselves with *urucum* and *genipapo*.

The sister who proved herself to be especially adept in the healing of skin diseases and the warding off of blood suckers transformed herself into *urucum*. Furthermore, it is surely no coincidence that she was the older, physically more mature of the two, after all, a concrete reference is established between the sisters and the plants which they transform into: The 'hairy' *urucum* capsules produce the dyestuff associated with blood. It is also significant that the two most important sources for the dyes used in Amazonian body painting are represented as sisters. The dyes are not seen separately, but in relationship to one another, just as López de Gómara, in his statement quoted at the beginning, mentions both dyestuffs in one sentence. When considering *urucum* as a paint colour, one shouldn't ignore *genipapo,* as both of them are closely related. Amongst the Brazilian Kayapó, the colour contrast is also reflected in the spatial application and the meaning of the colours: As already mentioned, red is applied to the 'peripheral' body parts, in contrast black is applied to the central parts, above all the torso, upper arms, thighs and cheeks. While red stands for the intensification of social contacts, black is a symbol for transitional areas and the suppression of 'animalistic' forces in the body (Turner 2012: 492f.).

A range of applications for *urucum,* as employed in Latin American folk medicine, which can be traced back to indigenous practices, have now been confirmed scientifically. It was found to have antibacterial, antifungal, fever-sinking, antioxidative, antiprotozoal, antimicrobial, malaria curative, blood pressure lowering and spasmolytic characteristics, as well as being effective against gonorrhoea, free radicals, radiation, staphylococci, snake venom, hepatitis and E. Coli; furthermore the plant plays a role in cancer research (see Barbosa et al 2014: 8; Venugopalan et al. 2011: 17ff.).

The oil and water soluble carotenoids Bixin (red) and Norbixin (orange) are extracted from the seeds, now also industrially, and used to colour cheese/cheese rinds (amongst others Cheddar, Red Leicester, Mamirolle, Reblochon), popcorn, snacks, biscuit fillings, sauces, dressings, juices, liqueurs, pudding, tomato sauces, cornflakes, smoked fish, butter, mayonnaise, sausages, pet food, soaps, textiles, leather, plasters, pill coatings, and not least, lipstick (Barbosa et al. 2014: 2; Venugopalan et al. 2011: 14ff., 19). Barbosa et al. even go as far as to say

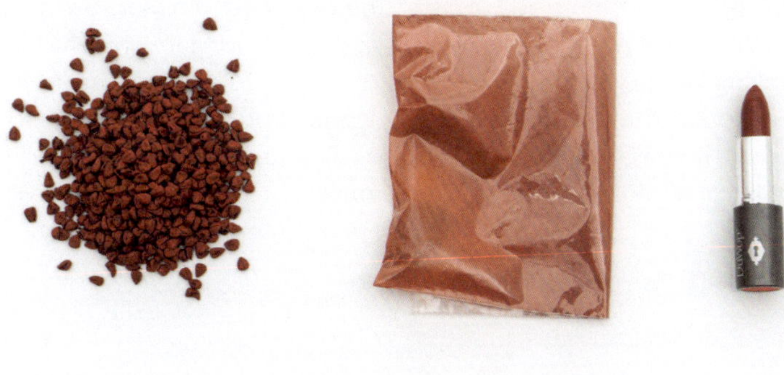

Fig. 5 l. to r. Seeds of the *urucum (Bixa orellana);* packet of *achiote* (dyestuff made from *Bixa orellana*) collected in Cuzco (Peru) in 1972 by Mark Münzel; lipstick, coloured with *Bixa orellana.*

that 70% of all natural dyestuffs consumed worldwide are obtained from *Bixa orellana L.* (2014: 1). The importance of *urucum* for the cosmetic industry is such that the plant is also known as the 'lipstick tree' in English (fig. 5). The reason for its popularity for consumer goods is not just its bright orange-red colour, but above all the proven non-toxicity of the plant and its dyestuffs. It is cultivated in various countries in Latin America, Africa and Asia, with an annual production of 14,500 tons in 2011. The biggest producer is Brazil, the biggest exporter Peru, with the main importers being the USA, Europe and Japan (Venugopalan et al. 2011: 13f.).

Thus *Bixa orellana* initially succeeded in attracting people's attention through the oily, fire red colour of its seed casings. And subsequently it was shown that this plant has far more to offer than a pretty dyestuff with a diverse range of applications. One has learnt to value its culinary and medicinal properties. When the Spanish conquerors encountered this knowledge they exported the plant to another tropical colony, the Philippines. From there it spread to India and Polynesia, while being simultaneously introduced into East Africa. The majority of European consumers are not familiar with *urucum/annatto/achiote,* although they have already been eating it for 200 years, primarily in the form of dairy products coloured with it. It has even been called the 'poor man's saffron' (Venugopalan et al. 2011: 14). Thus, a seemingly long journey has led from the body painting of the indigenous peoples to the food and pharmaceutical industry. However, at the latest, the journey comes full circle with lipstick. After all, what is colouring of one's lips red if not body painting, which, in addition to all its cosmological meanings, also serves to make the wearer more attractive?

1 Myths told by Buushimë, recorded by Bruce Albert.
2 E.g. Seeger 1975, Vidal 2007, Turner 2012.
3 For a critique of Viveiros de Castro's theories see Turner 2009.

References:

— **Barbosa, José Maria Filho et al. 2014:** 'Traditional Uses, Chemical Constituents, and Biological Activities of Bixa orellana L. A Review'. In: *The Scientific World Journal,* vol. 2014, article ID 857292, 11 pages. https://doi.org/10.1155/2014/857292 (29.05.2020)

— **Brabec de Mori, Bernd (ed.). 2013:** 'The Human and Non-human in Lowland South American Indigenous Music'. In: *Ethnomusicology Forum* 22 (3).

— **Brain, Robert. 1979:** *The Decorated Body.* New York: Harper & Row.

— **Casas, Bartolomé de las. 2006 [1875]:** *Historia de las Indias.* Edited by José Miguel Martínez Torrejón. Biblioteca Virtual Miguel de Cervantes. http://www.cervantesvirtual.com/obra-visor/historia-de-las-indias--0/html/d31cc52d-acd9-4776-a069-ee37b963f399_12.html (29.05.2020).

– **Descola, Philippe. 2011 [2005]:** *Jenseits von Kultur und Natur.* Berlin: Suhrkamp Verlag.

– **Grupp, Bernhard. Not dated:** *Unpublished manuscript on the body painting of the Canela-Ramkokamekrá.*

– **Humboldt, Alexander von. 2009 [1862]:** *Reise in die Äquinoctial-Gegenden des neuen Continents.* Vol. 3 (1799–1804). Bremen: Salzwasser-Verlag.

– **López de Gómara, Francisco. 1999 [1552]:** *Historia General de las Indias.* Biblioteca Virtual Miguel de Cervantes. http://www.cervantesvirtual.com/obra-visor/historia-general-de-las-indias--0/html/fef81d62-82b1-11df-acc7-002185ce6064_2.html (29.05.2020).

– **Nimuendajú, Curt Unckel. 1946:** *The Eastern Timbira.* Berkeley: University of California Press.

– **Schlerka, Annemarie. 2010:** *Die Farbe Rot in den Kulturen. Ein interdisziplinärer Vergleich im rituellen Kontext.* University of Vienna: Ph.D. Thesis.

– **Seeger, Anthony. 1975:** 'The Meaning of Body Ornaments. A Suya Example'. In: *Ethnology* 14 (3). 211–224.

– **Spix, Johann Bapt. and Carl F. Ph. v. Martius. 1828:** *Reise in Brasilien: auf Befehl Sr. Majestät Maximilian Joseph I., Königs von Bayern in den Jahren 1817–1820 gemacht und beschrieben,* vol. 2. Munich: Lindauer Verlag. https://reader.digitale-sammlungen.de/de/fs1/object/display/bsb10366760_00001.html (04.06.2020).

– **Swanson, Tod Dillon. 2009:** 'Singing to Estranged Lovers: Runa Relations to Plants in the Ecuadorian Amazon'. In: *Journal for the Study of Religion, Nature and Culture* 3 (1). DOI: 10. 1558/jsrnc.v3i1.36. https://journals.equinoxpub.com/JSRNC/article/view/6131 (04.06.2020)

– **Turner, Terence. 2009:** 'The Crisis of Late Structuralism. Perspectivism and Animism: Rethinking Culture, Nature, Spirit and Bodiliness'. In: *Tipití: Journal of the Society for the Anthropology of Lowland South America* 7 (1). 3–42.

– **Turner, Terence. 2012:** The Social Skin. In: *HAU: Journal of Ethnographic Theory* 2 (2). 486–504.

– **Vaz de Caminha, Pêro. 1500:** *Carta de Pero Vaz de Caminha.* Ministério da Cultura, Fundação Biblioteca Nacional, Departamento Nacional do Livro. http://objdigital.bn.br/Acervo_Digital/livros_eletronicos/carta.pdf (29.05.2020).

– **Venugopalan, Akshatha, P. Giridhar and G. A. Ravishankar. 2011:** 'Food, Ethnobotanical and Diversified Applications of *Bixa Orellana L.*: A Scope for its Improvement through Biotechnological Mediation'. In: *Indian Journal of Fundamental and Applied Life Sciences* 1 (4). 9–31. https://www.cibtech.org/J-LIFE-SCIENCES/PUBLICATIONS/2011/Vol%201%20No.%204/20-2-JLS-Giridhar.pdf

– **Vidal, Lux Boelitz (ed.). 2007:** *Grafismo Indígena: Estudos de Antropologia Estética.* São Paulo: SP, Studio Nobel.

– **Viveiros de Castro, Eduardo. 1997:** ‚Die kosmologischen Pronomina und der indianische Perspektivismus'. In: *Bulletin of the Société Suisse des Américanistes /Swiss Society of Americanists* 61. 99–114.

– **Wied-Neuwied, Maximilian, Prinz zu. 2001 (1820):** *Reise nach Brasilien in den Jahren 1815 bis 1817.* Edited by Hermann Joseph Roths. Vol. 1. Sankt Augustin: Gardez!-Verlag.

– **Wilbert, Johannes und Karin Simoneau (eds). 1990:** *Folk Literature of the Yanomami Indians.* Los Angeles: UCLA Latin American Center Publications.

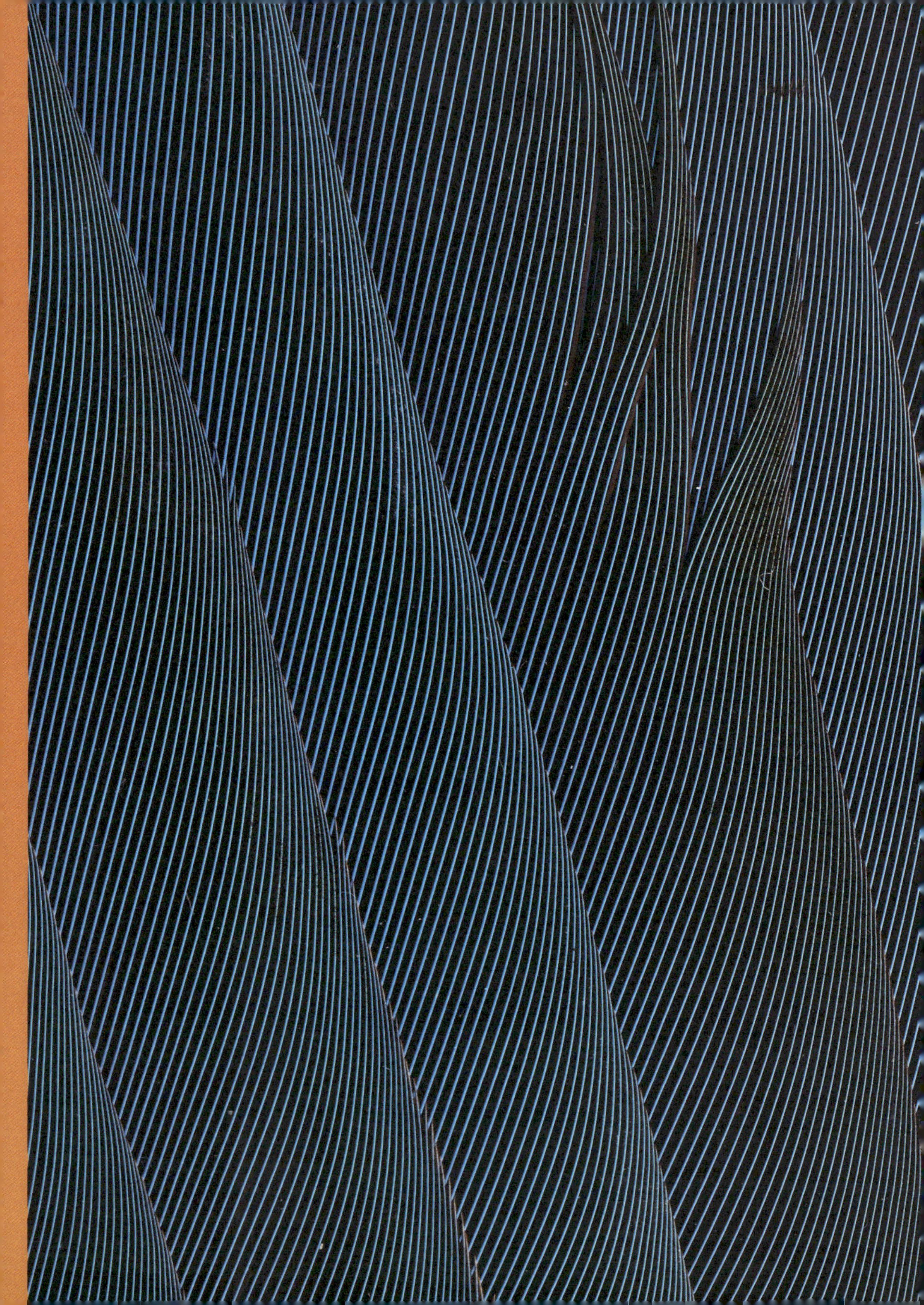

WORLD VIEWS

The headdress *krokrokti* is an image of the world. The centre of the village is occupied by the men's house (red feathers), encircled by the female sphere of the dwelling houses (blue feathers) and finally the transitional area leading to the wild world of the spirits, the forest (white feathers). At the same time this headdress is associated with the radiant sun and the human eye.
It is worn by men and women during specific ceremonies respectively. Cotton, tail and flight feathers of the Ara, eagle feathers. Kayapó Mekrãgnoti, Pará, Brazil. Collected by Luiz Boglar, before 1988.

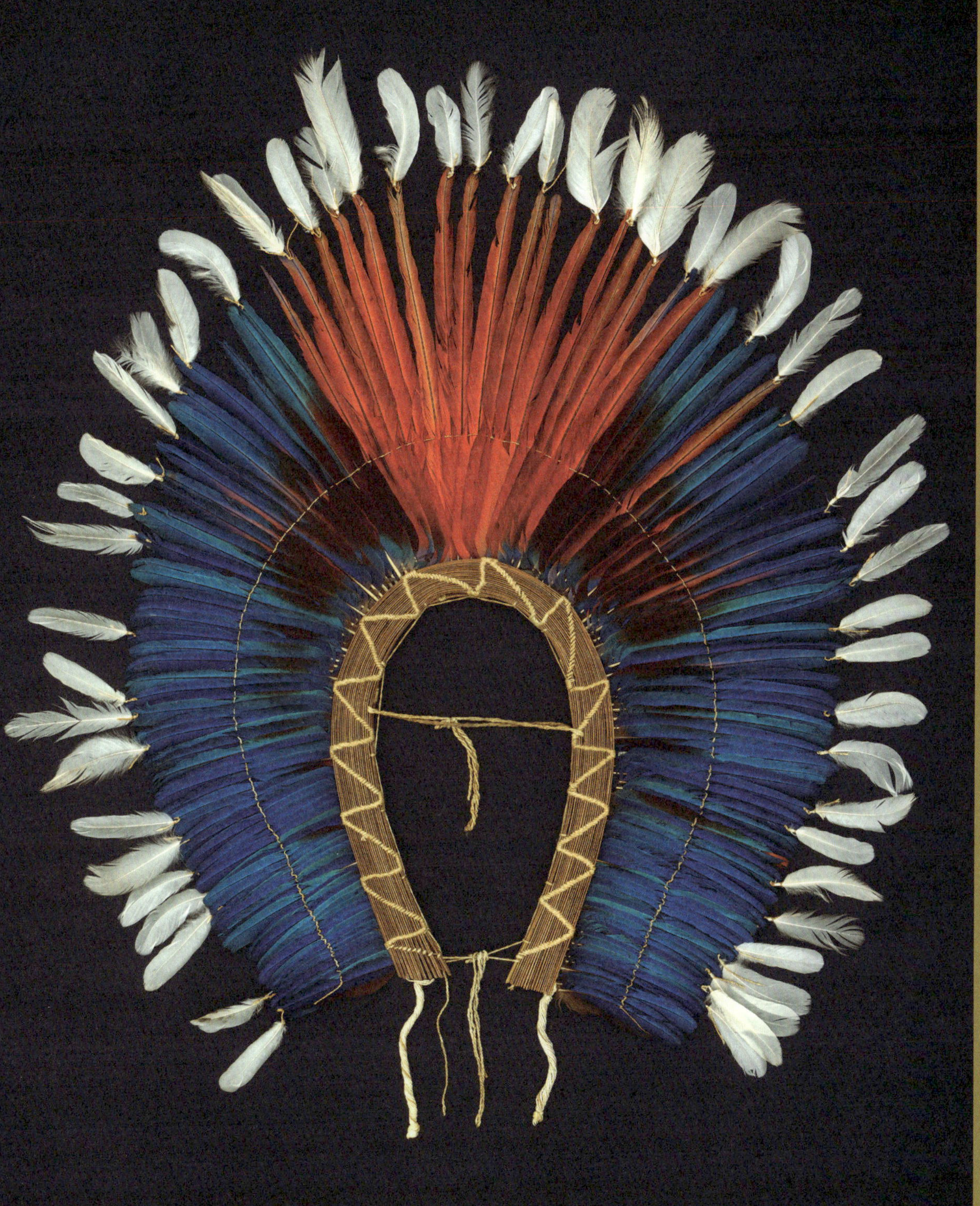

THE NIGHT, THE LIGHT AND THE BLOOD

The Colours of Creation in Polynesia

Matthias Claudius Hofmann

In the beginning, there was nothing. Accounts of the creation of the Polynesian islands start with a description of a seemingly infinite void, a limitless expansion into space. No substance has yet been given to the universe, it has no material quality – and what's more, there is no colour. The cosmos is situated in a deep darkness that envelops everything. There is neither sky nor firmament, neither ocean nor land. And yet the world emerges from this achromatic black nothingness.

At the heart of Polynesian creation mythology is the conception and birth of the world occasioned by gods and other mythical figures. This frequently occurs by means of what feels like an endless sequence of mythical matrimonial arrangements, which lead to the elements conceiving demonic beings, and it is from these that humans ultimately emerge. And so, consequently, people are genealogically linked with the cosmos and the creation (Williamson 1933: 1, 79–80).

Along with the birth of the Polynesian cosmos, colour also makes its way into the world as a meaningful element. Of particular significance here are black, white and red as symbols of the cosmic acts of creation. They establish an allegorical association between mythology, material culture and ritual practice. This essay will thus explore Polynesian colour symbolism, its roots in mythology, and how the different colours relate to each other.

The birth of the cosmos

The significance of this colour triad black-white-red is illustrated particularly well in the creation myth of the New Zealand Māori (Best 1924: 83–89).[1] It holds that the original state of the universe is a colourless nothingness, a primordial chaos from which the elements of the creation are formed: the sky father Rangi und the earth mother Papa. They lie closely intertwined in the seemingly endless night *(pō)*. Together they beget the gods, who remain entrapped within their mother's womb. Soon, however, their children attempt to escape the dark confinement of their parents' embrace: "There was no day and night to them, for all was darkness" (Best 1924: 80). This quest for light is described as the commencement of a birth. First of all, night itself experiences contractions, and then the gods battle their way through a narrow passage on their way to the world of light. This birth of the world is accompanied by incredible pain: when the gods attempt to separate the sky and the earth, they fail one after another because the primal couple are holding on to each other so tightly. Finally, Tāne orders his brother Tū to to cut off their parents' arms. This succeeds in loosening the embrace between the sky and the earth. Tāne lifts the sky up in the air and the gods are born from the night into *te ao mārama,* the 'world of light' (Best 1924:85) (fig. 1). As a distinction emerges between night and day, there is also the contrast between darkness and light, and along with this come the colours black and white. The resulting dualism divides the spheres into a world of gods – darkness/night – and a world of people – the light/day (Henry 1928: 412).

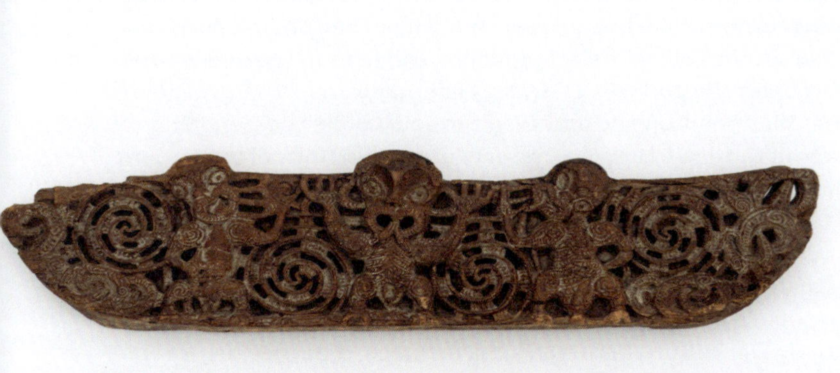

Fig. 1 This door lintel to a meeting house *(pare)* shows the separation of sky and earth. The spirals represent the encroaching light. The painted red clay is faded. Taranaki, New Zealand, Polynesia. Purchased by J. F. G. Umlauff, probably before 1910.

The allegorical use of black and white is supplemented by the presence of the colour red in the act of creation. As the sky and earth are separated, the blood of Rangi and Papa flows into the world as a sacred force. It is manifested in the sky as the red glow at dawn or dusk, which people scrutinise in an attempt to decipher prophecies and omens (Best 1924: 85). The alternation of day and night repeatedly reminds people of the creation myth from the mythical primeval era: we are born from the night, we bleed into this world, and it is in blood that we go back into the night – to death.

The creation of human beings

The blood of the earth mother is manifested as red clay, which is used by the Māori as a colouring agent for painting the carvings of mythical scenes and figures of the ancestors and gods. The red clay represents the reproductive primal force and the supernatural power of the divine sphere *pō* – the source of this otherworldly substance. The god Tāne, appearing here as a 'Polynesian Prometheus' who is associated with light and the colour white thanks to his role during the creation, forms the first woman from this magical red clay: Hine-ahu-one (Best 1924: 121ff.).[2] A very similar if somewhat less abstract version of this motif is related in the Samoan creation mythology. In this case, the seed *(fatu)* is planted in the fertile red clay *('ele)* and the male and female principles are created (Fraser 1892: 176). Just like in New Zealand, the red earth is used as a dye – principally for creating patterns on white barkcloths (fig. 2 and 3). In addition, according to Krämer, the earth is so fertile and "very beautifully red, fat and soft" that it is even eaten (1995: 353).

In the New Zealand myth, Tāne and his beautiful female golem now beget the first human, his daughter Hine-tītama. He takes her too as his wife, and becomes the founding father of the human race. But when Hine-tītama discovers the nature of her incestuous alliance she is appalled and flees to the underworld *(pō),* where she becomes the goddess of death: Hine-nui-te-pō – the 'great lady of the night'. From that point on she gathered the souls of her descendants to join her in the realm of the dead. Here, too, we encounter the trinity of the colours white, red and black, symbolised by Tāne (white), who uses red clay to form the first woman and their daughter, the goddess of the underworld (black). The dualism of night and day is always conveyed via the colour red – which represents blood. Thus the creation of human beings is directly – both causally and in terms of (colour) motifs – linked to the creation of the world, although it narratively inverts the creation. The culture hero Maui, for instance, a particularly prominent figure in Polynesian mythology, attempts to overcome death itself at the end of his life, thereby making eternal life possible for humans. He tries to crawl through Hine-nui-te-pō's vagina in order to reverse the birth process and

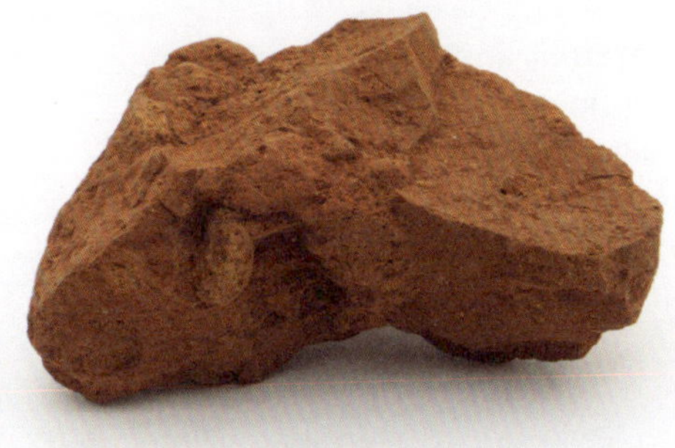

Fig. 2 In Polynesia, red clay *('ele)* is the blood of the earth mother, representing fertility and the female power of reproduction. Samoan Islands, Polynesia. Collected by Gerda Kroeber-Wolf, 1997.

Fig. 3 The white barkcloth made from bark fibres of the paper mulberry tree is dyed with a red clay pattern, which is then accentuated with black colour. *Siapo tasina*. Samoan Islands, Polynesia. Collected by Franz Linke, 1905–1908.

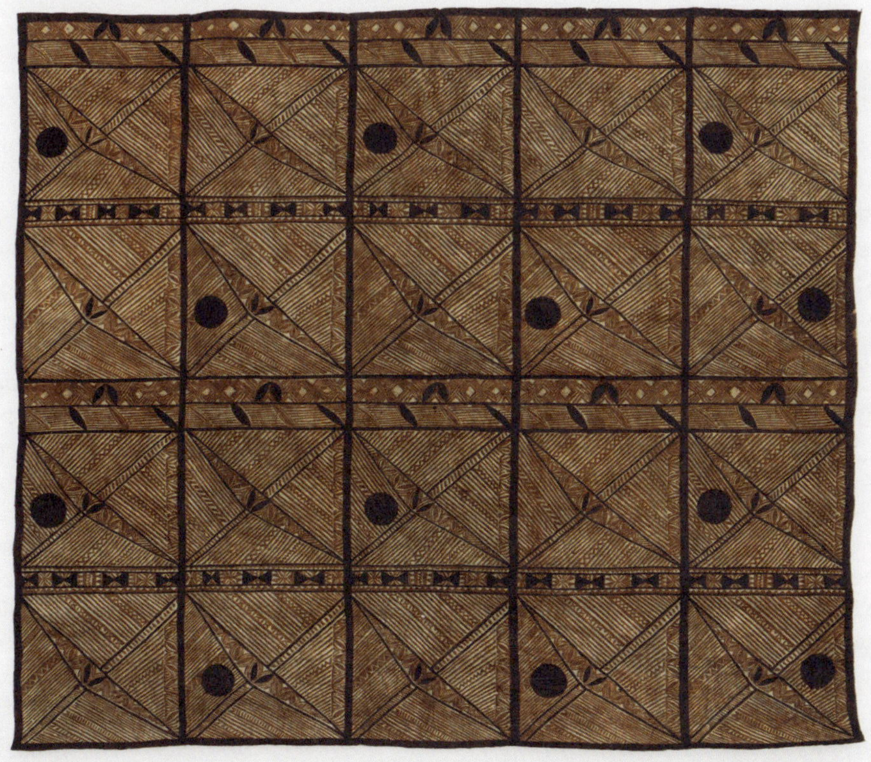

infiltrate the world beyond. But Maui dies in the attempt and has to stay in the afterlife (Orbell 1995: 57). The plan was doomed to failure because death is an inevitable part of the cosmic cycle. Just as people are born into the world in blood from the darkness of the divine night, at the end of their lives they have to return from the light of this world to the eternal night.

This colour symbolism with white, red and black is also apparent in the rituals carried out in Polynesian societies. It is expressed in a particularly dramatic manner with transitional rites, and especially mourning rituals. The deceased are often wrapped in and laid out on white barkcloth and mats. The missionary George Turner describes mourners keening as they rip the clothes from their backs in a frenzied manner and beat themselves on their heads with stones. The blood that flowed from this was described as an "offering of blood for the dead" (Turner 1989 [1884]: 144). Henry, too, explains that several of the women mourners injured themselves with instruments made of shark's teeth and then caught their blood on their white mourning attire, which is bequeathed to the family of the deceased as a "sacred token of love" (Henry 1928: 292). After the mourning rites were complete, the deceased was finally buried in the dark earth, covered with white mats and barkcloths (Turner 1989 [1884]: 148).

The colours of creation

As colours that can be physically perceived, black, white and red are worldly manifestations of a mythical reality, representing the cosmic night, the light of our world and the blood that accompanies birth. The transitional theme is of particular significance because it is always associated with birth, and the colour red symbolises the transition between the world of the living – i.e. the colour white – and the world of the dead – i.e. the colour black. It is possible to draw parallels between this colour symbolism and Victor Turner's ideas about transitional rites (1985), which comprises a phase of separation, transition and then re-integration. The transitional phase, which for Turner is particularly charged with magic, is situated at a half-way point in the dualism between the gods and humans: it enables not only the metamorphosis from one state of being to another but also the use of divine powers in this world. In his groundbreaking essay on the meaning of the colours black, white and red in a ritual context, Turner explains the interaction between these colours as symbolising an archetypal experience of elemental forces. The intention behind representing these forces as symbolic colours in a ritual or mythological context is to be able to control them for social purposes and make them subject to people's will (Turner 1967: 88–91).

In the Polynesian context, volcanic activity is the predominant elementary force. The Polynesian islands extend over an enormous expanse of Pacific Ocean, covering around 50 million square kilometres. Many of the islands are volcanic in origin and actually grew from 'nothing' as undersea volcanoes to join the realm of humankind. Other islands take the form of small coral atolls on the edge of the craters of undersea volcanoes, many of which are still active today. The infinite vastness of the ocean is an element that determines Polynesian geography as well as its cosmology, where it confronts us as creative chaos or the pitch-black night from which the creation of the world emerged.

In a Samoan version of the creation story of the universe, the god Tangaloa (as Tangaloa-a-langi, the personification of the sky) dwells amidst this primordial nothingness, wandering about aimlessly in its expanse until suddenly a rock *(papa)* rises up under his feet from the infinite emptiness of space. He cleaves the rock and couples with it. The cosmic womb becomes pregnant and bears the world. The elements issue from the rocky mother's womb one after the other in a genealogical series (Fraser 1892: 175–177). A version of this myth documented by Krämer conjures up the image of a volcano spitting fire: the burning red earth *('ele'elemū)* weds the brown earth *('ele'ele mea)* and their union produces the towering rock *(papatū)*. The latter marries the rocky earth *(papa'ele)* and their union in turn produces 'the white rock'. He then marries the rocky cave and this partnership produces song, melody, fetidity, the smell of sea water, and ultimately the fresh breeze. Genealogies of this kind usually result in the creation of demonic beings that arise from these natural forces (Krämer 1999: 24, 134f.). Localising this otherworldly setting in the depths of the ocean or within the earth can consequently be associated with the geological creation of the land through volcanic activity.

There is a deep impression of creative but threatening natural phenomena seared into this worldview. The creative energy pours out of the underworld, from inside the earth or deep down in the ocean, erupting into the world as a red glow. Moreover, the fertile volcanic earth establishes a connection to these creative forces. For this reason, in many Polynesian myths the red earth is associated with the female power of reproduction. It is very similar with the birth of human beings as a creative act of transition into life. Both are symbolised by the colour red as 'burning earth'.

Creation as ritual drama

This creative symbolism surrounding the colours black, red, and white was also a feature of the transitional rite that once accompanied aristocratic Samoan weddings; in the late 19th century, however, it was abandoned in the wake of cultural changes brought about by colonial influences and Christian missionaries. The mythical events take place here as a ritual drama. The culmination of the highly elaborate wedding ceremony, which was initiated with a red feather decoration being gifted to the bride's family, was the public ceremonial defloration of the bride. She would be led to the ceremonial ground where the wedding party was gathered. Around her loins she would wear a large, white fine mat with a magnificent edge of red feathers, her forehead would be adorned by pearl-white jewellery made of nautilus shells, and her hair was dyed with red clay (Freeman 1983: 231). In the myth, the creator god Tangaloa splits the rock with which he has coupled, and which subsequently gives birth to the universe. In this ritual drama, the bride represents the female rock (or the earth mother *papa*) in the myth, while the bridegroom is the creator god Tangaloa-a-langi (or the personification of the sky): "The lady [...] lays her hands upon the shoulders of the manaia [the bridegroom] and acts as if she were about to kneel. Hereupon the latter thrusts his index finger upward into the lady's sex organ. Now blood flows upon the mat that is spread out before the manaia [...] Everyone in the village sees the blood running down her legs. The manaia raises his hand and shows the blood on his index finger [...] The noise in the village is great, likewise the joy [...] They dance, loosen their lava lava, embrace and kiss the lady and sob for love" (Krämer 1999: 39).

After the deflowering, the blood is captured on a white bark cloth and presented in public. The white dress mat *('ie sina),* on which the wedding night will later be spent and which is part of the bridal clothing, is subsequently dyed with red clay: a further allusion to people being created from red volcanic earth. These dress mats are called *'ie o le pō* – 'the mat of the night' (Krämer 1995:342; Krämer 1999: 39).

The ceremony establishes a genealogical link between people and the cosmological basis of their ideological existence. Penetrating the hymen and publicly presenting the flowing blood reflects the process of creation, the union between the sky and earth, and anticipates its separation, i.e. the birth of the world. New life emerges from the mother's womb, the night, the creative chaos: 'born' through the blood into the light of the day.

The colours of knowledge

The meanings of the colours in the black-red-white trinity is also expressed in the Māori myth cycle of Tāne and the baskets of sacred knowledge, where they appear in the context of moral philosophy. The god Tāne has to ascend through the twelve heavens in order to retrieve the three baskets filled with sacred knowledge (cf. Best 1924: 99ff.; Orbell 1995: 73–74). Tāne, who, as described above, is associated with light and the colour white, wants to fetch these baskets from the highest point of the firmament and bring them to the people on earth. His opponent is his older brother Whiro, a trickster and evildoer who aspires to gain the sacred knowledge for himself. He is connected to the realm of darkness *(pō),* to which he retreats after his defeat with the aim of harming humanity henceforth. The classical fratricidal battle between Tāne and Whiro – the conflict between good and evil fought on behalf of the human race – is represented here in terms of colour symbolism as the dualism between light and darkness. Ultimately, Tāne wins the baskets of sacred knowledge for human beings. There is also a colour symbolism linked to these baskets: they are *te kete tuauri* (the black basket), *te kete tuaatea* (the white basket) and *te kete aronui,* the third basket, which due to its rather profane contents bears no colour coding in its name. It contains sympathy and empathy, as well as the capacity to bring about peace and a knowledge of the 'fine arts'.

The black basket contains knowledge of ritual songs and of the world of the gods and the creation – this corresponds to the secret knowledge of the priests. The white basket, by contrast, relates to the world of people. It reveals an understanding of evil and the capacity to carry it out, as well as a knowledge of malevolent sorcery, and it stands for dissatisfaction, conflict and dissonance between the people and gods (Best 1924: 103; Moorfield 2003–2020). As a symbol of the knowledge associated with this world, the white basket represents the realisation that discord and conflict are aspects of human nature, which makes them part of life.

The red house

As well as the three baskets, Tāne receives two red stones *(whatu kura),* which are charged with immense divine energy. They enable him to establish the sacred knowledge from the baskets as divine order in the human world. Tāne brings the baskets and the two sacred red stones into the 'house of learning', which is also called the *whare kura* or 'red house', and which he had previously brought down from the sky to the earth. Not only is it the prototype for the Māori meeting houses, it is also a representation of the universe (Best 1924: 104; Orbell 1995: 180). It is a place of learning because this is where sacred knowledge is passed on to the next generation. Moreover, its carvings are painted with the blood – the sacred clay – of the earth mother so that the house does indeed look red. Tāne placed the baskets of sacred knowledge in the rear part of the house. The two red stones mark the east and west sides of the house, designating sunrise and sunset. In this respect they refer to the colour red being linked to the day/night cycle and to the cosmic creation of the world.[3]

The example of the 'red house' shows that the colour red stands for the encounter between the supernatural sphere of the gods and the world of humans. It is here that people can come into contact with the transcendental and find the source of divine energy – symbolised by the black and white baskets of sacred knowledge and the holy red stones. Since the red house depicts the Polynesian cosmos, it is the place where traditions are passed on to the next generation. In contemporary *te reo Māori* this connotation in particular has been retained, so *kura* means not only 'red colour' but also 'treasure', 'school' and 'education course'. The dictionary also gives 'schoolhouse' as the translation of *whare kura* (Ryan 2004: 134).

This example shows that colour concepts are not merely limited to mythology but can also be found in language, rituals and of course in the material culture too. The colours black, white and red symbolise the three elements of the cosmos and their multifaceted meanings.

Fig. 4 Samoan tattoo: O le Tatau (3). Self-portrait. Gelatine print of a photograph by Greg Semu, 1995.

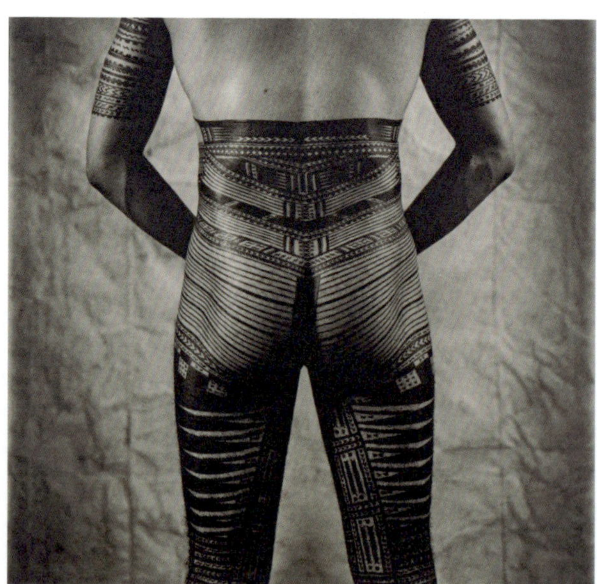

The colour of night

The colour black represents night and darkness, the time before the universe was created, the time before birth. It symbolises the underworld, the afterlife and the world of spirits and gods, but also the unknown and ignorance.[4] In Polynesian material culture it appears in the artistic patterns of tattoos (fig. 4); possessing knowledge of these is connected to the afterlife because culture heroes brought it to people from the underworld. The practice of tattooing is not connected solely with black, however, for as a rites of passage and symbolic transformation it is associated with the colours white and red. During this exceptionally painful and bloody procedure, the tattooing comb is dipped in a black ink that is made from the soot of charred candlenuts *(Aleurites moluccana L.)* and then driven into the skin with a chisel. The blood is wiped away with a white bark cloth. The pale skin is thus marked in blood with the colour of the afterlife. A Samoan tattooing song which is sung during the procedure highlights the meaning of this creative supernatural process as an analogy to women giving birth: "The colour is applied so that it may adhere [...] Like water flows your blood. Ah I feel pity for your condition [...] But this is the custom ages old. You constantly moan, but I sing. Women must bear children, man must be tattooed" (Krämer 1995: 73).

The colour of light

Black is a colour representing the afterlife, in opposition to white. The latter symbolises light and the day, the world of people and this life. It stands for knowledge, but to a certain extent also conflict and resentment. In the material culture, this is primarily apparent in the form of white barkcloths made from the inner fibres of the bark of the paper mulberry tree and in the bleached fibres of dress mats. Jewellery made from whale teeth, white snails and feathers also serve as tokens of dignity, status symbols and festive adornments for ritual occasions. One special feature of festive adornments among the nobility were nautilus shells, which had mother-of-pearl deposits that reflected the sunlight like a mirror; their iridescence would further enhance the status of whoever was wearing them. Interestingly, Krämer (1995: 332) mentions that by the late 19th century, European mirrors were increasingly replacing the mother-of-pearl shells in the ornaments worn on the heads of Samoan nobility. This emphasises once again the meaning of light and thus the colour white as a status symbol.

The colour of blood

The colour red symbolises birth and creation, the transition between a sacred and profane world. It represents blood and burning lava. It alludes to the power of creation, to divine or otherworldly potency, and to fertility and the reproductive powers of nature. In this respect it also stands for pain and violence. Red represents sacred governance, tradition and passing on knowledge. It is the divine element among the human race, and it allows them to make contact with the divine.

As explained above, red is manifested in the fertile red clay, but it is particularly apparent in the scarlet feathers of certain bird species. These were accorded an immense significance, and were regarded as being "among the most sacred natural products and seemed to have the property of activating those objects to which they were attached or which they covered" (Kaeppler 1998: 239). As early as the late 18th century, Georg Forster vividly described the high value accorded to red feathers by Polynesians: "A single little [red] feather was a valuable present, much superior to a bead or a nail, and a very small bit of cloth, closely covered with them, produced such extatic [sic] joy in him who received it, as we might suppose in an European, who should unexpectedly find the diamond of the Great Mogol" (Forster 1986: 383).

In a myth from the Society Islands, the creator god Tangaroa himself appears as a feathered anthropomorphic creature, who creates the world by shaking off his red feathers while his blood flows into the heavens and becomes the red sky at dawn and dusk (Henry 1928). Garments and prestige objects which were decorated with these sacred red feathers would place their wearers – the ruling classes and the nobility – in a relationship with the gods; they functioned as symbols of sacred governance which allowed their wearers to transfer divine energy upon themselves.

The colours of the cosmos

It is only when black, red and white interact that the meaning of the colours is revealed in Polynesian material culture, illustrating the connections to all parts of the cosmos. This colour trinity is found particularly in rituals. The ceremonial Samoan dress mats *('ie tōnga),* for example, with their bright white bleached fibres and blood-red feather borders (fig. 5), are worn over the mystical pitch-black tattooed drawings on people's hips and thighs, depicting a cosmological topography that represents the entire globe of creation and the elements of the Polynesian worldview. In this manner, these objects, which are exchanged as ceremonial gifts for the key transitional rites such as weddings, births, title inaugurations, and funerals, connect people in a creative genealogical association with the cosmos.

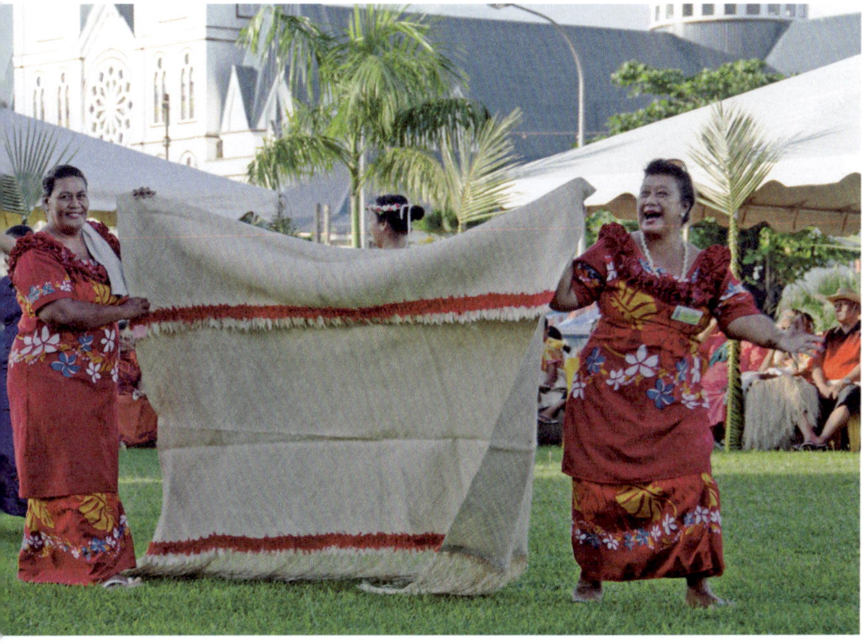

Fig. 5 Ceremonial presentation of fine mats *('ie tōnga)* in front of the government building in Apia, Samoa. Photo: Matthias Claudius Hofmann, 2015.

In Polynesia, the colours black, red and white do not stand for abstract colour concepts – a mere translation of the colour designations would therefore be insufficient. Their symbolic expressiveness as the colours of creation as well as their material nature means that they instead represent the complex whole of Polynesian culture.

1 A retelling of this central myth of the creation of the world and of the human race can be found in Reed's *Maori Myths and Legendary Tales* (1999: 11–21).

2 In Polynesia, Tāne represents masculinity and creation. In New Zealand, siring a child is thus regarded as an imitation of Tāne's act of creation (Orbell 1995: 180). In Samoa, *tāne* merely designates the man or husband (Pratt 1911: 319).

3 The mythological leitmotif of the 'red house' has its counterparts in other parts of Polynesia: In Samoa it is the *fale 'ula,* the residence of the creator god Tangaloa who, according to the myth, hands it over to the ruling family as their seat of government, thereby symbolising the divinely sanctioned nature of their sovereignty (Fraser 1892: 178 and Krämer 1999: 618 footnote 75); and in the Society Islands myth the creator god fashions a temple from his body which depicts a model of the construction of the universe (Henry 1928: 336).

4 Christian missionary work also influenced the traditional colour symbolism. The night is nowadays associated with the devil and with the heathen times before the missionaries came *(pōuliuli)* – as an era marked by lack of knowledge and ignorance – in contrast to the light of the gospel *(ao malama).*

References:

– **Best, Elsdon. 1924:** *Maori Religion and Mythology: Being an Account of the Cosmogony, Anthropogeny, Religious Beliefs and Rites, Magic and Folk Lore of the Maori Folk of New Zealand. Part 1.* Dominion Museum Bulletin No. 10. Wellington: Te Papa Press.

– **Forster, Georg. 1986:** *A Voyage Round the World.* Edited by Robert L. Kahn. Georg Forsters Werke. Sämtliche Schriften, Tagebücher, Briefe vol. 1. 2nd unchanged edition. Berlin: Akademie-Verlag.

– **Fraser, John. 1892:** 'The Samoan Story of Creation. A Tala'. In: *Journal of the Polynesian Society 1 (3)*: 164–189.

– **Freeman, Derek. 1983:** *Margaret Mead and Samoa. The Making and Unmaking of an Anthropological Myth.* Harvard: University Press.

– **Henry, Teuira. 1928:** *Ancient Tahiti.* Based on Material Recorded by J. M. Orsmond. Bernice P. Bishop Museum Bulletin 48. Honolulu: Bishop Museum.

– **Kaeppler, Adrienne L. 1998:** 'Hawai'i: Ritual Encounters'. In: Hauser-Schäublin, Brigitta and Gundolf Krüger (eds.): *James Cook. Gifts and Treasures from the South Seas. The Cook/Forster Collection, Göttingen.* Munich: Prestel. 234–248.

– **Krämer, Augustin. 1902 and 1903:** *Die Samoa-Inseln. Entwurf einer Monographie mit besonderer Berücksichtigung Deutsch-Samoas.* 2 Vol. Stuttgart: Schweizerbart.

– **Krämer, Augustin. 1995:** *The Samoa Islands. An Outline of a Monograph with Particular Consideration of German Samoa, Vol. 2. Material Culture.* Translated by Theodore Verhaaren. Auckland: Polynesian Press.

– **Krämer, Augustin. 1999:** *The Samoa Islands. An Outline of a Monograph with Particular Consideration of German Samoa, Vol. 1. Constitution, Pedigrees and Traditions.* Translated by Theodore Verhaaren. Auckland: Pazifika Press.

– **Moorfield, John C. 2003–2020:** *Māori Dictionary Online.* Online Version of Te Aka Māori – English, English – Māori Dictionary and Index. In: www.maoridictionary.co.nz (01.09.2020).

– **Orbell, Margaret. 1995:** *The Illustrated Encyclopedia of Māori Myth and Legend.* Christchurch, New Zealand: Canterbury University Press.

– **Pratt, George. 1911:** *Grammar and Dictionary of the Samoan Language.* 4th ed. Apia, Western Samoa: Malua Printing Press.

– **Reed, Alexander Wyclif. 1999:** *Maori Myths and Legendary Tales.* Auckland, New Zealand: New Holland Publishers.

– **Ryan, Peter M. 2004:** *The Reed Dictionary of Modern Māori.* 2nd ed. Auckland: Reed.

– **Turner, George. 1989 [1884]:** *Samoa, a Hundred Years Ago and Long Before.* Apia: University of the South Pacific.

– **Turner, Victor. 1967:** 'Color Classification in Ndembu Ritual. A Problem in Primitive Classification'. In: Turner, Victor: *The Forest of Symbols. Aspects of Ndembu Ritual.* Ithaka: Cornell University Press. 59–92.

– **Turner, Victor. 1985:** *The Ritual Process. Structure and Anti-Structure.* 4th ed. Ithaka: Cornell University Press.

– **Williamson, Robert W. 1933:** *Religious and Cosmic Beliefs of Central Polynesia, Vol. 1.* Cambridge: University Press.

BUDDHIST WORLDS OF COLOUR IN TEXT, PRACTICE AND ART

Eric Huntington

One particular Buddhist vision of the world, a maṇḍala, divides the cosmos into five directions (east, south, west, north and centre), each of which is governed by a Buddha of a different colour (blue, yellow, red, green and white). Dividing existence in this way, the five colours become a taxonomic framework for other features of the world that can be similarly analysed, not just its directions but also its landscapes, experiences, elements and more. A specific hue can thus reference almost innumerable topics of doctrine and ritual. In one of the most well-known such systems, that of the Vajradhātu maṇḍala (fig. 1), the colour red recalls the Buddha Amitābha, the western direction in which he resides (the top quadrant of the large, central square in the painting), the lotus symbol of his family, the affliction of desire, and the element of fire. Blue, in turn, calls to mind the Buddha Akṣobhya, the eastern direction (bottom quadrant), the affliction of ignorance, and so on. White indicates the principal Buddha Vairocana at the centre.

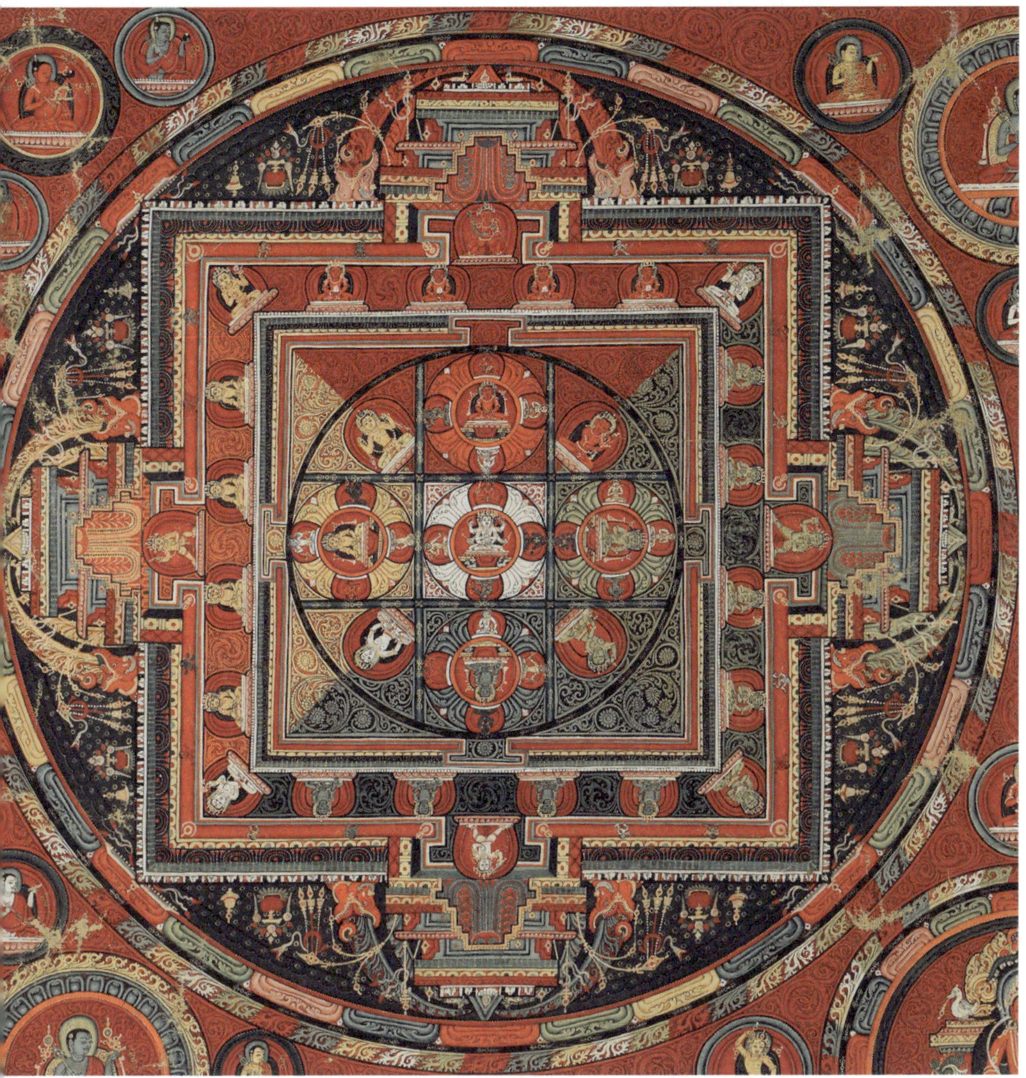

Fig. 1 Vajradhātu maṇḍala. Detail of the upper left quadrant of *Four Maṇḍalas of the Vajravali* Cycle. Ewam Choden Monastery, Tsang Provice, Central Tibet; 1429–1456. Pigments on cloth. Collection: Rubin Museum of Art, C2007.6.1 (HAR 81826).

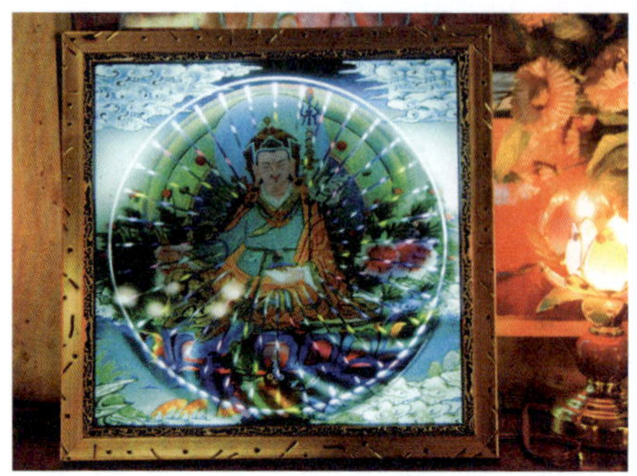

Fig. 2 *Padmasambhava* with moving coloured lights. Karma Chokhor Dechen Ling Nunnery, Sikkim, India. Photo: Eric Huntington, 2009.

But these relationships pertain mostly to related maṇḍalic systems, not to Buddhism universally. While in one maṇḍala, green may represent the element of wind, in another, it denotes the element of space (Gyatso 2004: 198–199). In an entirely different mapping of colour to cosmos, blue appears in the south primarily to reflect the blueness of the sky. Much of the significance of colour in Buddhism is context specific, depending on proximate function and convention as much as anything else.

At the same time, colours can also have significance that is deeply grounded in material or perceptual features. In many cultures, gold represents wealth, power and glory because of its rarity, malleability, corrosion-resistance, reflectivity and colour. The Buddha Śākyamuni (also called Siddhārtha or Gautama) is often painted with golden pigments precisely to indicate his special quality in the world (plate 48 and 49), and traditional texts list his golden complexion as one of 32 physical marks of his perfection (Walshe 1995: 441). These anatomical characteristics do not come by heredity or cosmetics, however, but as a result of his good actions, a sign of his moral attainment (Ohnuma 2007: 225).

A rainbow halo around the Buddha can also highlight his accomplishments (plate 48), based on a similarly infrequent and resplendent natural phenomenon. While metallic gold itself can actually be used as a reflective pigment, rainbows are transient and luminous in a way that paint cannot duplicate. Instead, a modern image of Padmasambhava uses rotating coloured lights behind glass (fig. 2). This object creates a far more spectacular impression of variegated radiance than most paintings could, simulating a powerful visionary experience.

Artworks such as these show that colours in Buddhist art are not only symbols or tools for taxonomy, they also participate in varied histories of materiality, technology, ethics and meditation. The examples below further reveal something of this complexity by comparing and contrasting several different theories and usages of colours in Buddhism. Taken as a whole, they suggest that luminosity, hue and materiality are among the key concepts necessary to understand colours. They also demonstrate that complementary historical, technical, ritual and doctrinal approaches are needed to fully appreciate Buddhist experiences and expressions of colour.

Colour binaries and luminosity

Light is a vastly important topic in Buddhism. Among many other things, it is associated with the Buddha's power to illuminate the world with his teachings, and it is often said to emanate from his body. In some sources, his foetus was even said to have glowed inside his mother's womb (Sasson 2009: 57). In other contexts, practitioners may take light sources such as the sun as objects of meditation, seeking visionary experiences (Turpeinen 2019: 133–134). More than bare luminosity, however, the contrast between light and darkness may be understood as a colour system.

Relationships of colour to luminosity go back to the earliest (pre-Buddhist) textual records available from South Asia. The *Ṛg Veda's* hymns (c. 1500 BCE) valorise deities for bringing light, and they explicitly oppose brightness against darkness. Both white and red are seen as bright and can be identified with light, fire and dawn (Elizarenkova 1994: 81). Black and other dark colours describe storm clouds, smoke and night.

Buddhist sources can use even more starkly binary language.[1] An early Tibetan chronicle known as the *Testimony of the dBa' Clan* (c. 11th century) uses terms for white and black to refer to Buddhist and non-Buddhist traditions, marking them as positive and negative (Wangdu and Diemberger 2000: 47n111). *The Mirror Illuminating the Royal Genealogies* (14th century) tells a story of the monk Lhalung Pelgyi Dorje assassinating king Lang Darma, who purportedly threatens Buddhism in Tibet.[2] The monk covers his white horse with black charcoal and wears a reversible black garment so that, when fleeing his crime, he can wash the horse white and reveal the white side of his clothing to disguise himself (Sørensen 1994: 432–434). Changing his appearance helps him evade capture, but it also reveals the dual nature of his action. On the surface, the killing is negative, in that all killing is wrong, but underneath, it is positive, in that it protects Buddhism.[3]

Not all colour binaries arise from contrasting luminosity, however. White and red can be paired based on biological materials, the contrasting male and female sexual fluids of semen and uterine blood.[4] In some understandings of conception, these two oppositional substances combine to form the physical basis of the body (Kritzer 1998). Their binary is thus not only mutually exclusionary

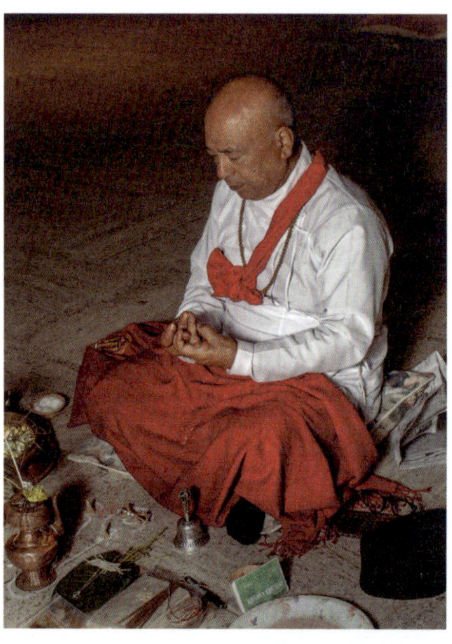

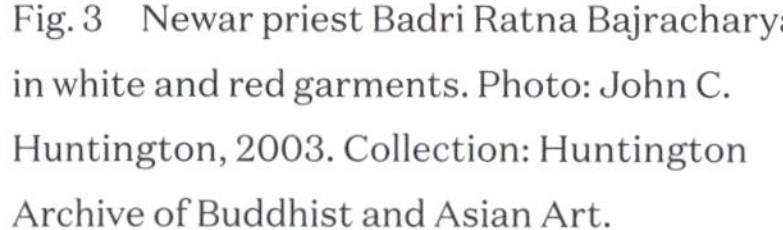

Fig. 3 Newar priest Badri Ratna Bajracharya in white and red garments. Photo: John C. Huntington, 2003. Collection: Huntington Archive of Buddhist and Asian Art.

Fig. 4 Mural of the *abhidharma* cosmos. Punakha Dzong, Bhutan. Photo: Eric Huntington, 2009.

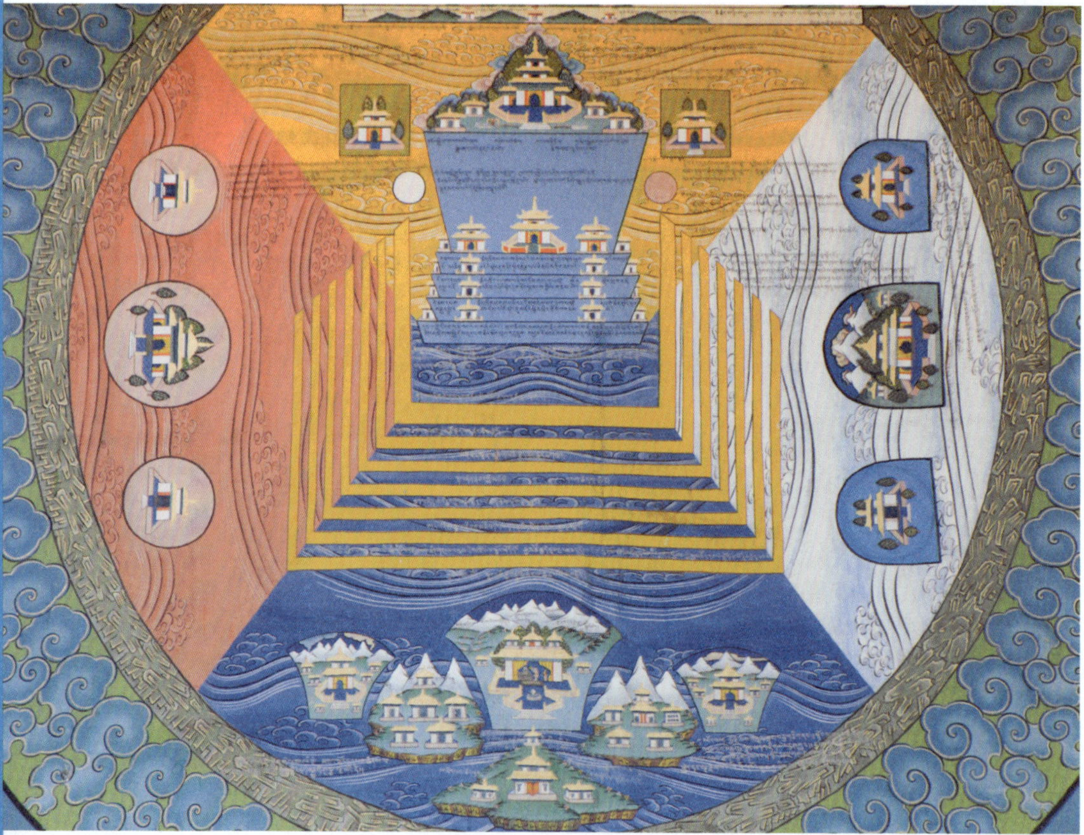

but also complementary. This relationship becomes central in Vajrayāna, symbolising among other things the union of compassion and wisdom in enlightenment. Building on these and other connotations, white and red are frequently paired in the rituals of Newar Buddhism in Nepal, including in the very garments that priests wear (fig. 3) (Locke 1980: 256). The white and red pairing also appears in paintings as the circular sun and moon (top of plate 46 and 47 and upper middle of fig. 4). Far from contrasting light against darkness, both white and red here characterise luminous bodies, as in the *Ṛg Veda*.

Hue, materiality and non-signification

Non-binary colour systems contrast hue in addition to luminosity, sometimes theorising colours based on specific approaches to materiality. Philosophically, colours may be understood as qualities of objects, independent entities or qualities of perception. In the practice of meditation, hues may be subjects in and of themselves, devoid of materiality or symbolism. Alternatively, colours in artwork may depend entirely on real pigments and evoke external objects by design.

The Sanskrit *Treasury of Abhidharma* (4th–5th century) philosophically describes colour in relation to objects of visual perception. Terms for the four primary colours are straightforward *(nīlaṃ, pītaṃ, lohitam,* and *avadātaṃ* approximate dark blue, yellow, red, and bright white), but other terms suggest colour only indirectly by comparison to light, darkness or things (for example, *ātapaḥ* is defined as the radiance of the sun, while *mahikā* describes fog or mist) (Filliozat 1974: 185; Vasubandhu 1998: 32). Going beyond linguistic relationships to ontological ones, another theory suggests that visual perception results from atoms of colour inherent in objects (Masaaki 1988: 37). Although these approaches are debated even within the *Treasury,* they show that it is possible to understand colour as ultimately material and objective.

In contrast, the Pāli *The Path of Purification* (4th–5th century) takes a practice-oriented approach, viewing colours as subjects for meditation. It lists ten *kasiṇas* (objects for complete meditative focus), including the four elements (earth, water, wind and fire), four colours (blue, yellow, red and white), light and limited space (Rhys Davids 1975: 172–174; Buddhaghosa 2010: 117, 162–166). Crucially, the purpose of considering these objects is precisely to avoid calling forth any symbolic meaning beyond the essences of the *kasiṇas* themselves (Shaw 2006: 86–87). Meditation on *kasiṇas* begins with actual physical materials, such as a circle of earth carefully arranged on a supporting cloth, then proceeds to mental images of the objects, and results in mental abstractions that produce calm, joy and, in some cases, insight (Shaw 2016: 125–128). Instructions for making *kasiṇas* emphasise care in not obscuring their essences. Elemental *kasiṇas* must exclude contamination by the four colours, and colour *kasiṇas* deconstruct coloured objects to make them less reminiscent of other things – for example, blue petals are removed from stems and stamens to make them less like flowers (Buddhaghosa 2010: 118, 164).

Meditators may also use pigments as colour *kasiṇas,* perhaps in part because pigments can be understood as colours stripped of objectness. Indeed, in figurative artwork at least, a pigment is precisely something that stops being the object that it once was so that it may represent another. For example, nuggets of gold are pulverised, mixed with a binder, applied to cloth, and burnished to become the Buddha's skin (Jackson and Jackson 1984: 85–87). Unlike in *kasiṇa* meditation, however, the original substances used in artwork are deeply considered. Buddhist texts explicitly encourage using more valuable pigments, such as gold and gemstones, to ensure the quality and efficacy of an artwork and ultimately to generate merit and blessings (Tayé 2012: 239; Skilling 2013).

Treatises on artistic technique describe colourants both in terms of theory and in terms of materiality and mixture. The Sanskrit *Commentary on Image-Making* (14th century) lists six primary colours/pigments (white, yellow, red, dark green, blue-black, and lamp black) in three colour groups related to three universal qualities of *sattva* (bright, cool, virtuous), *rajas* (red, hot, active) and *tamas* (dark, slow, obscure) (Marasinghe 1991: 161; Frazier 2018). Other Indic and Tibetan texts list primary colours not according to any abstract theory but in terms of materials that can be mixed to make other colours, including vermilion, minium, lac, orpiment and indigo (Jackson and Jackson 1984: 91; Nardi 2006: 125–126). These connections between pigment and hue are not absolute, however, since even a single substance can produce different colours, such as minerals that progressively lighten with finer grinding to produce several distinctly named tints (Jackson and Jackson 1976: 275).

Remarkably, even pigments that have not been shaped into a likeness can serve as figures. In some maṇḍala rituals, the main deities are invoked into small piles of colour placed on the image surface.[5] These heaps of dust may be understood not only as mere symbols of the deities but also as their actual presence, just as consecrated statues are considered living figures (e.g. Bentor 1996: 19). Insofar as different materials are allowed for creating the same hue, one might even argue that the colour itself substantiates the deity, not any particular kind of matter.

Colour, cosmology and symbolism

Outside of specialised rituals, colours can refer to external things in a variety of other ways, including natural connection, visual similarity, and arbitrary symbolism.

Perhaps the most direct way a colour can point to something outside itself is through causal connection. The *Treasury* attributes the blueness of our sky to reflection from the blue southern face of Sumeru, an enormous mountain at the centre of the world. Skies to the east, west and north of Sumeru reflect the different hues of other gems (Vasubandhu 1998: 401). Our blue sky thus manifests the presence of an external object (the blue face of the mountain) through a direct causal chain. Despite such specificity, however, even this colour system expands to include less rigorously connected things. The oceans and continents in the four directions can also be depicted as taking on the four colours (fig. 4, which despite some similarities has a different logic and arrangement than fig. 1), and, even more consistently, the divine kings who protect each direction. For example, the guardian of the western direction, Virūpākṣa, has red skin to match the mountain facet and sky of his quadrant.

Invoking another, more symbolic colour system, a painting of Virūpākṣa (plate 46) also uses a black background to emphasise his fearsomeness. Red or gold ground colours can similarly emphasise other qualities, such as power or wealth, although not entirely consistently. The most systematic explanation of such usage correlates the four primary colours (white, yellow, red and blue-black) with four kinds of ritual activity: peaceful, enriching, subduing and fierce (e.g. Skorupski 2001: 188–189). The relation to cosmology is not lost, however, as separate altars for these different types of rites can be placed in the four directions, occasionally even matching the arrangement of colours around Sumeru (Huntington 2018: 114).

Aside from the ground, the skin colour of deities can also have similar connotations, though again not consistently. In plate 48, just below the central Buddha appear four smaller figures with skin of white, yellow-orange, red and dark blue. As is clear even from their facial features, the white figure (Avalokiteśvara) is a peaceful deity associated with compassion, and the dark-blue figure *(Vajrapāṇi)* is a wrathful protector of the Buddha's teachings.

The skin of deities can also reference other deities of the same colour, essentially by visual similarity, but because of the potential for colour symbolism, the deities may also share similar meanings. At the top of the same painting, five multi-armed goddesses appear in the five colours of a full maṇḍalic system – white, blue, yellow, red and green. These goddesses are known as *Pañcarakṣā,* a popular group associated with worldly protection from disease and disaster. Even depicted in a line, such figures can represent the five directions of a maṇḍala, especially if they are arranged in opposing pairs around the centre (e.g. a linear order of south-east-centre-west-north pairs east and west around the centre at the interior and south and north at the exterior). This principle may or may not apply here, as the arrangement of goddesses in this painting is a bit different. There is evidence from the early history of these goddesses, however, that one may have changed skin colour from white to red precisely so that the set could match the system of five colours, five Buddhas and five directions (Mevissen 1992: 417). These goddesses are also associated with protections from dangers of the five elements (wind, fire, water, earth and space), but not in accordance with the pairings of colour and element in the relevant five-Buddha system, highlighting again the flexibility of these connections (Lewis 2000: 154).

Such systems of five colours become ubiquitous in later Himalayan and Tibetan Buddhism, often based on the symbolism of the maṇḍala but also adapted to other uses. Strings made of five-coloured threads, for example, help establish the influence of the five Buddhas in ritual objects. Tibetan-style prayer flags (fig. 5) appear in the same five colours and are variously associated with different deities, elements and mental factors, depending on whom one asks (Paul 2003: 63–73).

Conclusion

Colours may not always mean the same thing, and sometimes they do not mean anything at all. The significance of a colour may relate to real-world objects, materials or perceptual qualities; or it may not. In the abstract, colours may rest as the sole focus of meditation, or they may evoke disparate topics. In the concrete, artists use specific pigments to create spectra of hue, tint and shade and ultimately to portray recognisable figures.

To anyone who can see, imagine or apply them, colours manifest complex relationships between perception, signification and materiality. Using luminosity as a basis for valuation, hue seems less important. Alternatively, emphasising hue as a subject for meditation, its potential for symbolism is discarded. Or, interpreting colour as primarily symbolic, one may ignore the substance from which it is made. By contrast, a person creating art to generate merit must choose the very best pigments. Colours in Buddhism have all this potential for utility and meaning because they are natural features of visual perception, bearing significance that is not predetermined but that touches on nearly every aspect of experience and expression.

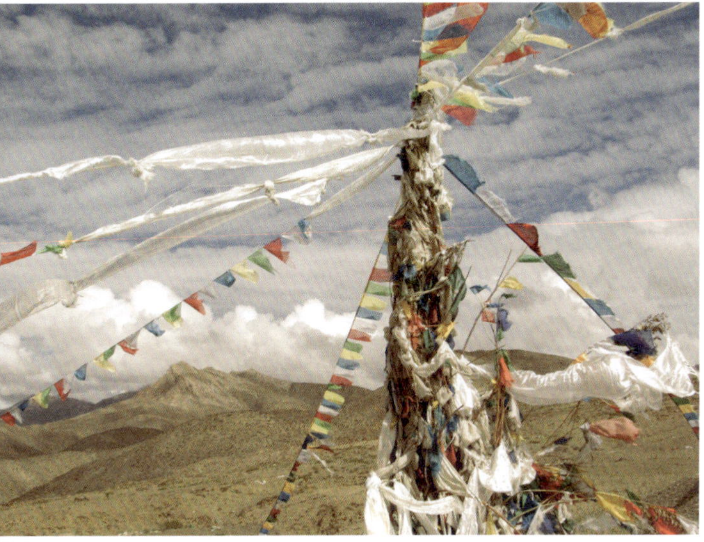

Fig. 5 Prayer flags. Tibet Autonomous Region, China. Photo: Eric Huntington, 2006.

1 Scholars debate whether and how the similar dualistic schema of different traditions may be connected historically (Kvaerne 1987: 171).

2 The historicity of this persecution is disputed (Dalton 2011: 47).

3 Such valuations of light and dark can also sometimes be correlated – problematically – to skin colour, ethnicity or social class (cf. Elizarenkova 1994: 84; Beck 1969: 559–560; Jackson 2011: 35).

4 For more on gender binaries and their problems in Buddhism, see Cabezón (2017).

5 Depending on the ritual and drawing style, this may be done before drawing a more complex image of the same deities or in place of such an image (Tayé 2012: 242; Kohn 1997: 383).

References:

— **Beck, Brenda E. F. 1969:** 'Colour and Heat in South Indian Ritual'. In: *Man* 4 (4). 553–572.

— **Bentor, Yael. 1996:** *Consecration of Images & Stupas in Indo-Tibetan Tantric Buddhism.* Leiden: Brill.

— **Buddhaghosa. 2010:** *The Path of Purification (Visuddhimagga).* Transl. by Ñāṇamoli. Kandy: Buddhist Publication Society.

— **Cabezón, José Ignacio. 2017:** *Sexuality in Classical South Asian Buddhism.* Somerville: Wisdom Publications.

— **Dalton, Jacob. 2011:** *The Taming of the Demons. Violence and Liberation in Tibetan Buddhism.* New Haven: Yale University Press.

— **Elizarenkova, T. 1994:** 'Notes on the Names of Colours in the *Ṛgveda*'. In: *Bulletin of the Deccan College Research Institute* 54/55. 81–86.

— **Filliozat, Jean. 1974:** 'Classement Des Couleurs et Des Lumières En Sanskrit'. In: Caillat, Colette et al. (eds.). *Laghu-Prabandhāḥ. Choix d'articles d'indologie.* Leiden: Brill. 185–192.

— **Frazier, Jessica. 2018:** 'Colors'. In: Jacobsen, Knut A. et al. (eds.): *Brill's Encyclopedia of Hinduism Online.* https://doi.org/10.1163/2212-5019_beh_COM_9000000172.

— **Gyatso, Khedrup Norsang. 2004:** *Ornament of Stainless Light. An Exposition of the Kālacakra Tantra.* Transl. by Gavin Kilty. Boston: Wisdom Publications.

— **Huntington, Eric. 2018:** *Creating the Universe. Depictions of the Cosmos in Himalayan Buddhism.* Seattle: University of Washington Press.

— **Jackson, David. 2011:** *Mirror of the Buddha. Early Portraits from Tibet.* New York: Rubin Museum of Art.

— **Jackson, David Paul and Jackson, Janice. 1984:** *Tibetan Thangka Painting. Methods and Materials.* Boulder: Shambhala.

— **Jackson, David Paul and Jackson, Janice. 1976:** 'A Survey of Tibetan Pigments'. In: *Kailash* 4 (3). 273–294.

— **Kohn, R. 1997:** 'The Ritual Preparation of a Tibetan Sand Maṇḍala'. In: Macdonald, A. W. (ed.): *Maṇḍala and Landscape.* New Delhi: D. K. Printworld. 365–405.

— **Kritzer, Robert. 1998:** 'Semen, Blood, and the Intermediate Existence'. In: *Journal of Indian and Buddhist Studies* 46 (2). 1031(30) –1025(36).

– **Kvaerne, Per. 1987:** 'Dualism in Tibetan Cosmogonic Myths and the Question of Iranian Influence'. In: Beckwith, Christopher (ed.): *Silver on Lapis: Tibetan Literary Culture and History.* Bloomington: The Tibet Society. 163–174.

– **Lewis, Todd. 2000:** *Popular Buddhist Texts from Nepal: Narratives and Rituals of Newar Buddhism.* Albany: State University of New York Press.

– **Locke, John K. 1980:** *Karunamaya. The Cult of Avalokitesvara-Matsyendranath in the Valley of Nepal.* Kathmandu: Sahayogi Prakashan.

– **Marasinghe, E.W. 1991:** *Citrakarmaśāstra Ascribed to Mañjuśrī. Being Volume II of Vāstuvidyāśāstra.* Delhi: Sri Satguru Publications.

– **Masaaki, Hattori.** 1988: 'Realism and the Philosophy of Consciousness-Only'. William Powell (transl.). In: *The Eastern Buddhist* 21 (1). 23–60.

– **Mevissen, Gerd J.R. 1992:** 'Transmission of Iconographic Traditions. Pañcarakṣā Heading North'. In: Jarrige, Catherine (ed.). *South Asian Archaeology 1989.* Madison: Prehistory Press. 415–424.

– **Nardi, Isabella. 2006:** *The Theory of Citrasūtras in Indian Painting. A Critical Re-Evaluation of Their Uses and Interpretations.* New York: Routledge.

– **Ohnuma, Reiko. 2007:** *Head, Eyes, Flesh, and Blood. Giving Away the Body in Indian Buddhist Literature.* New York: Columbia University Press.

– **Paul, Katherine Anne. 2003:** *Words on the Wind. A Study of Himalayan Prayer Flags.* The University of Wisconsin, Madison: Ph. D dissertation.

– **Rhys Davids, C.A.F. 1975:** *The Visuddhi-Magga of Buddhaghosa.* London: The Pali Text Society.

– **Sasson, Vanessa R. 2009:** 'A Womb with a View. The Buddha's Final Fetal Experience'. In: Sasson, Vanessa R. and Jane Marie Law (eds.): *Imagining the Fetus. The Unborn in Myth, Religion, and Culture.* Oxford: Oxford University Press. 55–72.

– **Shaw, Sarah. 2016:** 'Meditation Objects in Pāli Buddhist Texts'. In: Eifring, Halvor (ed.): *Asian Traditions of Meditation.* Honolulu: University of Hawai'i Press.122–144.

– **Shaw, Sarah. 2006:** *Buddhist Meditation. An Anthology of Texts from the Pāli Canon.* London: Routledge.

– **Skilling, Peter. 2013:** 'Rhetoric of Reward, Ideologies of Inducement. Why Produce Buddhist "Art"?' In: Park, David, Kuenga Wangmo and Sharon Cather (eds.): *Art of Merit: Studies in Buddhist Art and Its Conservation.* London: Archetype Publications. 27–37.

– **Skorupski, Tadeusz. 2001:** 'Jyotirmañjari of Abhayakaragupta'. In: *The Buddhist Forum* 4. 183–221.

– **Sørensen, Per K. 1994:** *Tibetan Buddhist Historiography: The Mirror Illuminating the Royal Genealogies.* Wiesbaden: Harrassowitz Verlag.

– **Tayé, Jamgön Kongtrul Lodrö. 2012:** *The Treasury of Knowledge. Book Six, Parts One and Two.* Transl. by Gyurme Dorje. Boston: Snow Lion.

– **Turpeinen, Katarina. 2019:** 'Luminous Visions and Liberatory Amulets in Rig'dzin rGod ldem's Great Perfection Anthology'. In: *Revue d'Études Tibétaines* (50). 132–149.

– **Vasubandhu. 1998:** *Abhidharmakośam.* Edited by Swāmī Dwārikādās Śāstri. Vol. 1. Varanasi: Bauddha Bharati.

– **Walshe, Maurice. 1995:** *The Long Discourses of the Buddha.* Boston: Wisdom.

– **Wangdu, Pasang and Hildegard Diemberger. 2000:** *dBa' bzhed: The Royal Narrative Concerning the Bringing of the Buddha's Doctrine to Tibet.* Vienna: Verlag der Österreichischen Akademie der Wissenschaften.

BLACK = NOBLE CHARACTER?

Colour Schemes in Wayang Kulit, Javanese Shadow Puppet Theatre

Vanessa von Gliszczynski

What makes the figures in *wayang kulit,* a Javanese form of shadow puppet theatre, so fascinating is their elaborate painting. A parchment made of water buffalo hide is first cut to the right size, then the patterns are punched out, and finally the puppets are painted and gilded. The body is depicted in one of the basic colours – gold, black or red – while the face might have a different colour. The garments worn by the figures are based on the colourful patterns of Javanese batik fabrics. But why are all these colours needed for shadow puppet theatre? According to the Indonesian cultural theorist Tyas Purbasari, the colours used for shadow theatre puppets actually play a crucial role:

> The colours of the *wayang* puppets are the key central element. It's in the colours of the figures that you can find each character's soul. (2011: ii)

Although the colouring is clearly extremely significant, it is often only marginally addressed in the extensive literature on *wayang kulit*. Understanding the main features of the colour symbolism in Javanese shadow puppet theatre requires a brief explanation of general *wayang kulit* concepts as well as the basic principles of Javanese colour symbolism.

The history and cosmological basis of wayang kulit

Today, *wayang kulit* is regarded as part of Indonesia's national cultural heritage, although it is found above all on the islands of Java and Bali.[1] Shadow puppet theatre existed on Java even before the 10th century, but the modern-day incarnation of *wayang* has been strongly influenced by India and – from the 13th century onwards – by Islam. We can clearly see this in the *wayang* stories, which are largely borrowed from the Indian epics Ramayana and Mahabharata. Over time the stories were partially changed and adapted to Javanese notions. Some figures, such as the popular jester Semar, do not exist in the original Indian versions and are rooted in Indonesian tradition (Djajasoebrata 1999: 17; Sabai Günther 2015: 109).

Wayang kulit is a reflection of humanity, explaining the Javanese view of the universe through the characters' actions and relationships. In this respect, *wayang* serves as a set of ethical guidelines, illustrating what is good and evil (Djajasoebrata 1999: 9, 16; Anderson 1996: 16; Mellema 1988: 8). An example of this are the Pandawa and the Kurawa, the main characters of the Mahabharata: two groups of cousins and their followers who battle each other to rule the kingdom of Astinapura. The Pandawa represent the good side, while the Kurawa embody evil. But the initial impression is deceptive because the dichotomy is actually much more complex than that; only around 1949 did it escalate into a symbolic battle of good against evil (Anderson 1996: 42).

> The division of the *kelir (wayang* screen) between Kurawa and Pandawa is often today taken to represent the conflict between Evil and Good. Yet the deeper complementarities and ambiguous interconnections of human existence are cunningly exposed by the irony that Left and Right are not absolute. Depending whether, at a *wayang* performance, one watches the puppets or the shadows, right becomes left and left right. Both are merely in the eye of the beholder. (Anderson 1995: 17)

However, *wayang* characters have both positive and negative traits and are thus traditionally not judged as being simply good or evil. It is much more relevant whether a figure properly performs its role or not. A knight *(satria)* is respected if he behaves in accordance with his code of conduct. As the 'evil' faction in the Mahabharata, the Kurawa are viewed negatively because they do not act in accordance with their role as knights, and not because they are fundamentally evil. The figure of Adipati Karna is positioned on the side of the Kurawa, but is regarded by the Javanese public as a role model because he acts in line with the knightly ideal. Each character in *wayang kulit* represents an archetype of society and can be selected as a role model by means of identification (Sabai

Günther 2015: 108; Anderson 1996: 18–19, 39). Nowadays, this identification of *wayang* figures – Arjuna as the ideal, delicate man or Bima (plate 41) as the strong warrior – is no longer as widespread. But the Pandawa brothers in particular are still much-loved characters who have turned up in advertising and comics (Dittrich 2001: 167–169). A Javanese adage hits the nail on the head: *'kuwi tontonan kang mawa tuntunan'*, namely that *wayang* is full of teachings and wise sayings rather than being merely entertainment (Purbasari 2011: 19).

Potent colours

The dichotomy between good and evil and between right and left is reflected in the way a *wayang* stage – which is also regarded as a depiction of the universe – is set up: the puppeteer *(dalang)* sits in front of a screen *(kelir)*, which is the sky. An oil lamp representing the sun hangs behind him, and in front of him lies a banana trunk *(gedebog)*, portraying the earth. The figures belonging to the 'good' side, such as the Pandawa, are set up to the right of the *dalang*, while the 'evil faction', including the Kurawa, is positioned on the left-hand side (Sabai Günther 2015: 112–113; Mellema 1988: 8). Elementary colour schemes are apparent here at a purely visual level, for the golden, black and white figures are positioned on the right-hand side while those who are golden, red and blue stand on the left (Purbasari 2011: 3).

Since around the middle of the twentieth century, it has been standard practice during a performance for the audience to move individually from the colourful side of the *dalang* to the shadow side, and vice versa. The realm of the *dalang* is traditionally regarded as being the more magically dangerous. After all, every performance is also the magical representation of a mythical tale. This is why *wayang* used to be exclusively staged as a ritual marking births or weddings, or after overcoming a crisis. The performance is supposed to restore equilibrium to the universe (Sabai Günther 2015: 103, 115; Mellema 1988: 8).

It used to be the case that only the organisers of shadow puppet theatre – who were for the most part aristocratic – were permitted to sit on the side of the *dalang* and enjoy the full splendour of the colours (Sabai Günther 2015: 115). According to the Dutch author R. L. Mellema, *wayang kulit* was once an initiation ritual, which is why only men were allowed on the *dalang* side. It was they who had exclusive access to the complete knowledge of mythology, and along with it the iconographic significance of the *wayang* figures. The women, in contrast, sat on the shadow side (Mellema 1988: 7). In both cases it is apparent that the intensity of the colours on the same side as the puppeteer is linked to the magical efficacy of the figures.

So the significance ascribed to the colours of *wayang kulit* figures is clearly more than just aesthetic. In fact, there is also a close link to general notions of colour in Javanese cosmology. Traditionally speaking, the entirety of Javanese life was based on the points of the compass, which in turn correlated with particular colours. Both were viewed as being closely related to the calendar, to stages of life, to nature and feelings. Black was associated with an imbalance, but also with stability. Red stood for greed and imperiousness, and yellow for boastfulness and vanity. The colour white, by contrast, supposedly represented purity, and thus the capacity to develop in all directions. However, the colour schemes mentioned have changed over time, in some cases considerably, and only have limited relevance for today's *wayang* (Djajasoebrata 1999: 42–43).

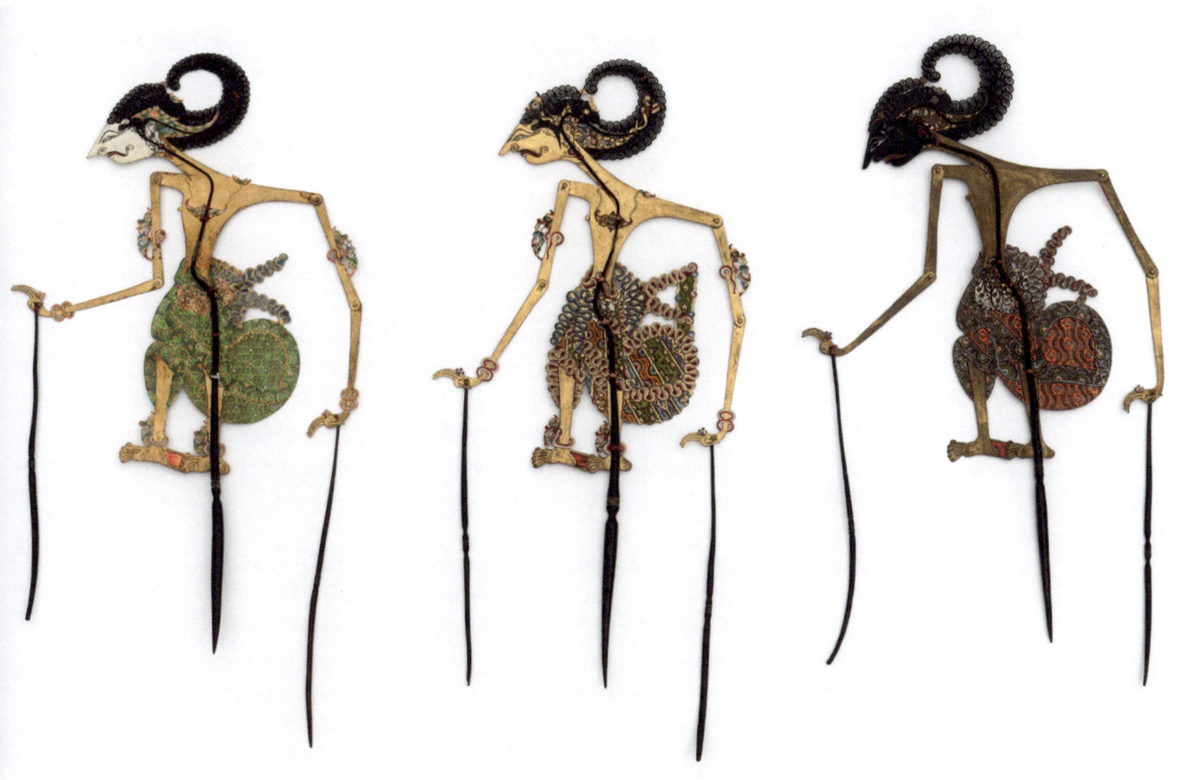

Fig. 1 The Pandawa prince Arjuna shown with assorted face colours – white, gold and black – which refer to different emotional states. Purchased by August Flick, 1989.

One important source for these colour codes in modern-day Java is the work of the Dutch ethnologist Rens Heringa, who explored the colours of Javanese batik in her field research. She discovered that the four main colours used in batik – white, red, yellow and dark blue – were associated with the day-and-night cycle and with the various stages of life: childhood, youth, the fertile years, then old age and death. This produces a kind of 'colour compass', which structures the world according to the four points of the compass. White thus symbolises birth and origins, as well as the east and the rising sun. The south is red and represents fertility. The colour tones from pink to dark red correspond to south-east on this 'colour compass' and are associated with adolescence. The transition from the 'fertile' colours of the south (red and orange) through to yellow stands for maturity. Nuances of yellow to green mark the west and the process of adults maturing into old people. Old age is accordingly positioned in the north-west and is symbolised by the transition from green to blue. The circle of life is completed in the north with blue tones through to black, which stand for paralysis and death. What is noticeable about this Javanese 'colour compass' is that the colours are always perceived as part of a series of colour tones (Heringa: 1989: 109; Libera 2018: 66–68).

This idea of the series, and of colours as harmonious resources, also surfaces in the way that *wayang* figures are manufactured. Around 1920, the Javanese puppetmaker Sukir wrote down detailed instructions which also included information on the colouring of the figures.[2] Sixteen colours are traditionally used, mixed from a basic colour palette of white, yellow, blue, black and red. Sukir underlines the importance of avoiding large areas of a single colour *(tumpuk)* when painting shadow puppets, and favours colour gradients *(sorotan)* instead (Mellema 1988: 30–34). According to the Javanese aesthetics of colour, moreover, not all colours are viewed as harmonious. A combination of two warm or two cold colours is described as an undesirable accumulation (Mellema 1988: 40). Sukir gives this as an example of 'friendly colours' *(kanti)* and emphasises that a maker of *wayang kulit* has to adhere to the rules of the Javanese aesthetics of colour:

> The reason is that each colour has its own specific friendly *(kanti)* colour, e.g. red has to be matched with green, and orange with blue. Should one match red with blue or orange with green then this would be called an error in the choice of the friendly colour. Should one juxtapose red to orange or blue to green, it would be called an accumulation *(tumpukan kantininpun).* (Mellema 1988: 40)

The stipulation that patches of colour should be avoided clearly does not refer to the colour used for the figures' bodies and faces, but rather just for their clothes and adornment. Such examples show that the figures' aesthetics and colour coding are subject to strict rules. These findings about the history of *wayang kulit* and Javanese cosmology allow us to draw conclusions about the relationships between colours and the characteristics ascribed to the figures.

Characters of Colour

The colours of the faces and bodies in *wayang* are an important means of characterising and identifying the figures. The latter is also relevant for the puppeteers, who have to distinguish between around 600 figures (Dittrich 2001: 57–58). Moreover, the shape of the eyes and nose, the size of the figure and the clothing and ornamentation all play a key role. The size of the figures indicates physical strength, for example, but whether the character is coarse or not is established by its colouring and the shape of the eyes (Dittrich 2001: 57–58; Djajasoebrata 1999: 39–42). These visual codes were widely known in Central Java as late as the 1960s:

> The universal affection and knowledge of this *wayang* mythology at all levels and in all areas of Java means that little village children from their earliest years are acquainted with the characters discussed above, not merely with their names but their physical, psychological, and ethical traits. And their acquaintance is not abstract but strongly visual. (Anderson 1996: 36)

Wayang kulit is still extremely popular today, although a detailed understanding of the figures' iconography is probably limited to expert circles. Yet the fundamental distinction between *alus* and *kasar* in the Javanese worldview remains vital. The desirable *alus* characters are refined and noble, associated with traits such as prudence, constancy and serenity. On the other hand, a character that is irascible, unstable and short-tempered is described as *kasar* or coarse (Djajasoebrata 1999: 39; Dittrich 2001: 59).

Distinguishing between the figures is particularly difficult because some characters appear in different forms *(wanda)* as they change over the course of time. In the Mahabharata there are, for example, eight versions of the belligerent Bima and thirteen forms of his brother Arjuna (Dittrich 2001: 58) (fig. 1). While the colour of the body mostly stays the same across the board, the face colour can change according to the situation. In addition to the figures' quintessential characteristics, it alludes to their state of mind and age (Mellema 1988: 59). The colours that feature most commonly on bodies and faces could serve to illustrate

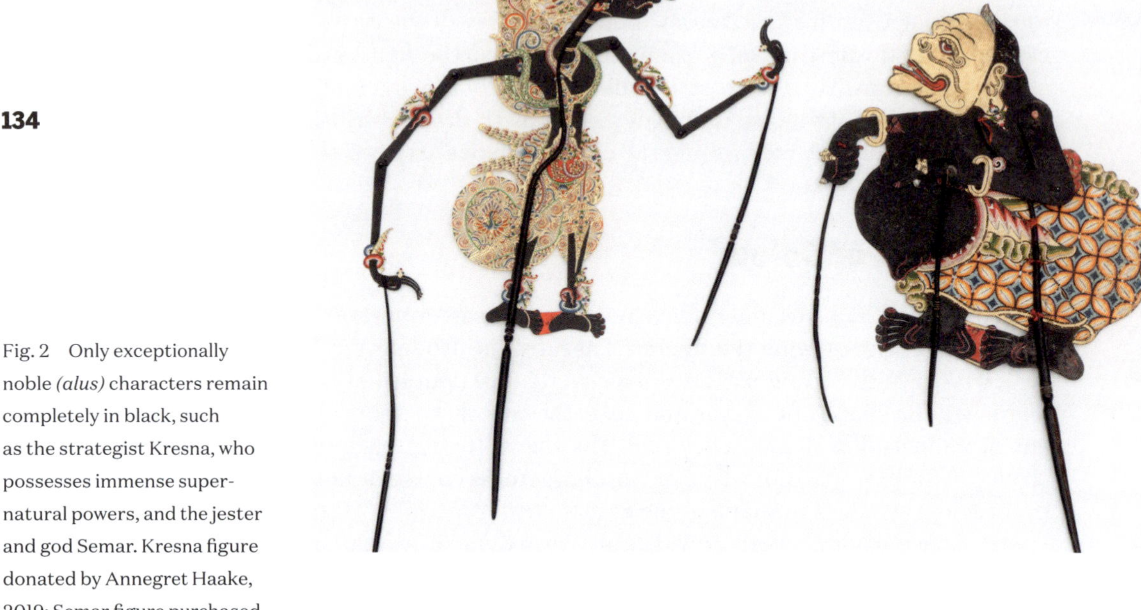

Fig. 2 Only exceptionally noble *(alus)* characters remain completely in black, such as the strategist Kresna, who possesses immense supernatural powers, and the jester and god Semar. Kresna figure donated by Annegret Haake, 2019; Semar figure purchased by August Flick, 1989.

the colour codes used in shadow puppet theatre. It should be noted that the colour of a figure's face has more symbolic power than the colour of its body (Purbasari 2010: 137).

Gold = young and beautiful?

Most *wayang kulit* figures have golden bodies. The applied gold leaf *(prada)* is viewed as yellow and associated with beauty, prestige and an aristocratic status (Djajasoebrata 1999: 42–43; Purbasari 2010: 134). This suits characters such as the aristocratic Pandawa brothers from the Mahabharata, whose bodies are often coloured gold. The 'womaniser' Arjuna, who is regarded as particularly attractive, is a good example of this. Golden yellow is sometimes also interpreted as the colour of youth and love, and so Arjuna in an amorous state is shown in gold (fig. 1). Female roles always have golden bodies, too (Dittrich 2001: 59). However, it is questionable whether this is linked to the attributes of beauty and youth, because with just a few exceptions the female characters in *wayang kulit* tend to remain in the background, and in some cases the negative characters also have golden bodies.

The high incidence of the colour gold means that it can almost be viewed as a basic colour or a default state. In fact, Tyas Purbasari, who conducted research in Central Java in 2010, confirms that the *wayang kulit* makers often choose gold for aesthetic reasons. In that case the meaning of the colour plays a secondary role. Yet the same is not true of the colour of the face, which is decisive for the figure's characterisation (Purbasari 2011: 134, 137). But there are exceptions to this too: Batara Guru, the highest divine being in *wayang,* is often shown completely in gold. The colour is intended to indicate his beauty, his divine size and his noble-mindedness (Purbasari 2011: 137).

Black = mature and noble?

Look at the characters who have a black face, and in some cases a black body too, and these will mostly be heroes and gods. Black is clearly reserved for noble characters who correspond to the Javanese ideal of the *alus.* The traits associated with the colour black are constancy, calm, an upstanding nature, honesty, a high degree of mental concentration as well as supernatural powers *(sakti)* that make it possible to vanquish mighty opponents. Moreover, black is linked to a mature character, adulthood or old age (Djajasoebrata 1999: 43; Dittrich 2001: 59; Purbasari 2011: 37). Very few characters are completely black, because this would indicate an entirely noble character. Kresna is the only figure who is totally black at every stage of life (fig. 2).[3] He is regarded as a great strategist, politician and diplomat. In the Mahabharata, Kresna is the trusted confidant of the Pandawa and stands at Arjuna's side in an advisory capacity. As an incarnation of Vishnu he is intrinsically divine and has enormous supernatural capabilities. He is extremely clever, upstanding and just. Moreover, he is responsible for implementing the divine plan in the Mahabharata: the final victory of the Pandawa over the Kurawa. Although he also applies cunning and intrigue to do so, in his case they serve a higher purpose (Anak Wayang 2013; Anderson 1996: 25–26). The beloved jester Semar is also completely black (fig. 2) – yet his face might be golden or white instead. With his huge girth, Semar is very much the opposite of Kresna. Moreover, like all jesters he is nominally one of the Javanese people. In reality, however, Semar is one of the highest-ranking gods, which explains his black colour. He is wise, honest and loyal, which makes him an important adviser to the Pandawa. The fact that he is not a knight means he can express himself openly and honestly and also give a critical opinion of the current political situation. That also explains why he is sometimes shown with a white (symbolising purity) or golden (symbolising high status) face (Anderson 1996: 37).

The figures frequently have a golden yellow body but black face. Arjuna's appearance is accordingly supposed to indicate supernatural powers, but also a grown-up and mature character. The young Arjuna, in contrast, generally has a golden or white face (see fig. 1). Arjuna's oldest brother Prince Yudhistira is purportedly unable to lie. The more mature Yudhistira, who has already been crowned king, is shown with a black face on account of his upstanding nature. The link between the colour black and maturity is particularly clear in the case of Gatotkaca, the son of the second-oldest Pandawa prince Bima and the giantess Arimbi. Not only is he extremely strong, he also has supernatural powers which means, for example, that he can fly. Gatotkaca is most frequently depicted with a golden body and a black face, but in the final battle of the Mahabharata he is at the height of his spiritual maturity and is therefore shown completely in black (Djajasoebrata 1999: 141; Purbasari 2011: 37–38, 132).

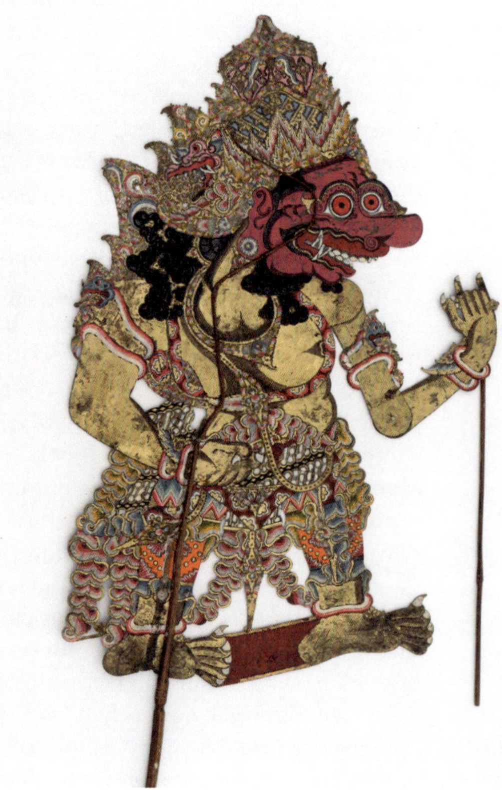

Fig. 3 The giant Kumbakarna is the brother of the demon king Rahwana in the Ramayana. Not only his red face colour but also his large eyes, broad nose and pointed teeth indicate a violent and uncontrolled character. Donated by Annegret Haake, 2019.

Red = mean and coarse?

The colour red is diametrically opposed to black:

> It appears that the red-rose face is found most of the time with those figures known as rough, ill-bred and violent, the general characteristic, for example, of the giants *(buta)*. It further appears that a black face is the proper characteristic of those figures which are calm, have their passions under control and are capable through spiritual concentration of scoring a final victory over these figures which can command even greater physical strength. (Mellema 1988: 64)

The association of red with power and uncontrollability comes from the colour being linked to energy and fertility. As described above, the giants – the *buta* and *raksasa* – bring together all the red characteristics: they are aggressive and violent, full of anger and wrath. Their nature is coarse *(kasar)* and they cannot control their mood. Many of these giants do indeed have a completely red body or, like Kumbakarna, a golden body with a red face (fig. 3).

Although these characteristics are viewed negatively in the Javanese world-view, there are still several highly-regarded figures with a red face. The Pandawa heroes Bima and Arjuna appear in several scenes with a red face, for example, to emphasise the vitality and strength of the powerful Bima. Arjuna can be given a red face in battle scenes in order to underscore the requisite fighting spirit – but such figures tend to be seldom. Thus red is associated not only with anger but also with courage. Particularly for figures who are generally not shown in red, it is notable that the eyes, nose and mouth are nonetheless characterised as *alus.* Almost all of the 'evil' Kurawa brothers have a golden body but a red face. This is not primarily because they are essentially *kasar,* but because they do not meet up to the knightly ideal and do not behave honourably in battle (Dittrich 2001: 58; Djajasoebrata 1999: 42–43; Purbasari 2011: 37–38). Thus, red cannot be viewed as an exclusively 'evil' colour. This is apparent in the example of Batara Brahma (plate 40), the god of fire. As a god he should actually have a black or golden face, but it is frequently red – just like his clothing (Purbasari 2011: 134). This indicates a close connection between fire and unbridled energies.

White = wise and pure?

With the exception of the monkey general Hanuman, white actually only appears as a face colour. As in many cultures, it is associated with purity, but also with beauty and wisdom. Some of the wise old hermits in *wayang* have a white face (plate 42). The fact that divine apparitions such as Sang Hyang Wenang (fig. 4) are mostly presented with a white face underscores the close link between spirituality and wisdom. Arjuna as a young man, however, is often shown with a white face (see fig. 1), which supposedly emphasises his chasteness and beauty. A white face also features on some of the female roles too, but the white faces of the jesters Limbuk and Cangkik denote their naively honest manner. As is the case with Semar, their comments on mythical and current political events are full of wisdom (Purbasari 2011: 37, 137; Djajasoebrata 1999: 42).

Blue = cunning and stupid?

Characters with a blue face are also occasionally found. A few isolated cases suggest that the colour tends to be assigned negative characteristics. According to Purbasari, blue characters do not stay true to their own position, and they are cunning, cowardly or foolish. Other 'blue' traits are supposedly pettiness, narrow-mindedness and an irresponsible attitude (Purbasari 2011: 134; Sujamto 1992). This is consistent with the character of the cunning Sangkuni, a Kurawa uncle and minister. Apart from this, very few concrete examples are to be found.

Antareja (fig. 5) is also sometimes shown with a blue face. He is the son of the muscular Bima and Nagini, a princess of the snake people. He is regarded as a positive character who is honest and faithful. He has a poisonous tongue and a protective scaly skin, which leaves him more powerful after each battle (Wayang Wordpress 2010). In this respect, Antareja does not conform to the interpretive pattern. Blue could possibly be derived from an association between snakes and water, in a similar way that the colour red is linked to the fire god Batara Brahma.

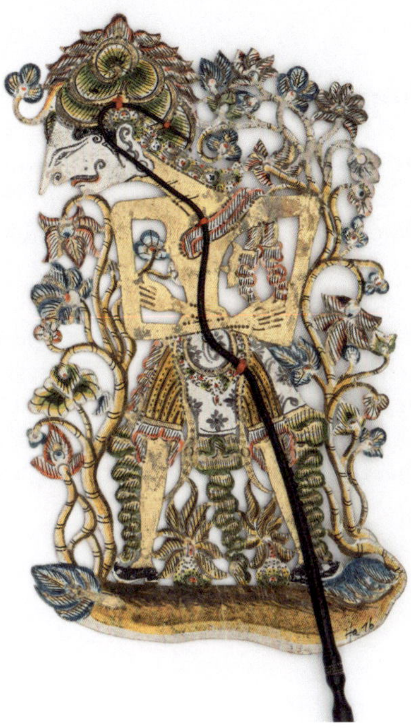

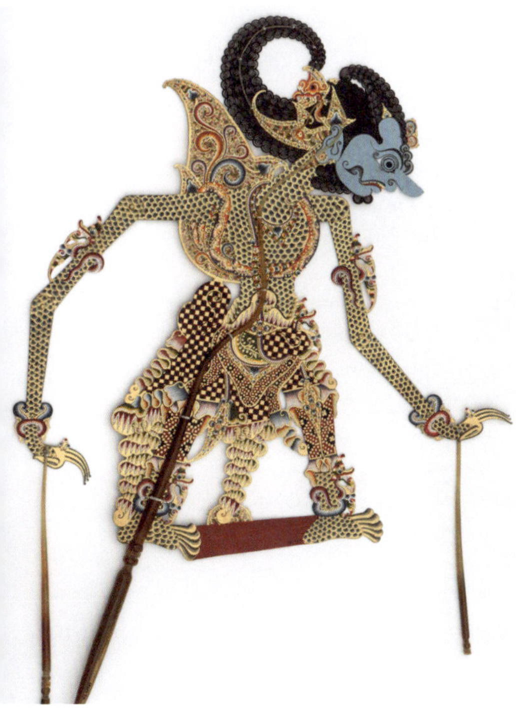

Fig. 4 Sang Hyang Wenang is a divine apparition who exists in Javanese shadow theatre but not in the Indian epics. The white face is an indication of spirituality and purity. Donated by Annegret Haake, 2019.

Fig. 5 Figures of Antareja have a black or blue face. The blue elements could refer to Antareja's relationship to the snake kingdom. Donated by Annegret Haake, 2019.

Fixed colour schemes?

The colour schemes outlined above illustrate the use of distinct codes in Javanese shadow puppet theatre to determine the colours of bodies and faces. These can be traced back to ancient core beliefs about cosmology that managed to assert themselves against Indian and Islamic influences. The colour schemes are not static, and in certain cases they have not been observed. Yet the colours used for the bodies and faces of shadow theatre puppets are helpful in making the characters more archetypal, understanding their traits and integrating them into Javanese cosmology. This means *wayang kulit* is much more than a 'theatre in the dark', serving instead as a social and cosmological guide which makes it possible to evaluate character traits in society and visually exemplify them as desirable or undesirable.

1 Balinese shadow theatre is presumably an old form of Javanese shadow theatre. Bali, however, unlike Java, was not subject to influence from Islamic scholars from the 13th century onwards (Djajasoebrata 1999: 16–17).

2 Sukir's original Javanese manuscript only became more accessible to a wider scholarly audience after it was translated by R. L. Mellema into Dutch and then later by ethnomusicologist Mantle Hood into English.

3 In Old Indic, Kresna actually means 'the black one', while Arjuna means 'the pale one'. See also the essay by Eystein Dahl in this volume.

References:

– **Anak Wayang. 2013:** *Mengenal karakter dan watak para tokoh pewayangan.* http://anakwayan9.blogspot.com/2013/06/mengenal-karakter-dan-watak-para-tokoh.html (24.6.2020).

– **Anderson, Benedict R. O'G. 1996:** *Mythology and the Tolerance of the Javanese.* Cornell Modern Indonesia Project no. 37. Ithaca: Cornell University.

– **Dittrich, Iris. 2001: Wayang kulit:** *Mythos und Provokation im indonesischen Schattenspiel.* Europäische Hochschulschriften, Reihe XXX: Theater-, Film- und Fernsehwissenschaften, vol. 77. Frankfurt am Main: Peter Lang.

– **Djajasoebrata, Alit. 1999:** *Shadow Theatre in Java: The Puppets, Performance and Repertoire.* Amsterdam: The Pepin Press.

– **Heringa, Rens. 1989:** 'Dye Process and Life Sequence: The Coloring of Textiles in an East Javanese Village'. In: Gittinger, Mattiebelle (ed.): *To Speak with Cloth: Studies in Indonesian Textiles.* Los Angeles: Museum of Cultural History, University of California. 107–130.

– **Libera, Svetlana. 2018:** *Historische und soziokulturelle Aspekte der indonesischen Batikkunst: Die Bedeutung von Farbsymbolik und Musterung, Herstellung und Verwendung in Kerek und Tuban.* Schriften zur Kulturgeschichte, vol. 48. Hamburg: Verlag Dr. Kovač

– **Mellema, R. L. 1988:** *Wayang Puppets: Carving, Colouring, Symbolism. Translated by Mantle Hood.* Amsterdam: Royal Tropical Institute.

– **Purbasari, Tyas. 2010:** *Kajian Aspek Teknis, Estetis, dan Simbolis Warna Wayang kulit Karya Perajin Wayang Desa Tunahan Kabupaten Jepara.* Jurusan Seni Rupa. Fakultas Bahasa dan Seni. Universitas Negeri Semarang. https://lib.unnes.ac.id/5300/1/7681.pdf (22.6.2020).

– **Sabai Günther, Jasmine Ii. 2015:** 'Schatten und Farbe: Das indonesische Wayang'. In: Sabai Günther, Jasmin Ii and Ines de Castro (eds.): *Die Welt des Schattentheaters: Von Asien bis Europa.* Stuttgart: Linden-Museum Stuttgart. 102–123

– **Sujamto. 1992:** *Wayang dan Budaya Jawa.* Semarang: Dahara Prize.

– **Wayang Wordpress. 2010:** *Raden Antareja (Anantareja).* https://wayang.wordpress.com/2010/07/22/raden-antareja-anantareja/ (24.6.2020).

THE COLOUR PRAXIS OF THE ABELAM AS PART OF A CULTURE-SPECIFIC AESTHETICS

An Example from Papua New Guinea

Brigitta Hauser-Schäublin

Introduction

In 1912 the ethnologist Richard Thurnwald was the first European to cross the region between the Sepik River and the north coast in the north east of the island of New Guinea (at the time the German protectorate of Kaiser-Wilhelmsland). On his journey he encountered the Abelam, an ethnic group that had settled in the southern foothills of the Prince Alexander Mountains and who lived from the cultivation of tubers (above all yams). The ceremonial houses of the Abelam – he called them "festival halls" – left a deep impression on him (1914: 82). He described them as "heaven storming" as they were built to a height of almost 30 meters and their magnificent gable fronts were almost completely painted. 50 years later Gerd Koch visited the Abelam region (also known as the Maprik region), establishing a large ethnographic collection for the Museum für Völkerkunde in Berlin. Writing about the sculptures and paintings, he stated: "The intensive colouration (above all the yellow, rare in other parts, and the bold red) lends [...] these works, together with the clear arrangement of lines and surfaces with their strict stylization, a very special agency, which is intensified in the extreme, thus making the Maprik art something highly special in the wider oceanic region" (1968: 28–29).[1]

Fig. 1 Ceremonial house in the hamlet of Yambusaki, Kalabu village, with towering gable and painted façade. In the background the gable peaks of other ceremonial houses can be seen. Photo: Brigitta Hauser-Schäublin, 1980.

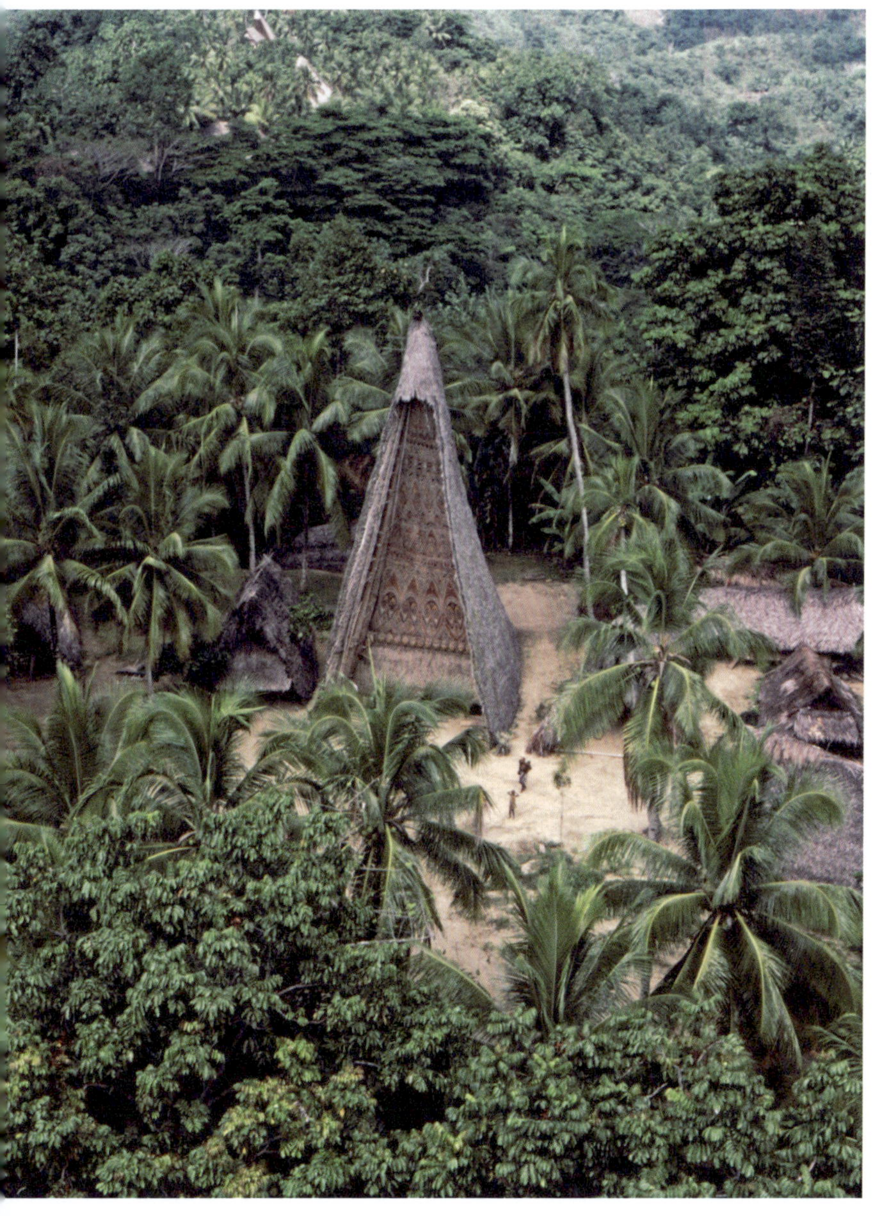

Alfred Bühler, who also travelled the Abelam region and collected for the Museum für Völkerkunde Basel, spoke of the "lavish painting" of the sculptures and described the paintings as "monumental forms" of façade decoration (1960). The most impressive of all are the triangular, richly painted gable fronts of the imposing ceremonial houses, which were generally built at the highest point of the settlement (fig. 1, cf. plate 44) (Hauser-Schäublin 2016).[2]

In terms of form and execution, the anthropomorphic sculptures, generally conceived as symmetrical frontal views, appear clumsy compared to the often extremely filigree carvings of their southern neighbours. The strong impression which the figures nevertheless leave on the observer is due to their intense painting. The Abelam refer to an unpainted sculpture as 'just a piece of wood' if they want to emphasize the significance of the colour. It is only when it is painted black, white, red and yellow that the 'wood' becomes animated. That is why all the sculptures are completely repainted before they are displayed in a ritual held in the ceremonial house. They thus become living beings from the beyond (ancestors and spirits), or rather their temporary seats. In the past, when initiation rites were performed in the ceremonial house sculptures, paintings, shell rings and stones, as well as flowers, were combined to create an entire ensemble. This resulted in veritable visual orgies of colour, which, in the dim light of torches, drew the novices under their spell.

For the Abelam, as mentioned, the primary colours consist of black, white, red and yellow. They have their own theory of colour, although it is formulated neither orally nor in written form. Instead it is a *colour praxis,* which consists in the selection of colours and their material characteristics, as well as the combination of individual colours and their arrangement to form motifs and patterns. Artists pass on their knowledge and skills to talented young men through learning by doing, not theoretical lessons. The use of colour is regimented and not everyone is (or more correctly, was) free to paint and use motifs or change them at will, although master painters always enjoyed a certain scope of action. Painting – what we would generally refer to as 'art' – was framed by basic cultural parameters.[3] As the anthropologist Anthony Forge concluded, who studied the art of the Abelam in the mid-20th century, and who also compiled a large collection for the Museum für Völkerkunde Basel, the visual art of this ethnic group is of a "ritual character" and forms a central component of rituals (2017a [1962]). The paintings directly affect the observer in a fashion that cannot be expressed in words as the images are connected to a world of experience beyond the everyday.

Theories of colour: From Goethe to the Abelam

Theories of colour are not universal. The emotions and sensations associated with colours are also learned and depend on cultural evaluations and meanings. Johann Wolfgang von Goethe identified the fundamental principle of human colour perception and its corresponding evaluation in the polar opposite of light ("Licht") and dark ("Finsternis") (1810). He termed yellow, blue and red as the pure colours (primary colours), to which the human eye formed the complementary colours. He organised these colours within a colour circle. He marked it with a plus sign on the one side and a minus on the other and associated them with corresponding effects on our sensations ("warm", "cold"). Wassily Kandinsky (1866–1944), like Johannes Itten (1888–1967) and Paul Klee (1879–1940), was a teacher at the Bauhaus. They all made an intensive study of colours and forms, however each in their own way. The basic forms of Bauhaus teaching were the yellow triangle, the blue circle and the red square. The psychological dimension – sensations that are associated with colours and forms – played an important role for all these artists. Kandinsky, for example, spoke of an "inner sound" that colours are able to evoke, that is, associations with things and appearances (1911). This effect is intensified when they are embodied in certain forms. Colours thus had an outside – the colour itself – and an inside, which appeals to sensations and meanings (associations). Itten also proceeded from three primary colours and spoke of "secondary" and "tertiary" colours (twelve in total) generated by the mixing or superposition of the primary colours. He used this to develop a system of seven colour contrasts, i.e. different forms of the juxtaposition or combination of different colours, which he also illustrated using a colour circle.

As in a number of other colour theories, for Itten colours were "colourful", and he considered black and white to be "non-colours" (Itten [1961] 2009: 17).[4] Paul Klee wrote the following on the meaning of colours and motifs: "Art does not reproduce the visible, instead art makes visible" (1920: 28). As we will see, this also applies to the Abelam. What their paintings show are not reproductions; instead, in the first instance, they make relationships between meanings visible.

But now let us move on to the principles of the Abelam paintings. I will discuss a number of the aspects of European-Western colour theories sketched above from the perspective of the Abelam: the concept of the non-colours, the idea of the primary colours and their equivalence, the mixed colours (secondary and tertiary colours), the combination of colours with one another and the relationship between colour and form. A further, especially important point, refers to the relationship between the outer and the inner dimension of the colours, as Kandinsky called it, in other words, questions of associations, sensations and meanings.

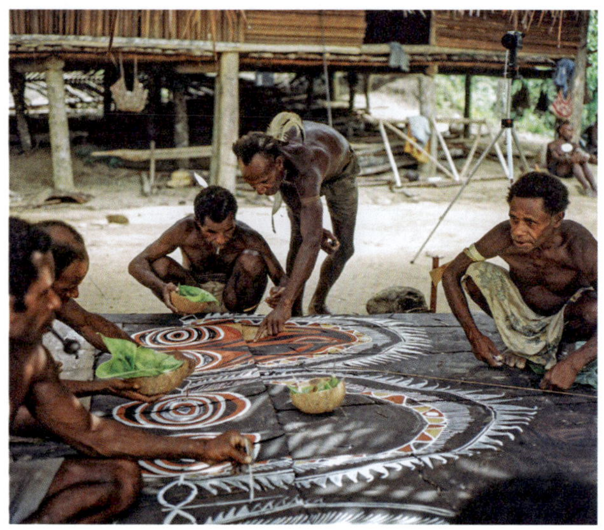

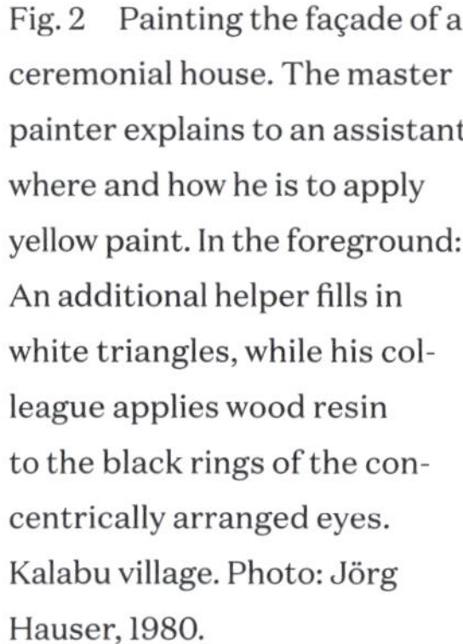

Fig. 2 Painting the façade of a ceremonial house. The master painter explains to an assistant where and how he is to apply yellow paint. In the foreground: An additional helper fills in white triangles, while his colleague applies wood resin to the black rings of the concentrically arranged eyes. Kalabu village. Photo: Jörg Hauser, 1980.

The assumptions which European colour theories operate with are especially apparent in the case of the 'non-colour' white. It is well known that canvas and paper are white (or whitish) – and these are the most important bases which European artists have painted on. These base materials appear to have been implicitly understood as a neutral background. Thus the aforementioned colour theories present the colour circles they have developed against a white background. Amongst the Abelam white never serves as a background, instead it is the most important paint colour. The naturally given background colour amongst the Abelam is brown. All picture carriers – smoothed palm leaf stalks, wood, skin (for body painting) and yams (especially large cultivated examples) are brown or brownish. Brown does not exist as a paint colour. As already mentioned, the primary colours used in painting are black *(wuinkipma),* white *(sabyo),* red *(waimba)* and yellow *(paalkipma);* here the names are those of the corresponding pigment. These colours do not fit into the schema of European colour theories; above all the colour blue is missing, which, from an optical-physical perspective, is also one of the primary colours. This may be due to the fact that no blue colour pigments, i.e. earth pigments, are to be found on New Guinea. Of course the colour blue – as well as green – occurs in nature. However, abstract terms for these colours appear to be missing, as it is the composition or materiality – bird feathers, butterfly wings, flowers and leaves – that is in the foreground. Even the – ephemeral – cult images made from flowers and leaves consist exclusively of the aforementioned colours, although theoretically different coloured materials are available. Furthermore, the Abelam never mix their primary colours, therefore they have not manufactured any 'secondary' or 'tertiary' colours.

The materiality and spirituality of the colours

When imported oil paints became available in the middle of the 20th century the Abelam also began to experiment with blue and green. Sometimes they employed blue for those parts which they had previously painted black. They used the same name for blue and black; the same applied for green, which was sometimes used to replace yellow. In the 1970s the Abelam returned to the traditional colours. Whether this was on the advice of the many European collectors who, as far as possible, wanted to buy 'authentic' painted artefacts, or on the initiative of the Abelam themselves, as colours are not just colours, is not completely clear.

Many painted gables, which now adorn the fronts of churches, schools and community centres – the majority of the Abelam are now Christians of various denominations, which is why hardly any ceremonial houses are built or initiations conducted – still display the traditional patterns and colours.[5] Coupaye (2007) reported that since the end of the 1980s only industrially produced colours were used. However, in terms of hue – in contrast to the first wave of modernisation – they largely correspond to the traditional colours.

During my research amongst the Abelam, black, white and yellow were exclusively pigments which occurred naturally at certain locations in the area and which were traded regionally as small clumps. These pigments were cleaned of little stones and employed without adding any further ingredients. Another black paint, which is not used for priming but for painting small areas, is still manufactured from soot to this day, which is chewed together with certain leaves. The black juice is then spat out and used. Red was the most complex colour as it was composed of different components, also of a magical nature. The starting material was a type of earth only occurring in one place. This was then finely grated and mixed with the bark of the *ndigu* tree and red flowers. At the time some men stated that the piece of bark must be collected by a menstruating woman in order for the colour to exert its full power (Hauser-Schäublin 2007). The mixture was then burnt and stored in powder form in a small bamboo tube. This red powder displayed slight variations in colour, depending on the manufacturing process. Master painters placed great value on having the 'right' paint powder, and they preferred to go in search of another 'supplier' rather than use one that did not meet their expectations.

The colour red is – or more accurately, was – not just a colour as is the case in Western colour theory, but a special, magical substance which refers to a series of multi-layered meanings, including those from religious contexts. Red is associated with vitality, menstruation and birth. These, at least at first sight, are dangerous areas for men, as they are understood as uncontrollable female powers diametrically opposed to the ritual world controlled by men. Nevertheless, the colour red plays a dominant role in the ritual lives of the men, as it means vitality and ritual heat. The sculptures, predominately painted red, awaken associations with animated bodies pulsing with blood, with vitality par excellence (cf. plate 43). After uttering a magic formula over it and mixing it with further ingredients, yam farmers gave red paint to their seedlings to make the tubers grow as big and beautiful as possible. It was also administered to novices and sacred images during initiation ceremonies. In these contexts it was no longer a colour for painting but a magic substance *(urakus)* which could be extremely dangerous if it landed in the wrong hands. It transformed the people and objects into powerful, sacred protagonists (which was termed *maira* 'sacred-miraculous').

Depending on the cultural context in which it was used this red substance was given different names. Today, as even the Abelam lead an increasingly globalised lifestyle and use industrial paints, a secularisation process seems to have also taken place with respect to the colours: For many of them red has become a mere colour or material, which is still assigned a certain power, but as a secondary property, so to speak. However, that which previously possessed neither an 'inside' nor an 'outside,' as it was referred to in some colour theories, but instead, all in all, was a potent substance, is now subject to a corresponding division.

None of the other colours display this potent-dangerous substance character like the red earth pigment, whose manufacture and usage included secret knowledge and the observance of many taboos. The example of red shows that this colour cannot be assigned either a plus or a minus sign in order to evaluate the impressions and feelings, as is the case in some colour theories. Red encompasses both: vitality, extreme life force – and deadly danger. However there is another difference to the European colour theories: The Abelam associate some of the colours with sex, i.e. *gender.* Thus red refers to women and womanliness. However, this gender allocation can be transformed through powerful actions, as occurs in the male cult when a magic spell is cast over the colour red and it becomes a magical masculine substance.

In contrast to red white has a male connotation. White refers to bones, the skeleton. As an inner structure it lends the body its form, that which is enduring in a human being. In accordance with the Abelam's ideas on reproduction, the male contribution to procreation is responsible for the formation of the bones, the female for flesh and blood. Both of them, blood and bones, are the seat of 'souls,' of which the human individual possesses three different ones. When a person dies the 'soul' associated with blood functions as a frontier crosser, moving between the here and now and the beyond, until the funeral rituals are completed and the 'blood soul' remains in the hereafter. The bones are the seat of a 'soul' which continues to exist after the funeral rituals. The 'bone soul' is associated with stars and shooting stars. Accordingly, the 'bone soul' has an almost eternal character. Large, smoothly polished shell rings (gouged from the giant clam *Tridacna gigax)* are considered valuables. They are also used to decorate the lower section of the front of a ceremonial house on the occasion of its inauguration, and are also considered to be an aspect (or a manifestation) of stars, which decorate the everlasting firmament – the cosmos. Thus white is also a colour that connects different materials with one another. Red and white do not have a single, clearly defined meaning. Instead they point to a whole series of phenomena associated with one another, or more precisely, to relationships between them (cf. Forge 2017b [1970] and Losche 1995). Put simply, red is associated with fertility, earthliness and transiency, white with light/sun, the ethereal, as symbolized by white feathers, and immortality. However, for the Abelam, these boldest of colour contrasts are not opposites but complementarities and form an indivisible whole.

Combinations of colours and forms in the painting

This complementary relationship is also apparent in the painting process, which is traditionally a sacred activity carried out shielded from everyday life. There are regional and local differences regarding the painting process, the motifs and patterns, and even the 'signatures' of the master artists differ from one another. In 1980 I was able to follow the painting process in detail – the painting of a gable façade – in the village of Kalabu. The following remarks are based on this (cf. Hauser-Schäublin 2016).

The gable front of a ceremonial house is tailor made, its size is determined by the building's dimensions. It is constructed from the lower sections of Sago palm sheaths, which are sewn together. These palm sheaths, pressed flat to produce an extremely smooth surface, are first primed with a dark grey or black earth pigment, piece by piece, and from top to bottom. This produces a surface onto which the earth pigments can adhere. At the same time the priming is understood as the first step in the transformation of the natural substrate into a sacred image. The main artist – as the leader of a whole team of painters – traces the first line with a bird feather dipped in white paint, beginning at the tip of the gable triangle laid out on the ground. The white paint is the form-giving colour; it has precedence over all other colours and is therefore reserved for the master artist. He does not partition the gable front into different sections for the respective horizontal pattern bands. He successively paints the outlines of the motifs from the tip of the façade such as swirls, vegetable and animal elements, figures with bent arms and legs, bodies, faces with flat triangular headdresses and white feather bands as well as net bags as attributes of the figures.

The pattern bands are generally arranged symmetrically and are composed of characteristic motifs. The main artist continues from the point where he has previously completed a pattern band. Horizontal lines are rare, and the vertical connecting lines do not play a dominant role in the overall composition. The majority of lines are curved. A number of the motifs are composed from several closely aligned lines drawn in parallel. Sometimes they form hatching or zig-zag lines. Spiral forms are composed from white lines, on whose outer edges feather-like triangles in white are often placed. Occasionally, white bands of triangles are positioned on the circumference of circles, as can be seen at hip height on some anthropomorphic sculptures. White lines also determine the size of the figures' eyes composed of concentric circles, for example on the bottom row of faces on a gable façade. Sometimes two artists work simultaneously on the same motif, one on the right hand side, one on the left.

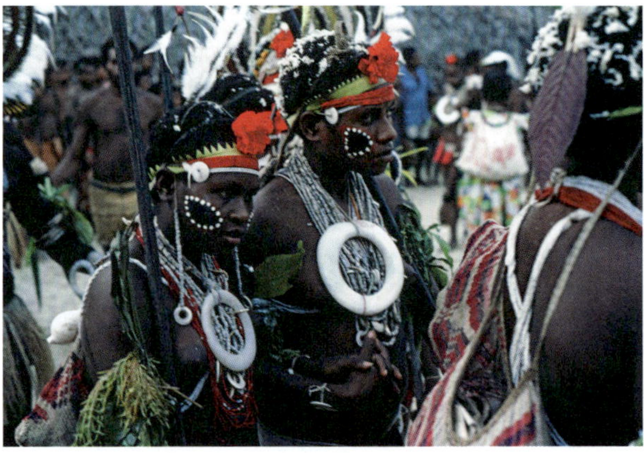

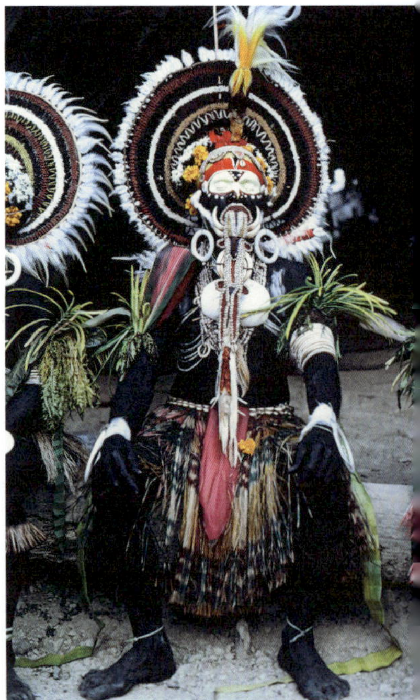

Fig. 3 left Young women adorned with shell ornaments and face painting; they accompany their brothers during a ritual dance. Lonem village. Photo: Brigitta Hauser-Schäublin, 1980.

Fig. 4 right Ritual dancer emerging after an initiation: His entire body is first painted black and then decorated with ornaments made from a wide variety of materials. The eye area is completely covered with paint; he is not allowed to open his eyes. Between his teeth he holds a boar tusk ornament as a symbol of prowess. Lonem village. Photo: Brigitta Hauser-Schäublin, 1980.

In a second step stripes of red paint – generally applied with a brush-like instrument – are painted by the main artist's assistants. Red nestles seamlessly against the white lines, subordinating itself to them. In contrast to the white lines the red stripes are often wider, more extensive. Red and white are the most important, high-contrast colour combinations in a painting. They result in what can be described as white lines in a sea of red (Hauser-Schäublin 2007).

Red stripes often border larger black core areas (i.e. the painted substrate). However, the clashing of red and black is offset or moderated through rows of white dots. These circular spots are dabbed onto the edge between red and black and form, as Kandinsky had already determined, both a border and a bridge between different coloured and form-giving elements (1969 [1926]: 21). These points follow an imaginary line, however they nevertheless form a type of staccato – each point an element in itself – in relation to the curved white lines and their red frames. At the same time, these points frequently convey the almost perspectival impression of an edge which borders a dark chasm. In fact black is sometimes used for intermediary or (imagined) cavities. It is frequently also used for hairy body parts: Facial hair, but above all male and female genitalia, which are depicted in the form of a black pubic triangle surrounded by a red line dotted with white points. This form-giving combination generates a dynamic tension between the elements of point, line and area, surface, edge and depth.

It is rare that red and black are immediately juxtaposed. This occurs in the case of parallel lines, not areas of colour, as can be occasionally seen in head silhouettes or concentric circles.

At many points in a painting the red border of black core areas is only an intermediary step, as many of the black intermediary spaces are ultimately filled with yellow paint. Above all this is done with faces or parts of faces, where yellow is used to mark areas of skin (cf. Mc Guigan 1992: 244) that do not display any bodypainting. In these paintings yellow plays a mediating, appeasing, two-dimensional role. The combination of yellow and red is harmonious. Sometimes the two colours almost seem to merge, when they are not separated from each other by a white line. In a final step in the painting process, those areas which are left black are painted over with a white tree resin. This dries crystal clear and lends the black a light gloss. The sheen, the brilliance of colours and colour combinations, is a quality that the Abelam value highly.

Conclusion

The combination of colours and forms sketched here – the repertoire of forms must be systematically discussed in a further analysis[6] – also appear in the decoration of male and female dancers, yam tubers, which are displayed during a festival, as well as on carvings and plaited masks (fig. 5). The idea of white lines as the primary colour and structuring element is central. However, beyond the white painting colour, they are also realized using other materials, for example the sun-bleached string from which women produce patterned net bags, or the light-coloured plaiting material for male basket masks or rear headdresses. Despite the variety of materials, similar or identical combinations of colours and forms are always employed, and thus refer to interrelated meanings.

The colours and colour combinations form a system. The colour praxis of the Abelam, as I have attempted to show, possesses a culturally immanent logic and system of meaning which cannot be explained using European colour theories, let alone understood. The colour praxis, and the basic rules of their combination and form-giving, are central parts of the Abelam's aesthetic and are embedded in comprehensive relationships of meaning.

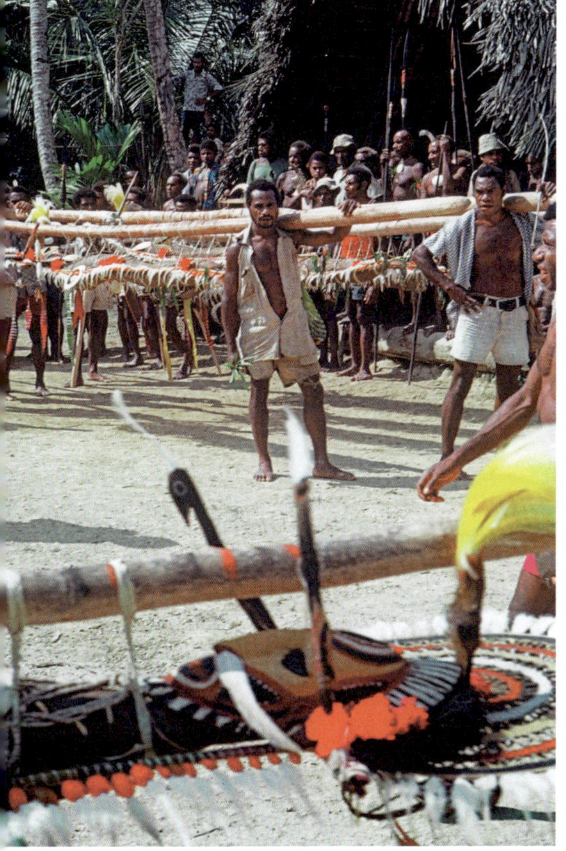

Fig. 5 The magnificent specimens of long yams, bound to bamboo poles and decorated with masks and plaited rear headdresses, are carried to the competition at the ceremonial ground. Lonem village. Photo: Brigitta Hauser-Schäublin, 1980.

1 The Abelam collection of the Museum der Weltkulturen was established by Meinhard Schuster and Eike Haberland on the occasion of the Frobenius New Guinea Expedition of 1961.

2 The author of this essay undertook research in the Abelam village of Kalabu between 1978 and 1985, together with her husband Jörg Hauser. She visited the village again in 2015 (cf. Hauser-Schäublin 2017).

3 Today much has changed, not least as a result of the Abelam's conversion to Christianity. Consequently, painting is no longer embedded in ritual and subject to the corresponding taboos. Nevertheless, I employ the present tense in order to convey a livelier picture than would be possible with the past tense.

4 The painter and art theorist Philipp Otto Runge (1777–1810), a contemporary of Goethe, already described black and white as a "different class, opposed to the chromatic colours" (quoted according to Keller Tschirren 2011: 55).

5 In 2012 an exhibition was held in the Queensland Art Gallery & Gallery of Modern Art in Brisbane, which also invited Abelam artists to paint an on-site gable façade (using plywood panels and modern acrylic paints) and build the front side of an Abelam ceremonial house. Here too the artists restricted themselves to the traditional colours white, red, yellow and black, cf. the illuminating report on this successful project from McDougall (2015).

6 For the repertoire of forms cf. Hauser-Schäublin 1989.

References:

– **Bühler, Alfred. 1960:** *Kunststile am Sepik.* Basel: Museum für Völkerkunde.

– **Coupaye, Ludovic. 2007:** 'Des portraits Abelams'. In: *Arts & Cultures* 7. 258–275.

– **Forge, Anthony. 2017a [1962]:** 'Paint. a Magical Substance'. In: Forge, Anthony: *Style and Meaning. Essays on the Anthropology of Art.* Edited by Alison Clark and Nicholas Thomas. Leiden: Sidestone Press. 43–49.

– **Forge, Anthony. 2017b [1962]:** 'Learning to See in New Guinea'. In: Forge, Anthony: *Style and Meaning. Essays on the Anthropology of Art.* Edited by Alison Clark and Nicholas Thomas. Leiden: Sidestone Press. 123–137.

– **Goethe, Johann Wolfgang. 1810:** *Zur Farbenlehre.* 2 vol. Tübingen: Cotta.

– **Hauser-Schäublin, Brigitta. 1989:** *Leben in Linie, Muster und Farbe. Einführung in die Betrachtung außereuropäischer Kunst am Beispiel der Abelam.* Basel: Birkhäuser Verlag.

– **Hauser-Schäublin, Brigitta. 2007:** 'Weiß in einem Meer von Rot. Die bemalte Giebelwand des Abelam-Kulthauses'. In: Schmid, Anna and Alexander Brust (eds.): *Rot. Wenn Farbe zur Täterin wird.* Museum der Kulturen Basel. Basel: Christoph Merian Verlag. 190–194.

– **Hauser-Schäublin, Brigitta. 2016:** *Ceremonial Houses of the Abelam, Papua New Guinea. Architecture and Ritual – a Passage to the Ancestors.* Goolwa, SA: Crawford House Publishing.

– **Hauser-Schäublin, Brigitta. 2017:** 'Looking back. Abelam Art and some of Forge's Theses from a 2015 Perspective'. In: Forge, Anthony: *Style and Meaning. Essays on the Anthropology of Art.* Edited by Alison Clark und Nicholas Thomas. Leiden: Sidestone Press. 255–267.

– **Itten, Johannes. 2009 [1961]:** *Kunst der Farbe. Subjektives Erleben und objektives Erkennen als Wege zur Kunst.* Freiburg: Christophorus Verlag.

– **Kandinsky, Wassily. 1911:** *Über das Geistige in der Kunst. Insbesondere in der Malerei.* Munich: Piper.

– **Kandinsky, Wassily. 1969 [1926]:** *Punkt und Linie zu Fläche. Beitrag zur Analyse der malerischen Elemente.* Bern-Bümpliz: Benteli.

– **Keller Tschirren, Marianne. 2011:** *Dreieck, Kreis, Kugel. Farbenordnungen im Unterricht von Paul Klee am Bauhaus.* University of Bern: Ph.D. Thesis. https://archiv.ub.uni-heidelberg.de/artdok/2073/1/Keller_Tschirren_Dreieck_Kreis_Kugel_2012.pdf. (1.9.2020)

– **Klee, Paul. 1920:** *Schöpferische Konfession.* Berlin: Reiß.

– **Koch, Gerd. 1968:** *Kultur der Abelam. Die Berliner Maprik-Sammlung.* Berlin: Museum für Völkerkunde.

– **Losche, Diane. 1995:** *The Sepik Gaze. Iconographic Interpretation of Abelam Form.* In: *Social Analysis* 38. 47–60.

– **McDougall, Ruth. 2015:** 'Material Matters. Commissioning Contemporary Artworks from Papua New Guinea for the 7th Asia Pacific Triennial of Contemporary Art'. In: *AICCM Bulletin* 35 (1). 14–21. DOI: 10.1179/bac.2014.35.1.002 (05.08.2020).

– **Mc Guigan, Noel Damascus. 1992:** *The Social Context of Abelam Art. A Comparision of Art, Religion and Leadership in Two Abelam Communities.* University of Ulster, Belfast: Ph. D. Thesis.

– **Thurnwald, Richard. 1914:** 'Vom mittleren Speik zur Nordwestküste von Kaiser-Wilhelmsland.' In: *Mitteilungen aus den Deutschen Schutzgebieten* 27 (1). 81–84.

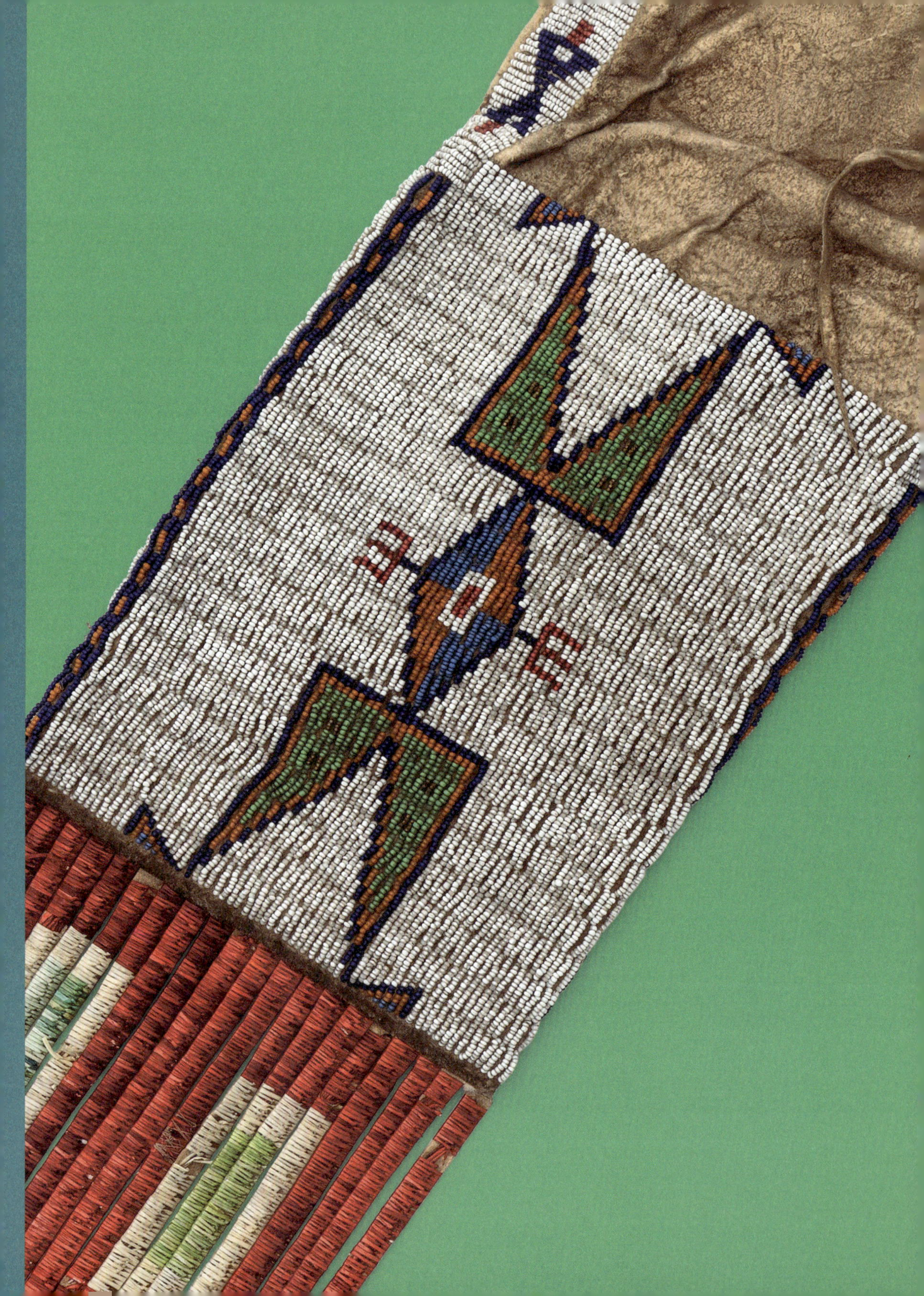

CHANGE

This tobacco pipe pouch unites two epochs: Up until the middle of the 19th century red-white-green embroidery employing flattened, coloured porcupine quills was the predominant method of embroidery amongst many indigenous peoples in North America. From around 1830 glass beads of European manufacture were increasingly used. Being easier to work with they led to an embroidery boom, above all on the plains. Leather, glass beads, metal, porcupine quills. Sioux, plains and prairies, USA. Collected by Robert W. M. A. Lotichius, 1930.

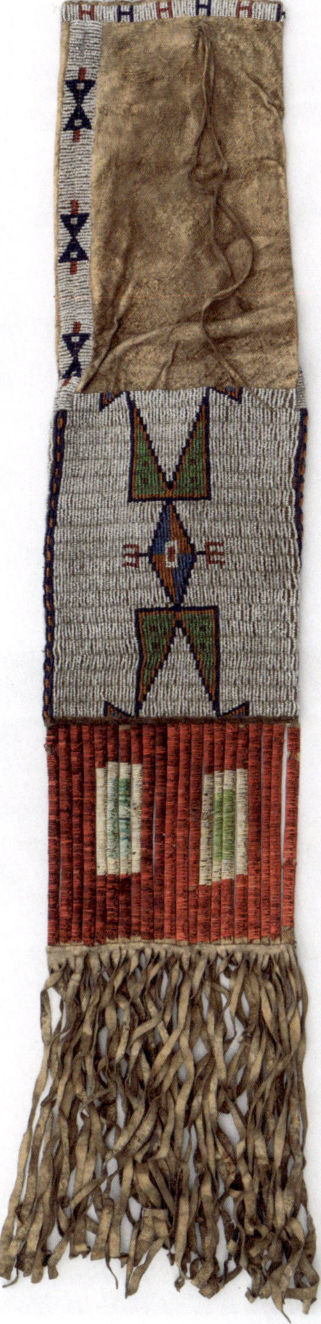

THE COLOURS OF AMAZONIA

René Fuerst in Conversation with Chantal Courtois

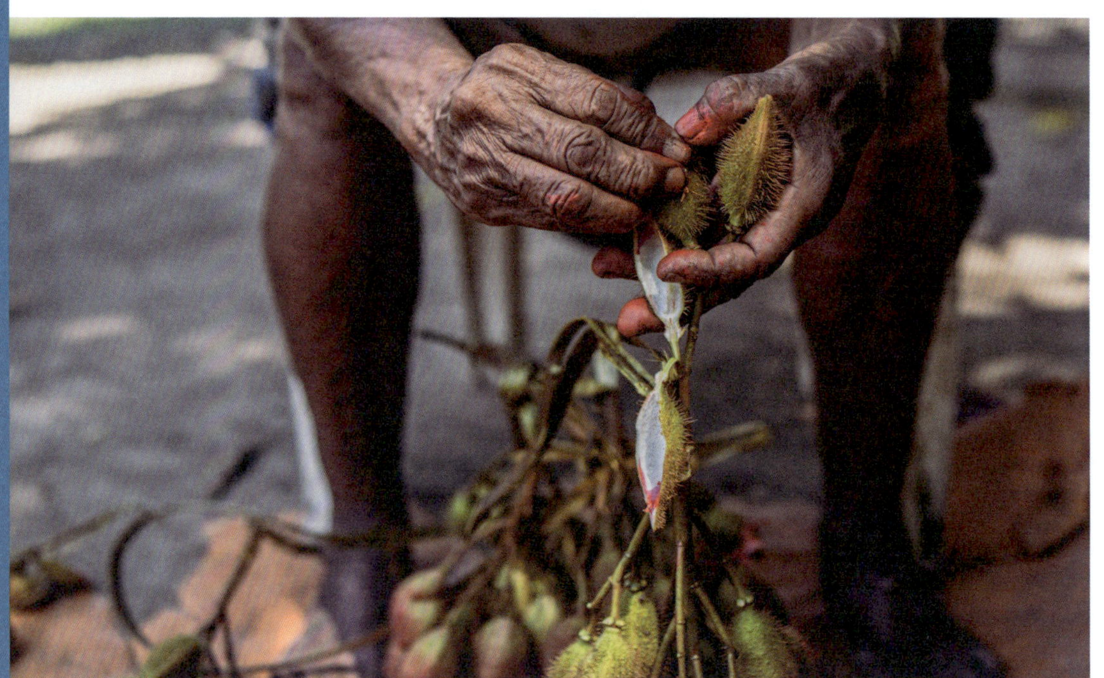

Fig. 1 Opening of the *urucum* capsules. Kayapó Xikrin, Cateté, Pará, Brazil. Purchased from the photographer in 2015. Collection: Musée d'ethnographie de Genève. Photo: Aurélien Fontanet, 2013.

Chantal Courtois (CC): The Weltkulturen Museum, Frankfurt am Main, invited you to participate in the exhibition GREEN SKY, BLUE GRASS in order to report on your experiences with the phenomenon of colour in Amazonia – your area of expertise. Thereupon, you enthusiastically seized the opportunity to discuss a theme within the framework of the project that is clearly close to your heart. What convinced you, as an ethnologist and specialist for Amazonia, about this ethnological approach to colour?

René Fuerst (RF): Somehow the theme of colour has always accompanied me, somewhere in the back of my head, on all my research expeditions. Penetrating the Amazon rain forest also means immersing oneself in nature and its dazzling wealth of colour, which one cannot escape as it is also reflected in all of the everyday objects of the people who live there. I myself have never approached the theme of colour from an ethnological perspective, and by the way I don't see myself as an ethnologist but as a proponent of indigenism. My research activity between 1955 and 1975 was primarily conducted in central Brazil, in the federal state of Mato Grosso and deep in the interior of Amazonia. This research was not the logical consequence of a corresponding education at a university, but was based on the desire to get to know indigenous peoples still living freely, or who had just recently been contacted, above all the Kayapó, the Nambikwara and the Yanomami. My ethnographic research and collection activities on behalf of the Geneva Museum of Ethnography (Musée d'ethnographie de Genève) and other European institutions ended when the Brazilian authorities expelled me from the country, amongst other things because I took part in a ground-breaking study of the International Red Cross and criticized government policy towards the indigenous peoples. I mention this as an aside to make clear that my thoughts on colour amongst the peoples of the Amazon region are not the result of detailed scientific research but are the fruit of all that I experienced through my contact with these people. In my opinion, up until their first contact with white people, the relationship of the indigenous peoples to colour was primarily of an intuitive and sensuous nature. When it comes to their colours I always think how exciting I found the stories about the 'redskins' as a child. And beyond all the clichés, I later discovered that the colour red plays a predominant role in the culture of the indigenous peoples of South America. Here we have cinnabar and iron oxide, there it is the *urucum* bush (fig. 1). And with this we are once again referred back to the close bond between the indigenous peoples and Mother Nature with her great wealth of vegetable and mineral colours.

CC: Your first words already conjure up in the mind's eye that world of colours which you are so familiar with. Why did you decide at the time to record this world in the form of black and white photographs?

RF: First of all, photography is my primary means of expression for documenting the world of the indigenous peoples. I decided on black and white photos because, from a technical perspective, they produce better results and more precise details than colour photographs. In my opinion colour does not capture the essential aspects. My photos are an expression of my view of things and my perception of a world that Europe's colonisers called a 'new' world, in order to simultaneously marginalise its original inhabitants. One sees how an unspoiled nature and culture was shattered by the ignorance and self-complacency of those who considered themselves to act and think in a civilised fashion. Of course there were exceptions: Men and women who devoted themselves to their work locally and bore witness to it in text and pictures.

CC: A number of these researchers, both men and women, virtually celebrated colour, especially in the forests of the Alto Xingu, which you also visited in your early years and called a 'paradise on earth'. Could you provide us with a few examples?

RF: Indeed! First and foremost there were the brothers Claudio and Orlando Villas-Bôas, who I often mention in my texts, from whom I learned the tools of my trade, and like them, how to be at the service of the indigenous peoples. The texts in the book *XINGU* from Maureen Bisilliat, a photographer and friend of mine, also originate from them. She captured the indigenous people, their bodies and their jewellery and the play of colours wonderfully in her pictures.

CC: It's like I can see the book before me. The realism and the extraordinary blaze of colour found in her photos are really overwhelming. Which colours have left the deepest impression on you when you think back on the life in Xingu?

RF: Overall, the life of the people there was very colourful, however their red, black and white left the deepest impression on me: the deep *carvão* – or charcoal black – the *urucum* red of the Annatto bush and the white of the light clay. These colours are used for body painting, which depicts a whole universe of signs and symbols. When the Kamaiurá mixed their colours for painting in preparation for a celebration, I asked them to paint the same motifs on paper which I had brought from Geneva for that purpose. For the first time ever the Kamaiurá executed a series of motifs on this unusual material, without altering anything else about their technique. I can still see them before me today, how they drew the patterns with a little wooden stick using paint from crushed wood charcoal and the juice from the *mangaba* fruit or Annatto bush (fig. 2). Before travelling the headwaters of the Xingu I was lucky enough to encounter the Xavante. These people, still uncontacted at the time, were the actual reason for my decision to travel to Brazil. The Xavante were not as richly adorned, and their colours were nowhere near as impressive. It was only later that I connected them both to their living environment. In accordance with the savanna and its brown and grey tones, the Xavante warriors were painted with ash and decorated with eagle feathers. This was completely different in the case of the Kalapalo, the Yawalapiti, the Waujá and the Kamaiurá in the tropical rain forest of the Alto Xingu with the lavish contrasts of their multi-coloured feather ornamentation. I only gradually came to understand the symbiotic relationship of the indigenous peoples to nature during the course of my repeated encounters with them, and anyone in my position would have experienced it the same. Other factors played a role, amongst others the exchange with fellow specialists. In the 1960s I began collecting for the Geneva Museum of Ethnography (MEG) and similar institutions in Europe, and this was associated with a different approach to the peoples and their material culture.

CC: During these years you met the anthropologist and botanist Borys Malkin at the Museum Goeldi, who as a collector had specialised, amongst other things, in the culture of the Ka'apor. As this people had already been pacified, the barter with them proceeded without difficulty. You once described the feather ornamentation of the Ka'apor as the most beautiful of all.

RF: Their colours are simply unbelievable: blue, turquois, cinnabar red, light yellow or gold-yellow, and their combinations are also unusual. The feather art of the Ka'apor, called Urubu by the Brazilians, is really unique. I have brought a few specimens with me, which you can see in the MEG in Geneva (fig. 3). I can also recall the first publication on the theme, it was a little masterpiece, written and illustrated by a couple of friends and a talented illustrator.

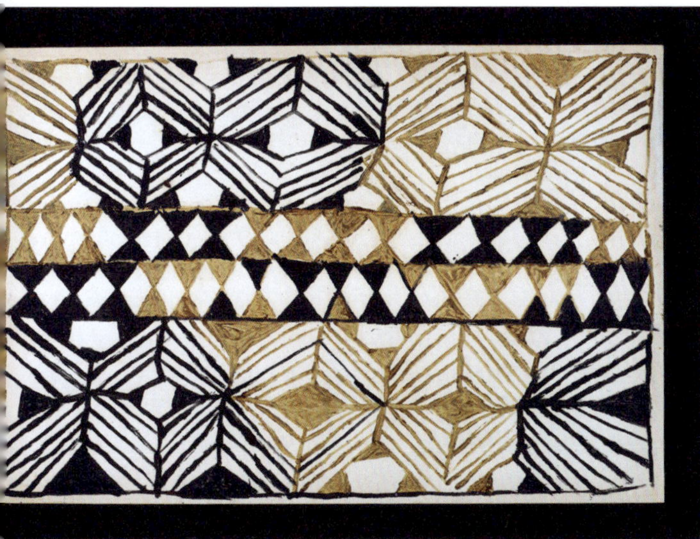

Fig. 2 Body painting motifs. Wood charcoal and Annatto on paper. Kamaiurá, Alto Xingu, Mato Grosso, Brazil, 1956. A gift from René Fuerst, 1956. Collection: Musée d'ethnographie de Genève. Photo: Johnathan Watts, 2016.

CC: How did you acquire these objects and all the other objects you collected?

RF: One usually acquires them by exchanging them for things that the indigenous people need: knives, axes, nylon thread and hooks, but also glass beads which we bought from the Lebanese traders in Rio. I knew from the Villas-Bôas brothers that the first thing I had to do was buy kilograms of glass beads in the Rua da Alfândega in order to get around in Alto Xingu, and to even get there in the first place.

CC: Overall, a continuation of customs that have been cultivated since the first contact with Europeans in this region in the 18th century, including the glass beads as a constant factor. However, these industrially manufactured glass beads break down the cosmic connection of the indigenous peoples to their colours, or do you see this differently?

RF: I was always fascinated by the fact that these beads proved so irresistible to the indigenous people, especially the women. I would love to have researched the history of the *misunga* – as I call them – from the point when they first arrived in Amazonia onwards. During my first encounters with those groups, who had remained uncontacted until that time, these beads still functioned like an 'open sesame'. I tried to understand what they found so desirable about them: the size, the colour? No one wanted yellow and green beads. The most coveted were the blue beads, the red with various colour nuances, white... The beads appeared desirable to the indigenous people because they brought new colour into their lives, and on top of that were easy to work with. As they served practical and ritual purposes, over time these objects became incorporated into the symbiotic relationship between the people and the universe, especially as their colours blend into nature's colourful spectrum.

CC: During this time you got to know, one after the other, the Yanomami, the Kayapó on the Xingu and finally the Xikrin from Cateté – 'your tribe' as you like to call them. Your book *Xikrin. Hommes oiseaux d'Amazonie* ('The Birdmen of Amazonia') is richly illustrated with photographs and drawings and the text explicitly addresses the Kayapó's colours.

RF: Yes, the encounter with the Kayapó, especially with the Xikrin, was formative. Documenting them is akin to my life's work. Who would still say that black is not a colour after seeing the Kayapó? Black is definitely their most distinctive feature. A sub-group of them even call themselves Metukti, the 'completely black people'. They literally paint their whole body black, only their head and feet are painted red. That they choose this second colour for body parts which are closest to the elements earth and sky respectively, says a lot about the significance

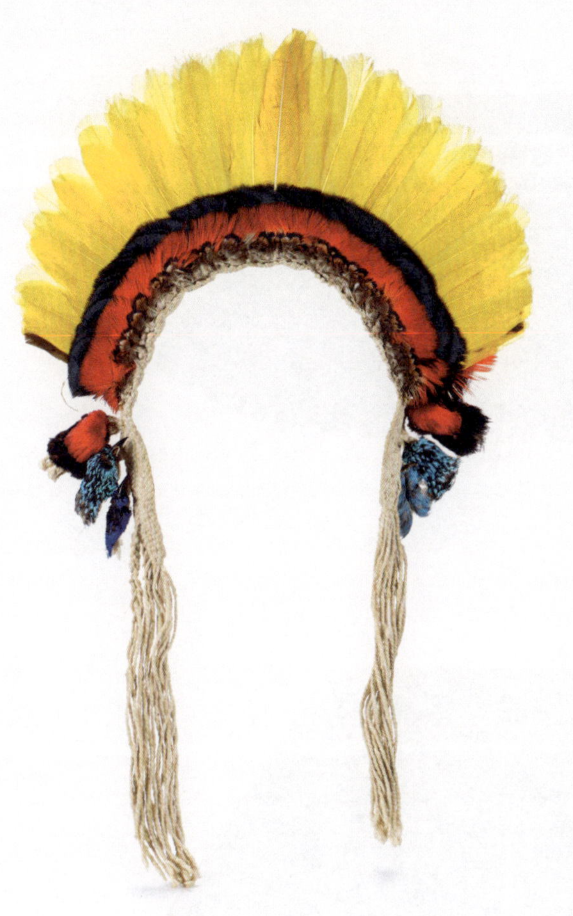

Fig. 3 *Wirara* or *akangatar* headdress. Ka'apor, Javaruhu village, Rio Gurupi, Maranhão, Brazil, middle of the 20th century. Yellow feathers from the oropendola *(Psarocolius)*, black of the great curassow *(Crax rubra)*, red of the scarlet macaw *(Ara macao)*, pigeon down, plumage of the spangled cotinga *(Kotinga cayana)*, cotton. Purchased in 1966 through the anthropologist and biologist Borys Malkin. Collection: Musée d'ethnographie de Genève. Photo: Johnathan Watts, 2016.

of the colour red, which is found amongst all the peoples of Amazonia. I brought them black beads as their body paint made from the pigment from the *Genipapo* fruit turns bluish when dry. They liked these black pearls, they were a genuine novelty for them. Since then they have integrated other colours, in particular the green and yellow of the Brazilian national flag, into their feather ornamentation. What can one say?

CC: I would like to show you a tanga (loincloth) from the Weltkulturen Museum which will be shown in the exhibition. We call it the 'blue tanga' (fig. 4). It was initially in the possession of Johann Friederich Gustav Umlauff (1833–1889), who in 1868 in St. Pauli, which was a suburb of Hamburg at the time, ran a family business which, in addition to natural products from overseas, also imported

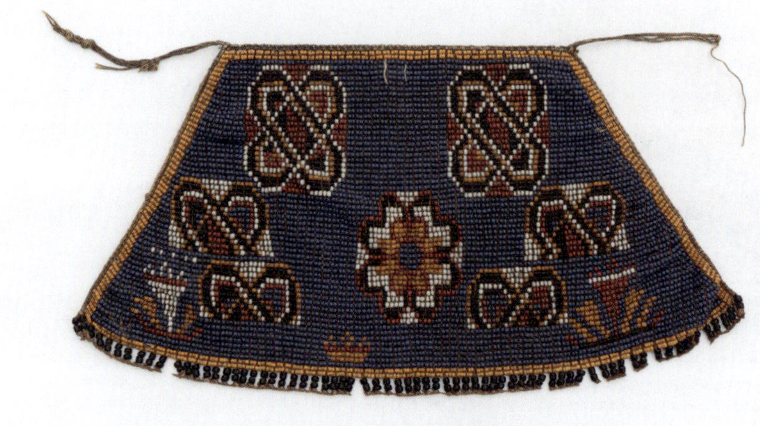

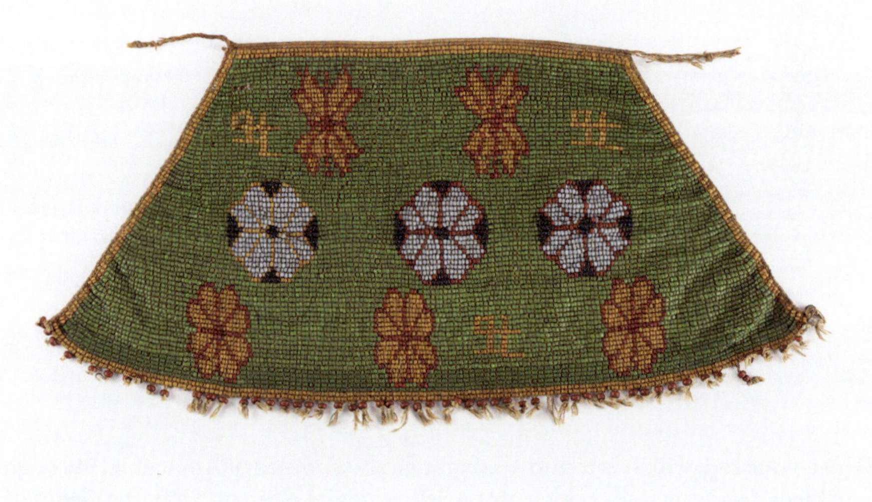

Fig. 4 above *Tanga* (woman's loincloth). Presumably Arawak, Guyana, 18th century. Glass beads. Purchased from the trader Johann F. G. Umlauff, 1908.

Abb. 5 below *Tanga* (woman's loincloth) with European motifs. Kalina, Guyana, beginning of the 19th century. Woven cotton and glass beads. A gift from Capitaine César-Hippolyte Bacle to the Musée académique, 1874. Collection: Musée d'ethnographie de Genève. Photo: Johnathan Watts, 2013.

ethnographic rarities and exhibited them in the manner of a cabinet of curiosities. This specimen was purchased from the Umlauff Company in 1908 and originates from Guyana, although it was not known from precisely which tribe.

RF: I have seen this type of hand-woven tanga decorated with beads, but I don't know anything more about it as the uncontacted peoples that I researched did not wear loincloths of this type. One finds them from the 18th century onwards, above all amongst the Karib peoples along the coast. However, this piece is similar to a number of bead loincloths in the collection of the Ethnography Museum in Geneva.

CC: That is true. In the historical collection of the MEG there are a number of woven bead tangas which originate from Guyana's coastal peoples and the period between the end of the 18th and the middle of the 19th century. A number of them were acquired from César-Hyppolite Bâcle (1794–1838). Bâcle was a former officer under Napoleon and was a similar type to the seller of the 'blue tanga'. He traded in exotic plants and animals. In addition, he also imported hundreds of specimens, such as the one in Geneva, including women's loincloths decorated with beads, above all from Brazil and the Caribbean. They have the same form, a similar colour composition and the same European flower motifs and rosette as the 'blue tanga'. Only the background colours and the execution of the patterns differ slightly (fig. 5). An analysis of the style concluded, on the basis of the weave, that they must have originated from an Arawak group. Accordingly, the 'blue tanga' probably comes from Surinam, where precisely this group was dominant. The Ethnological Museum Herrnhut in Saxony, founded by the Evangelical Unity of Brethren, possesses a number of similar specimens. They were collected in Surinam in the second half of the 18th century during the course of the missionary work of these liberal Protestant brethren (Oehrl 2019: 24).

RF: On the one side, I find such objects, and the beads as such, fascinating. On the other side, they also make me sad. I am fascinated by the power of seduction which they have exerted over centuries, and by the manner in which the women have integrated them into their weaving, appropriating them in ever new creations. What is sad about it is that when one traces their journey one is confronted by the whole history of conquest and subjugation which shook this continent. On the basis of these two merchants, who participated in the colonial adventure, we become aware of the missionary work and its acculturation of the indigenous population. And what is the situation today? Everything has only got worse with the activities of the Evangelical sects, who have been rampant in Brazil over the last fifty years. One can hardly believe it but in fact the person responsible for the isolated indigenous peoples at the National Indian Foundation (FUNAI) is an evangelist, in other words a pike in the carp pond. We look on impotently as the government, with a total disregard for life, promotes the destruction of the forests in the interest of agribusiness. Today it is more necessary than ever to fight alongside the peoples of the great Amazon rain forest.

CC: My dear René, my heartiest thanks for this conversation! You have ended with an angry appeal, which cannot be otherwise if, like you, one has campaigned so hard for the cause of the Indigenous peoples of Amazonia. At the same time we have not left the theme of colour. The passion with which you fight for the cause of the peoples of the Amazon rain forest contributes to preserving the wealth of colour in this forest and many other areas of the world.

RF: I hope so with all my heart.

References:

— **Bisilliat, Maureen; Claudio and Orlando Villas-Bôas. 1979:** *Indiens du Shingu*. Paris: Editions du Chêne.

— **Fuerst, René. 1964:** 'La Peinture Collective des Femmes Xikrin. Contribution à l'Étude des Indiens Kayapo du Brésil Central'. In: *Völkerkundliche Abhandlungen* 1. Hannover. 117–130.

— **Fuerst, René. 2006:** *Xikrin, Hommes Oiseaux d'Amazonie*. Milan: Cinq Continents.

— **Fuerst, René. 2019.** *Indiens d'Amazonie. Vingt Belles Années 1955–1975*. Milan: Cinq Continents.

— **Ribeiro, Darcy; Ribeiro, Berta G. and Georgette Dumas. 1957:** *Arte Plumaria dos Índios Kaapor*. Rio de Janeiro: Seikel.

— **Oehrl, Michael. 2019:** 'Beaded Aprons of the Coastal Peoples of the Guianas'. In: *BEADS. Journal of the Society of Bead Researchers* 31. 58–73.

WHOSE AESTHETIC IS AUTHENTIC?

The Colour of African Masks Between Cultural Practice and Commercial Appropriation

Frauke Gathof

Masks are among the objects that many people intuitively associate with art from African countries. Not only are they omnipresent in private collections, museums and exhibitions, they are also regarded as some of the most stereotyped and iconicised objects (Forni 2016: 38).

On the international art market, the search for 'authentic' items in 'original condition' plays a dominant role in assessing the value of objects.[1] But the condition of the masks in many collections today is often not representative of their condition when used in the societies of origin. In some cases, the objects looked quite different before being sold to the (mostly foreign, European or North American) clients. This is because the producers themselves or local intermediaries or foreign dealers have changed the appearance of the masks by adapting them to the collectors' notions and expectations of what comprises an 'authentic-looking' object, in an attempt to make them more attractive as a purchase (Eisenhofer and Guggeis 2002: 11, 23; Junker 2017: 15). But what are the consequences of this notion of 'authenticity' which dominate the international trade in art?

The use and aesthetic of masks

Masks have many different meanings and applications among various African ethnic groups.[2] Often they refer directly to a transcendental creature with precisely defined physical features, clothing and demeanor.[3] In this respect, masks fulfil various social functions in certain rituals, while their wearers perform specific tasks and roles. The outward appearance of masks also varies widely. Those with inside knowledge can identify the function of the masks through certain stylistic elements such as their proportions, imitation scarification or in particular the application of paint (Thurner 1997: 92). These criteria, which are aesthetically adapted to the role in question, are of central importance because only specific painted designs lend the mask its significance in rites and ceremonies. Without these the masks would not be worn (Bouttiaux 2009: 58; Heißenbüttel 2006: 71; Herold 1970: 16).

One example of this are the *kifwebe* masks of the Songye and Luba in the territory of the modern-day Democratic Republic of the Congo. These masks were worn in the *kifwebe* secret society for occasions such as inaugurations, initiations, circumcision rites or burials (Neyt 1994: 201). Their appearance typically features concentric decorative grooves which are painted white and black (fig. 1). This colour combination refers to the connection between the world of the living and the world of the dead (Agthe 1983: 17). White is associated both with benevolent dead spirits and with healing. Black is linked to destructive magic, and its use on masks is viewed as providing protection against this kind of sorcery (Hersak 1993: 156).

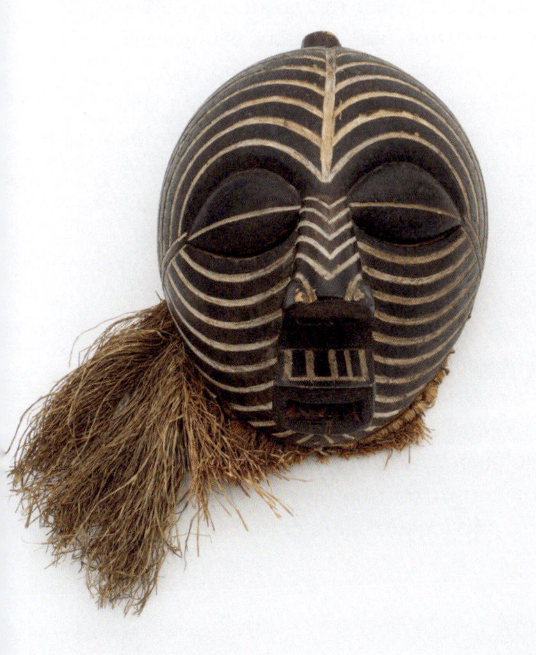

Fig. 1 The *kifwebe* masks of the Luba are oval or (more seldom) round. The wood of this mask was blackened, then the concentric grooves were painted white. Acquired from Guillaume De Hondt, c. 1940.

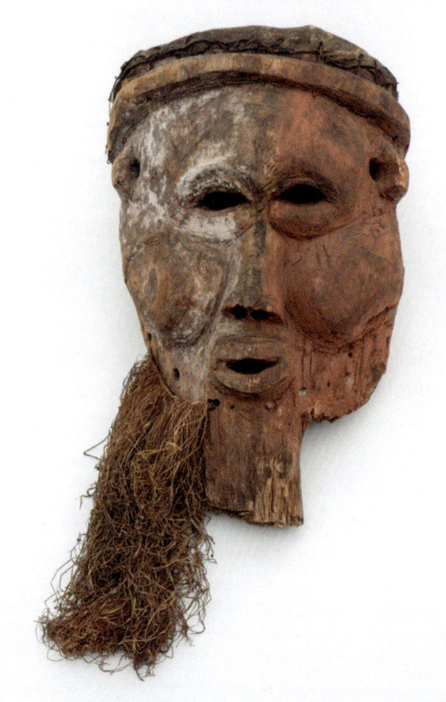

Fig. 2 The *kakungu* masks of the Suku are impressive with their notable size (this one is 65.5 cm, but in many cases they can be up to 90 cm), prominent cheeks and jutting chin. Acquired from Guillaume De Hondt, 1941.

Similarly, the *kakungu* masks of the Suku and Yaka (situated in today's Democratic Republic of the Congo and Angola) not only display a uniquely identifiable shape, but were also painted exclusively in white and red (fig. 2). Red here symbolises blood (as the colour of life), revenge and evil; wearing the mask would ensure that the latter kept its distance from all those present at the ritual site. White stands for health and benediction, as *kakungu* masks were supposed in particular to protect young men from evil influences and magic before and during circumcision and initiation. These masks were also present at the healing of initiates (Bourgeois 1980: 42–44; 1985: 13–14).

The masks on the European art market

The ritual use of masks meant that within a relatively short space of time they became prestige objects which were popular for trading purposes and as diplomatic gifts. From the early 20th century onwards they were also given to Europeans who were conducting research in a particular region or had settled in that area. This allowed some kinds of masks to spread beyond their original region and also attracted the attention of European travellers (Forni 2016: 40–41). From the late 19th century onwards, large quantities of African masks were being systematically collected and brought to Europe by employees of European colonial governments, as well as by researchers and missionaries (Heißenbüttel 2006: 74–76).[4]

Over the course of the 19th century, the terminology changed from 'curiosities' to ethnographica, then to museum exhibits, and ultimately to works of art (Thurner 1997: 81). This upgrade in value to *objets d'art* was triggered by the enthusiasm for African ethnographica shown by modernist artists such as Pablo Picasso, Henri Matisse and Wassily Kandinsky in the early 20th century. They were, however, solely interested in the form the objects took, while the context in which they were created and used was ignored (Eisenhofer and Guggeis 2002: 8–9; Thurner 1997: 81).

After World War II, 'African art', as it was known, became ever more popular in Europe and North America and also became accessible to a broader section of society. People decorated their homes with masks and they were marketed in films and magazines as an interior design feature. At the same time, increasing numbers of people were able to travel to African countries, where they would acquire objects as souvenirs or goods for trading. This led to a huge growth in demand (Crowley 1981: 66; Himmelheber 1967: 18). Businesses opened up in many African cities to target this new market, and indeed dealers still offer their wares in these shops today, with goods coming not only from their own area but also from neighbouring regions and states. This is done via intermediaries who acquire the goods from smaller villages (Crowley 1981: 67; Thurner 1997: 79–80).

The rise in demand for masks influenced their production, too. It became more market driven, with a stronger emphasis on displaying and selling goods to foreign customers. This created opportunities for the societies producing the goods to actively exploit the financial advantages of international demand (Forni 2016: 38). Parallel to this, masks were – and still are – produced and used for their traditional purposes. Objects which display signs of use, however, are particularly popular on the international art market because they are perceived as being 'more authentic'. For this reason, masks which are intended for actual use are also traded (Kasfir 1992: 45). In some cases this happens illicitly because members of many societies that produce masks still used for ceremonial purposes would not themselves sell them; moreover, some societies have imposed sanctions to prevent these objects being traded (Turner 1997: 80).

How the colours of masks have changed

On the whole, the tourist market has had no influence on how the masks produced by various African ethnic groups have changed; nonetheless, these changes were later adjudged to be 'inauthentic' on the international market. It has always been the case that new materials, tools and techniques have made their way to Africa via trade with other global regions, and upon arrival they have been integrated into local production methods. One example of this is the introduction of sandpaper from Europe. While carvings in the tropical regions of Africa had hitherto been rubbed down with raw *Ficus asperifolia* leaves, the frequent use of sandpaper subsequently enabled larger surface areas to be finished in less time and generally produced softer contours (Himmelheber 1967: 15). Materials brought in via trade also left their mark: most notably, glass beads, synthetics and oil paints were directly absorbed into the material culture of many ethnic groups. In some cases, prestigious but expensive materials were replaced by goods that were imported in large quantities and could thus, over time, be acquired more cheaply and easily. The *ku'ngang* masks of the

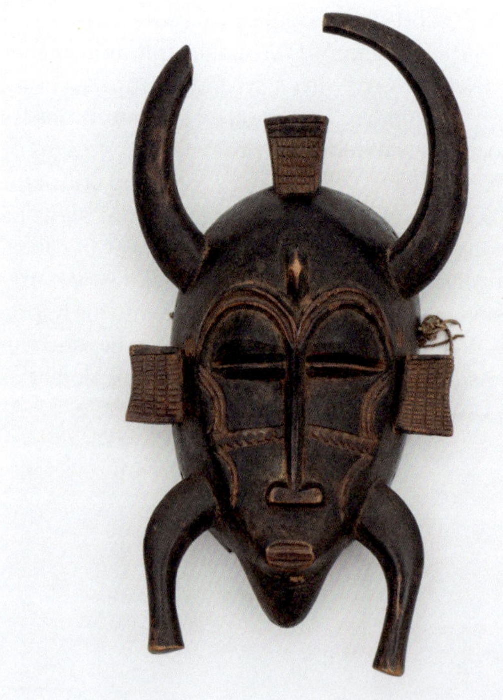

Fig. 3 The horned *kodal* mask is covered with a classical black-brown patina. When the colouring is polychromatic, the Senufo respect the dynamics of the shape, for instance along the curved lines of the decorations or horns. Acquired from E. Le Veel, c. 1927.

Bamileke people in Cameroon, for example, were traditionally decorated with cowrie shells. More recent masks of this type are increasingly adorned with white buttons or a combination of buttons and cowrie shells (Forni 2016: 43–46; Thurner 1995: 226).

The introduction of industrially manufactured paints from Europe was particularly significant for the cultural production of masks. The paint used for masks had previously been extracted from mineral-, plant- or animal-based raw materials. The colour red, for example, was produced from red ochre, redwood powder and sometimes from animal blood; white paint came from kaolin, pale clay, flour or ground mussels. Black paint could be extracted from coal, while some objects were blackened by being held over an open fire (Gröning 2001: 114–116; Himmelheber 1967: 23). The introduction of oil paints expanded the colour spectrum as well as the number of options for varying colours, which meant that groups such as the Baule and the Guro (in present-day Côte d'Ivoire) began painting their masks in colours that were noticeably more vibrant and wide-ranging. Moreover, oil paints are more durable than other colouring agents. This is why, for example, the Guéré (Côte d'Ivoire) use oil paint primarily to adorn masks with particularly significant hues. The greater durability of the paints makes it possible to utilise the objects for a longer period of time (Himmelheber 1967: 16–17).

Aesthetic changes in the name of 'authenticity'

Yet it was precisely this use of industrially produced paints to apply colour that many dealers found problematic. Even today, the majority of their foreign customers prefer objects that look used and old (Forni 2016: 39). Although oil paint has been imported to Africa and used on the continent en masse since the late 19th century, many collectors view its use as 'inauthentic', or even 'un-African' (Eisenhofer and Guggeis 2002: 11; Thurner 1995: 228). This leads to some dealers stripping the paint from masks ahead of sale and re-varnishing them "in order to correspond to western visual practices and projections" (Eisenhofer and Guggeis 2002: 11). Attention is paid neither to the aesthetic notions of the ethnic group that produced the masks nor to the significance of the colours for these people. The sole priority is the economic objective.

Yet it is not always the case that the colour is simply removed from the mask. The predominantly matte tones found at tourist markets and in galleries are supposedly reminiscent of natural paints. The Guro masks traded at markets exhibit these kinds of hues. However, the masks which are actually used by this group today feature bright and glossy colours (Bouttiaux 2009: 57; Thurner 1995: 228). A totally different kind of painting is added for other masks. The Senufo people from Côte d'Ivoire mostly paint their *kodal* masks with a single colour which used to be black or red-brown (fig. 3), whereas today there are also examples in more striking hues. *Kodal* masks for sale at the tourist markets, by contrast, are painted in matte red and yellow horizontal stripes. This contradicts Senufo aesthetics, according to which the painting has to enhance the structures of the carving; horizontal stripes, however, achieve precisely the opposite effect (Thurner 1995: 232).

The masks being traded are supposed to reflect not just the notions of European customers, but also their aesthetic sentiments, thereby making them better suited to urban European lifestyles and interior design. There have been cases where this has been achieved pre-sale, for example, by removing patinas that have formed as a result of sacrificial offerings (Crowley 1981: 67; Junker 2017: 18). Ironically, however, at the same time other means are also used as a way of artificially producing signs of use and age.

One significant aspect of the definition of 'authenticity' used here is that masks are actually used in rites or for other traditional purposes before they are circulated on the foreign market (Majeed 2019: 5). Thus two masks of the same quality and by the same carver might be valued differently if one of the masks bears no traces of use – and it is irrelevant here whether both masks were destined to be used in rituals or not. This clearly shows that the mask's value is adjudged not on the basis of the object itself, or its purpose, or artistic quality, or the level of artisanal skill it required, but rather in connection with unrelated characteristics that have been externally determined (Thurner 1997: 82). In order to meet the demand for supposedly used objects, dealers – along with the manufacturers themselves – have developed a range of methods to make the masks appear older and more used (Himmelheber 1967: 21).

One of these methods is to bury the mask in the ground for a while; the resulting damp, friction from grains of sand and damage from hungry insects create the requisite aged appearance. Then there is the application of fire, deliberate damage and breakages – some masks are even rubbed with shoe polish. Dyeing either an entire mask or just one section also supposedly fakes an antiquated look. The back of the mask is dyed a darker colour and then rubbed hard in order to simulate many years of being used. At the same time, partially removing paint can mimic intensive usage (Himmelheber 1967: 23; Eisenhofer and Guggeis 2002: 23).

Market-driven manipulation

Within a system determined by economics, any changes made to masks of African ethnic groups purely serve the purpose of making them more attractive for the European market and adapting them to suit the customers' wishes and ideas. 'Authenticity', which has evolved into being the most important criterion on the market, is defined not by the actual state of the object but instead by stereotyped notions of African art from a European perspective. There is the idea of an historical 'African art', an 'original condition' that never existed as such because masks have always been subject to change. The international market ignores these changes and relies on a concept of authenticity that depicts a stereotypical and distorted picture of cultural production in Africa rather than the recent situation (Thurner 1995: 225–226, 235). Nonetheless, these ideas are paramount when trading African objects on the international art market. Coming to a conclusion about an object's 'authenticity' is directly connected with making a judgement about its value. 'Authentic' means good and valuable, while 'inauthentic' signifies bad and worthless (Kasfir 1992: 44).

The preferred antique status of masks refers not just to the date when an object was made, but also to the aesthetic and immaterial notions upon which form and function are based. Artists such as Picasso and Matisse, but also August Macke und Emil Nolde, were enthusiastic about this art from Africa. They saw it as encapsulating art in its 'original state' (Heißenbüttel 2006: 78). A similar assumption underpins the before/afterwards scenario of colonialism, which long went unquestioned by dealers, collectors and indeed scholars as the basis for distinguishing between 'authentic' and 'inauthentic'. Objects from the pre-colonial era were deemed 'authentic' because they were free of western influences, something that could be seen, for example, in their use of colours from natural and locally obtained materials. Moreover, there was the belief that African societies had existed in relative isolation from each other in pre-colonial times and featured a high degree of internal coherence, i.e. they were not influenced by other African ethnic groups. Everything produced during or after the colonial era was thought to be 'inauthentic', because, for example, the introduction of a monetary economy supposedly led to a different set of interests and, in addition, new aesthetic ideas had been spread by missionaries, colonial employees and tourists (Kasfir 1992: 41–43). Although colonialism did bring about changes in the population and thus their cultural practices too, this before/after scenario about the colonial era can by no means be regarded as useful in appraising African masks. Long before colonialism there had frequently been developments and influences which were also reflected in mask production. These include the proliferation of new technologies such as weaving and brass casting and the spread of religious beliefs such as Islam. If the history of African societies and the changes they have undergone is restricted to the colonial era, there are two consequences: firstly, it denies their internal capacity for development without European influence, and secondly it produces a "timeless past" which implies that there were no changes for centuries prior to colonialism (Kasfir 1992: 43).

These views make it difficult for producers to sell their wares if they reflect the current local aesthetic. And then there are the contemporary artists who tried to develop new artistic approaches after many African countries attained independence, but who have experienced difficulties in some cases if their art is not explicitly devoted to issues – or does not follow an aesthetic – perceived on the international market as 'African' (Heißenbüttel 2006: 80).

In addition, dealers and collectors long equated 'authenticity' with anonymity. Ignorance of the specific names of whoever made the masks was not regarded as a consequence of the collection's context. This meant that for a long time, (intermediary) dealers as well as researchers and scholars abstained from recording the artist's name and asking them questions about the use and aesthetics of the objects. This predominant anonymity was acknowledged as an inherent aspect and feature of 'authentic' objects (Heißenbüttel 2006: 74–76; Kasfir 1992: 44). What this comes down to is that the notion of an artist who creates a work by exploring an aesthetic system with individuality and creativity does not fit in with images of a 'backward' and homogenous society where the individual only 'instinctively' follows the stipulations of the group (Majeed 2019: 21; Thurner 1997: 85–86; Vogel 1986: 5). As far as removing or altering the paint on masks is concerned, this viewpoint leads to any trace of an individual artist being eradicated from the object. The impression thereby created is that the painting on all masks is identical – a perspective that ignores and eliminates not only key aspects of the society's preferences regarding aesthetics and content, but also the artist's individual decisions. When the creator is not identified as a specific individual, there is no need to consider the ideas and concepts that form the basis for their work, meaning that these can be changed.

What is 'authentic'?

To summarise, it has been established that the appearance of African masks has changed repeatedly over time. These alterations were long confined to the choice of tools and materials. However, contact with Europeans over the last two centuries has meant that masks have come to be perceived and evaluated differently. When they became a popular product in Europe and North America they were ascribed new meanings through collecting and dealing practices. They ceased to be ritual or other cultural objects and were turned instead into commodities and then ultimately pieces of art in European galleries and households (Kasfir 1992: 47; Thurner 1997: 88). The fact that masks as commercial collectibles have dropped their ritual application, and are thus no longer subject to the aesthetics and function stipulated by a particular ethnic group, can legitimate a change in appearance. But this only holds as long as the masks are also perceived as art in the sense of artificial rather than 'authentic' objects. It does not change the fact, however, that the artist's original intention has been negated.

Generally speaking, there is an inherent contradiction in the international market relying on an understanding of authenticity that ultimately requires the masks to be changed in order to conform to these notions. This means there can be no mention of the masks being 'authentic'. Clearly, their modified appearance simply serves to uphold an idea that is fair neither to the societies that produced them nor to the individuality of the people who created them. At the same time, the notion of 'authenticity' sustains a market with real financial clout that also benefits local actors and producers.

When assessing and describing African masks it is ultimately of vital importance to ask questions about who is defining the parameters of cultural 'authenticity' and to what end, as well as querying the basis upon which these assumptions are made and the principal criteria for designing masks in the societies where they are made (Vogel 1986: 7).

1 According to the dictionary, 'authentic' means "genuine; based on facts; accurate or reliable" (Oxford 2020); in this essay the word is placed in single quotation marks to indicate its usage with a different definition. This is based on stereotyped notions of art and society in African countries that come from an external perspective.

2 Masks are produced and used in many but by no means all African ethnic groups. Groups with a nomadic or semi-nomadic lifestyle, such as the Maasai in Tanzania and Kenya, do not have masks as part of their material culture (Göltenboth 1987: 42).

3 Whenever masks are mentioned here, only the part covering the face is meant. The entire mask ensemble also includes specific clothing and characteristic accessories (Eisenhofer and Guggeis 2002: 19).

4 This collecting occurred in a variety of ways. Some of the objects were purchased or exchanged for money or other goods; in other cases, however, they were illicitly obtained.

References:

– **Agthe, Johanna. 1983:** *Luba Hemba. Werke unbekannter Meister.* Frankfurt am Main: Museum für Völkerkunde.

– **Bourgeois, Arthur P. 1985:** *The Yaka and Suku.* Iconography of Religions. Sec. VII, Africa. Leiden: Brill.

– **Bourgeois, Arthur P. 1980:** 'Kakungu among the Yaka and Suku'. In: *African Arts* 14 (1). 42–46.

– **Bouttiaux, Anne-Marie. 2009:** 'Guro Masked Performers. Sculpted Bodies Serving Spirits and People'. In: *African Arts* 42 (2). 56–67.

– **Crowley, Daniel J. 1981:** 'African Crafts as Communication'. In: *African Arts* 14 (2). 65–71.

– **Eisenhofer, Stefan and Karin Guggeis. 2002:** *Afrikanische Kunst.* Munich: Deutscher Kunstverlag.

– **Forni, Silvia. 2016:** 'Masks on the Move. Defying Genres, Styles, and Traditions in the Cameroonian Grassfields'. In: *African Arts* 49 (2). 38–53.

– **Göltenboth, Dieter. 1987:** 'Massai, die Vermarktung des "edlen Wilden"'. In: Pollig, Herrmann (ed.): *Airport Art. Das exotische Souvenir.* Stuttgart: Cantz.

– **Gröning, Karl. 2001 [1997]:** *Geschmückte Haut. Eine Kulturgeschichte der Körperkunst.* Munich: Frederking & Thaler.

– **Heißenbüttel, Dietrich. 2006:** '"Afrikanische Kunst". Europäische Annährungen an eine komplexe Realität'. In: *Tribus* 55. 67–89.

– **Herold, Erich. 1970:** *Afrikanische Masken.* Prague: Odeon.

– **Hersak, Dunja. 1993:** 'The Kifwebe Masking Phenomenon'. In: Herreman, Frank and Constantijn Petridis (eds.): *Face of the Spirits. Masks from the Zaire Basin.* Ghent: Snoeck-Ducaju & Zoon. 145–161.

– **Himmelheber, Hans. 1967:** 'Fälschungen und andere Abweichungen von der traditionellen Kunst in Negerafrika'. In: *Tribus* 16. 15–34.

– **Junker, Dirk. 2017:** 'Über den "Originalzustand" bei afrikanischen Objekten'. In: *Kunst & Kontext* 13 (1). 15–22.

– **Kasfir, Sidney Littlefield. 1992:** 'African Art and Authenticity. A Text with a Shadow'. In: *African Arts* 15 (2). 40–53.

– **Majeed, Risham. 2019:** *Get Real. Seeking Authenticity in African Art.* Ithaca: Handwerker Gallery, Ithaca College.

– **Neyt, Francois. 1994:** *Luba. To the Source of the Zaire.* Paris: Musée Dapper.

– **Oxford Online Dictionary. 2020:** https://en.oxforddictionaries.com/definition/authentic (15.09.2020).

– **Thurner, Ingrid. 1997:** 'Kunst als Fetisch. Zur westlichen Rezeption afrikanischer Objekte'. In: *Mitteilungen der Anthropologischen Gesellschaft in Wien* 127. 79–97.

– **Thurner, Ingrid. 1995:** 'Airport Art aus Westafrika'. In: *Mitteilungen der Anthropologischen Gesellschaft in Wien* 125/126. 225–247.

– **Vogel, Susan Mullin. 1986:** *Aesthetics of African Art. The Carlo Monzino Collection.* New York: Center for African Art.

THE ART OF MAKING MYTHS AND SPIRITS

Avim Paintings between 1961 and 2019

Tomi Bartole

In 1961, German anthropologist Eike Haberland embarked on a collecting trip to Papua New Guinea. Amongst his journeys, he travelled to the Upper Karawari river and visited the Avim village in the Arafundi area, where he collected 26 paintings, or rather 26 panels with 12 different motifs from the men's house (Haberland 1966: 33; 1987: 31, 34).[1] It was 58 years later, in 2019, that a Slovenian anthropologist and the author of this text – who has spent a total of 16 months doing field research in Avim acquired a number of Avim paintings showing 18 motifs on 18 sheets of paper.

The Avim people, who are speakers of Tapei, a Papuan language, and Tok-Pisin, the lingua franca of Papua New Guinea, have experienced a series of significant transformations since Haberland's visit, most notably the introduction of Christianity and a change in their relationship with the spirits. The two series of paintings allow us to observe some of these changes, but also the continuities. It is noteworthy, for example, that despite the influence of Catholic missionaries since 1963 (ABN 1963: 10), which put an end to initiation rituals in 1977 and caused the eventual abandonment of the men's house, in 2014 the Avim people still possessed their spirit flutes, now hidden in the gardens. Moreover, in 2019 the number of painted motifs had not decreased but rather increased by a third (Haberland 1966; Gabriel and Gorecki 2014; Sullivan 2012; Sullivan n.d.; Roscoe and Telban 2004).

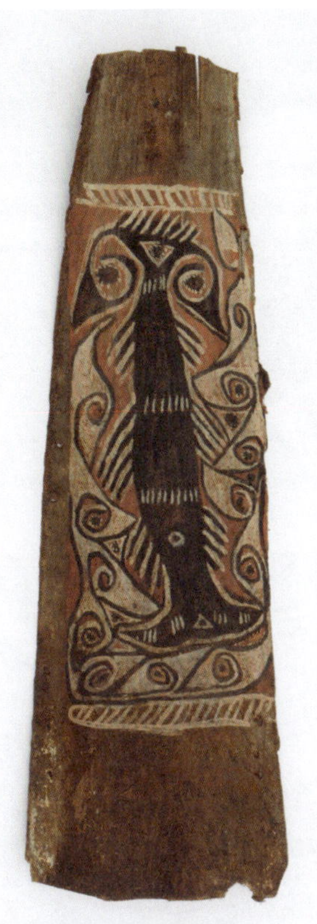

Fig. 1 Sago palm sheath with the motif *Kinin Kumnya* ('Mother of Fish'), Avim, Upper Karawari, New Guinea. Collected by Eike Haberland, Sepik Expedition, 1961.

Fig. 2 *Kinin Kumnya* ('Mother of Fish') painted by Sebastian Katuk in 2019. Avim, Upper Karawari, New Guinea. Collected by Tomi Bartole, 2019.

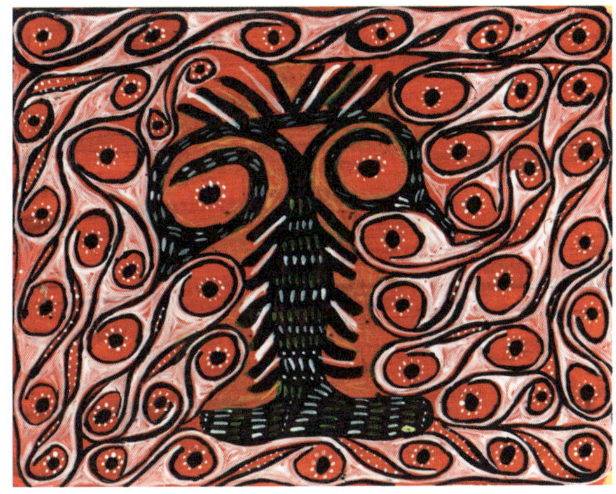

The material employed in the painting process has certainly changed. Haberland's series, and some subsequent series from 1987 and the late 2000s, were painted using the colours red and white, which were made of natural pigments, as well as black, which was made of charcoal and two other ingredients that remain a secret to non-initiates. These colours were applied onto flattened-out sago petioles, the lower end of the palm leaf stalks. The recent series, by contrast, was painted with acrylic paints on larger sheets of paper, and a fourth colour, namely yellow, has been added (cf. fig. 1 and fig. 2).

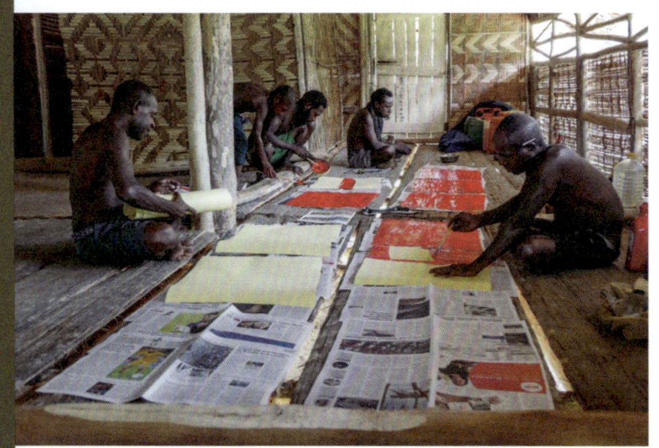

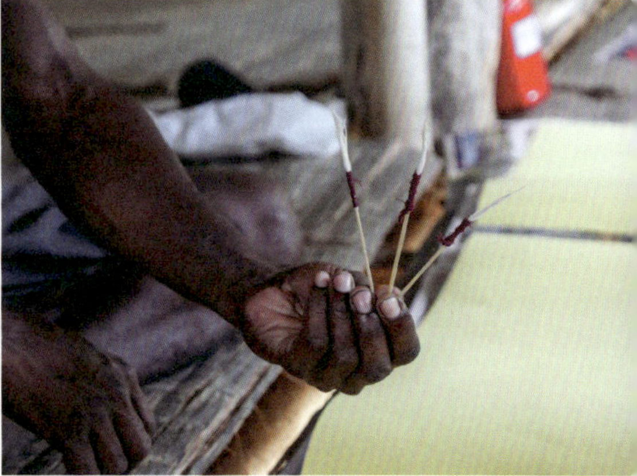

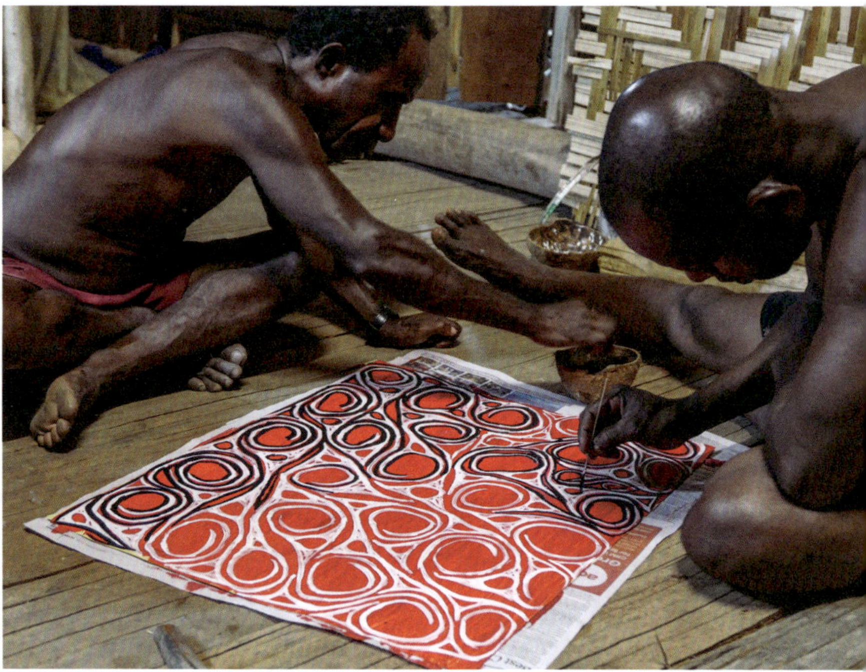

Fig. 3 First stage of painting with the colour red. Photo: Tomi Bartole, 2019.

Fig. 4 Traditional paintbrush made of bird's feathers. Photo: Tomi Bartole, 2019.

Fig. 5 Painting of the second pattern, identical in shape but different in colour and meaning from the first pattern. Photo: Tomi Bartole, 2019.

The difference in the material used partially accounts for the fact that the earlier motifs were painted multiple times as a single panel, a diptych, or even a triptych, while in the recent series a single motif is captured on one sheet of paper. The repetition of motifs in the 1961 series might stem from the fact that new artists, or the initiates in the men's house, had to paint and thus repaint the motifs in order to "learn to see" them (Forge 1970). While the paintings Haberland collected played a key role not just during initiations but also generally throughout the men's lives, because these paintings tell myths and are spirits themselves, this acquisition initiated an era in which Avim artists would paint for visitors.

The colours of patterns

In 2019, I documented the two-week-long process of painting the 18 motifs. First, the painting surface was painted entirely red, a colour that is associated with blood and initiations, but is also said to be the skin colour of New Guineans (fig. 3). While the paint was drying, the artists made their own paintbrushes from birds' feathers (fig. 4), the heads of which were soft and hence curved, thereby making it possible to spontaneously produce a curvilinear pattern and achieve the requisite degree of accuracy. Depending on the motif, the first curvilinear pattern was painted either in white or black. White pigment is also applied to people's skins, either to cool down their bodies on a hot day or within the context of mortuary rites. The colour black is similarly related to the body because it is made in a person's mouth, where a process of emulsification occurs between charcoal, a leafy green vegetable, and saliva. The painted curved lines should not 'touch' each other, as this would interrupt the open-ended pattern. The second pattern, which to our eyes seems identical in its form to the first one, is painted with the colour that has not been chosen for the first pattern (fig. 5). This second pattern is different, because by filling the spaces created by the first one it is said to 'round-up' the first pattern, creating closed circles but without compromising the first pattern, that is, without affecting its open-endedness.

Precision is crucial because if someone were to fail to paint a spiral and instead paint a circle, it would mean that "the two lines would be joined when they should not be touching each other", the lead artist Sebastian Katuk commented, adding that "once asked for assistance in battle, for example, the spirits would have no power and we would be sure not to succeed in our endeavours". The design affects the spirits it depicts as well as the spirit's powers, which are their abilities to affect and interact with humans. Indeed, the quality of a painting and the skills of an artist are judged according to the criterion and precepts inherent to the pattern itself. A master artist is able to paint the first curvilinear pattern continuously without interrupting the line. An inept artist, however, would complete the design by way of "joining smaller portions of lines together" instead. This is because joining is a function of the second design, the curvilinear pattern that 'rounds' and makes round things.

The first curvilinear pattern is called *manganem;* the second curvilinear pattern is called *manga. Manganem* is composed of the word *manga,* which signifies both the fruit and the seed, and the suffix of the verb being. I have translated the first pattern as 'work of the heart' in order to emphasise its active aspect, but also to distinguish it from the second pattern, which I have translated as 'heart'. Both patterns and concepts represent two distinctive ways of approaching living beings, either human or non-human, in the Avim world.

The 'heart' pattern functions as a container that, when held in the chest, stores kinship and customary knowledge. When *manga* names the joints of the body, it holds the body parts together, but it also makes it possible to see, for eyes are *manga* as well. On the other hand, the 'work of the heart' is made of innumerable folds and layers. This heart is tactile, and thus best approached by and understood through touching. Some trees have a heart, people say, because when felling them one might feel the specific softness of the tree's skin, flesh, heart and bone; and similarly, when asked what Avim people touch with, they would say with the skin, flesh, heart and bones. The 'work of the heart' expresses the uninterrupted unity of persons and things, and when people fold certain materials they gain control over the circulation of things and their consumption. If people are cautious when giving, it is because they are giving themselves.

Manga and *manganem* are the content that is conveyed in the process of painting, and together they account for the spirits' agency and capacity to affect. The two patterns visualise the way in which spirits are at once connected to and disjoined from humans: connected, because humans can be affected by them, and disjoined, because humans neither know their thoughts nor are able to control their will. Despite the many years of Christianity being actively practiced in the village, even today considerable care and attention is put into securing the spirits' will and affective capacities, as well as in conveying the messages these paintings hold, namely that the spirits are like humans, and their two 'hearts', a feature they share with the humans, is proof of that.

The colours of mythology

If the two main patterns are heavily governed by tradition, and space for innovation is thus scarce, changes and alterations are undeniably pronounced when it comes to the paintings' relationships to mythology and meaning. Avim people claim to have only recently migrated from the mountains to the lowlands, where their ancestors acquired a riverine lifestyle. Incidentally, migration and the acquisition of knowledge are also two themes addressed by two main Avim myths: that of Api and that of Kondom. All paintings are associated with at least one of these myths, at times with both. Once placed within the context of the two myths, the paintings become human-like and nomadic, for they too inhabit the tension between mountain, represented by Api's myth, and river, represented by Kondom's myth.

The myth of Kondom

The myth of Kondom tells the story of a man who descended through the Karawari river into the underworld, which was an exact copy of the world above. There he acquired the knowledge associated with the men's house, most notably an understanding of how to paint, and he subsequently brought this skill back to his village (cf. Sullivan 2012: 11–12; Sullivan n.d.: 8–9). In descending into the underworld, Kondom passed through *Putuku,* which is not only a painting but also a spirit that takes the form of water bubbles. *Putuku* is known to hide other spirits from human gazes by surrounding them with his water bubbles, like the 'Mother of Fish'. Three paintings of the 'Mother of Fish' or *Kinin Kumnya* (cf. fig. 1 and 2) are interchangeably associated both with the myth of Kondom and that of Api. When linked with Api, the 'Mother of Fish' is said to reside in a pond high in the mountains, where all fish were first created. A second 'Mother of Fish' is proof that there are many varieties or, as people say, many families of fish. When the 'Mother of Fish' is associated with Kondom, however, she is said to rest in certain parts of the river, and when she leaves these behind, the river dries out and all the fish disappear. Finally, the third 'Mother of Fish' gives birth to saltwater fish. In 1961, only two versions of this motif existed, but in 2019 there were three. One of the two collected by Haberland was painted by Fidelis Apot (plate 35), the only artist of that period still alive today and creator of the painting named *Waman* in 2019. The other motif of the 'Mother of Fish' had not been painted between then (fig. 1) and 2019, when Sebastian Katuk, a recognised authority in matters of tradition, decided to paint it again (fig. 2). He made it clear that in order to remain faithful to the original motif he would have to make use of a fourth colour, which is not present in the majority of other paintings: yellow. A quick look at the motif painted by Yaie Pasuwaing in 1961, however, reveals that the colour yellow is used neither in his painting nor in any other collected by Haberland. Sebastian's commitment to originality and tradition led him to take an innovatory step by changing the motif. This innovation occurred despite the fact that Fidelis was present, and although Sebastian and other artists had access to prints of the paintings collected by Haberland that they had received in the late 2000s (fig. 6).

188

A motif that does not feature amongst the paintings collected in 1961 but does appear in 2019 is the painting and spirit of 'Wild Sago Foliage'. This motif is said to have been brought by Kondom from under the water, where the wild sago stood in front of the men's house (Gabriel and Gorecki 2014: 35). The painting is at once an indication of the surface on which Avim artists paint as well as a monument to sago as a giver of life, for it provides them with their daily staple food. *Ook 1* and *Ook 2,* or simply 'Ook' and 'Ook's Mother', are also recent. Again, 'Water Bubbles' appears in the paintings, but this time within these spirits, where he is said to rest. The powerful *Ook* spirits are likened to octopuses or snakes and appear as whirlpools that can kill humans or capsize their canoes; for these reasons 'Ook's Mother' usually stands at the front, while 'Ook' is placed at the rear entrance of the men's house as their guardians.

The painting and spirit *Memanja* also only appeared at a late stage. In Tapei, *mema* is a spirit of the dead, but *Memanja* is a spirit of the dead who belongs to the underworld, which is populated by water spirits (plate 37). The painting is indicative of something that Kondom became aware of very soon after descending into this world, namely that the world below was the exact copy of the world above, and that spirits there also died and in turn became spirits of the dead (spirits).

'Kondom's suspension hook' is one of the most pronounced motifs in Haberland's series, appearing three times: once in a diptych, part of which was painted by Fidelis Apot in 1961, and twice as a standalone painting. This hook is unlike any other of its kind, for instead of being used to suspend baskets and string bags, it serves to hang the two bamboo flutes – considered spirits in their own right – in the underworld men's house. As humans could not claim Kondom's hook for themselves, at least they could paint it. Before Kondom brought the image of the hook from the underworld, Avim people did not know how to carve these objects. Between 1961 and 2019, another motif of the suspension hook appeared which belongs exclusively to humans and was at times also associated with Api's myth (Sullivan n.d.: 15, cf. Gabriel and Gorecki 2014: 34).

Tokopai is another notable motif from the 1961 series that features once as a triptych (plate 36) and twice as a standalone panel. While some paintings are interchangeably associated with one myth or the other, this painting consistently traverses both. As the 'Creation Pot' from which humans and spirits are said to have originated, *Tokopai* formed the central element of male initiations – the ritualised letting of penile blood into the clay pot, where it was mixed with sago and then consumed (cf. Gabriel and Gorecki 2012: 33; cf. Sullivan 2012: 19, n.d.: 15).

The myth of Api

The second myth tells the story of Api, a spirit who migrated, encountered humans, married and had children. Api is compared to the Christian God because he provided humans with genitals and anuses; moreover, he created the men's house in a mountain cave called Kopau. While Kondom brought the 'Creation Pot' from the underworld to the men's house in the world above, Api's relationship to the 'Creation Pot' is unmistakable because he also filled a number of creation pots with his penile blood, and it was from those pots that humans and spirits subsequently emerged. The colour red has a strong association with Api, for every painting is analogous to a creation pot: the curvilinear patterns give form to the colour of blood, but also skin, thereby creating the spirits.

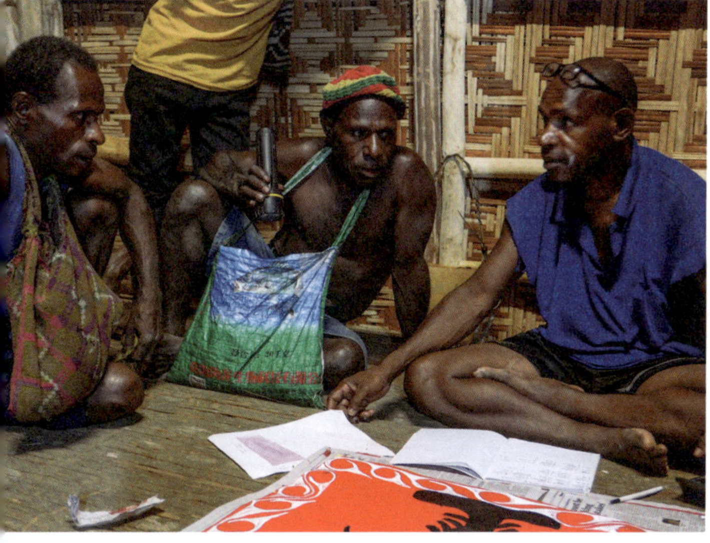

Fig. 6 Avim people consulting each other during the painting process about prints of the paintings collected by Eike Haberland in 1961. Photo: Tomi Bartole, 2019.

Once Kopau became overpopulated, however, people left the mountain cave and migrated to the lowlands, taking with them one of the pots and, in other versions of the same myth, the whole world. Yet some people are still trapped in the cave and can inhabit today's world only as spirits (cf. Roscoe and Telban 2004: 107; cf. Sullivan 2012: 10–11; cf. Sullivan n.d.: 7–8; cf. Telban 2001: 12–14).

Some of the paintings are painted by Api within the myth itself, such as a painting that Avim artists recognised as the 'Suspension Hook' in 2011 (Sullivan 2012: 17) and as 'Kondom's Suspension Hook' in 2019. Within a nomadic context, the suspension hook might have first appeared in Api's myth and then migrated into Kondom's story and territory, while the introduction of a suspension hook exclusively owned by humans might have accounted for the empty place created by this migration.

Api also painted 'Pendam's Father' and 'Pendam's Family and Clan', which constitute half of a mini-series along with 'Pendam and His Son Nikumunga'. This series is particularly cryptic. Firstly, although the Pendam motif was painted in 1961, it was last seen in 1987, and it does not feature in the 2019 series. In 1987, the story behind the Pendam motif had either already been forgotten or was being kept secret, while in 2019 it was claimed that Pendam did not possess a painting of his own, but that he was nevertheless present within the other three. Moreover, 'Pendam and His Son Nikumunga' from 1961 appear identical, and when Haberland collected them from the men's house they stood side by side. The Avim people have declared, on the one hand, that Pendam and his son have the exact same painting, without specifying whether that means there are two motifs or only one (Gabriel and Gorecki 2014: 32), yet they also state that the two panels are in fact two paintings (Sullivan 2012: 17). Although lacking a mythological account of his own, Pendam is an important spirit of warfare, while his father is also knowledgeable in peace-making and rhetoric; in addition, his family/clan provides the necessary strength by evoking kinship relations to become an army when needed.

Intermittently associated with Api (Sullivan 2012: 11) and at other times with Kondom (Gabriel and Gorecki 2014: 35), *Etoka Enunga* (plate 38), or the stomach of the bamboo arrow shaft, is a spirit who resides inside weapons and slit drums. When its design is carved onto weapons it enhances their reach and destructive power, and when it is carved onto the slit drum that is used to communicate across distances, it becomes possible to immobilise wild boar during hunts. In both cases the spirit operates in the same way, because in Tapei, communication is referred to in the register of hunting language.

Another motif associated with Api is *Waman*, a powerful water spirit who lives in mountain springs, creeks and ponds, and who is likened to a spider or scorpion due to his ability to poison his victims (see Sullivan n.d.: 15). *Waman* also confers his powers upon musicians in the men's house, thus preventing them from running out of breath while playing the flutes. In 1987, however, residents of

Avim said *Waman* was the creation pot that Kondom had brought from the underworld (Gabriel and Gorecki 2014: 33). And in 2019, a different painting, depicting the sago palm frond that is utilised in the process of washing the fibrous residue of the sago pith in order to extract the starch, was also said to represent the creation pot still hidden in Kopau, the mountain cave.

Conclusion

When Avim paintings are seen as representations of myths and real objects, instances of innovation and tradition are present in equal measure. However, when the paintings are approached from the perspective of their two lead patterns – that is, as a closed system of communication, as if unrelated to myths and things (Forge 1970) – convention reigns supreme. In 2019, Avim artists introduced certain innovations to the motifs by comparison with the paintings from 1961. In painting the two patterns they sometimes exchanged the primary and secondary colours, namely white and black. What had been painted in black in 1961 was painted in white in 2019, and vice versa. The value of the colours white and black is not intrinsic but stems instead from their relationality, in other words they only truly acquire their value in relating to each other as the two patterns. These two patterns, contraposed to and complementing each other with the help of the colours black and white, are a function of the spirit's capacity to interact with humans. But the same function is also exercised by the recently introduced colour yellow, which was applied to chosen motifs, the artists claimed, for the very same reasons.

Space for innovation is provided not by the value of authenticity, but rather by originality. Indeed, artists are obliged to paint the spirits *not* as they truly are, because only a disguised spirit presents the opportunity for a safe interaction. This soon became obvious during a discussion that emerged about the motif of 'Mother of Fish' (fig. 2). Avim artists said they knew very well that she is not a fish, but rather a woman living underwater. In order to see her true self, however, a heavy price had to be paid. Anyone seeing this true self would be instantly seduced, tricked, and sent insane, meaning that they would become unresponsive to humans because an exclusive relationship with the spirit had been created. The freedom to improvise the overall motif thus counterbalances the strictness of the two patterns, as if balancing out two claims, namely that spirits are, on the one hand, like humans, yet on the other hand they are nothing like them. However, even when the form is heavily governed by tradition, colours nonetheless still offer space for innovation.

What remains a constant in Avim painting and their usage of colours is the colour red, which is situated under all the other colours. The colour red, incidentally called *papua* in Tapei, reminds us that humans and spirits, including not only the writer of this essay but also the reader, share a common ancestor, namely, the spirit Api, who led Papua New Guineans and Europeans alike out of the mountain cave Kopau.

1 The men's house was a dwelling reserved for the exclusive use of initiated males which also served as a bachelors' dormitory. It was, most notably, the place where young men underwent initiation rituals, during which time they learned the skills of adulthood and were introduced to the spirits.

References:

- **ABN. 1963:** *Amboin Patrol Report No. 2, 1962/63.* Port Moresby: National Library and Archive.
- **Forge, Anthony. 1970:** 'Learning to See in New Guinea'. In: Mayer, Philip (ed.): *Socialization. The Approach from Social Anthropology.* London: Tavistock Publications. 269–291.
- **Gabriel, Jennifer and Paul Gorecki. 2014:** *The 'Karawari Caves Precinct' of the Sepik River Basin, Papua New Guinea.* Cairns: The Cairns Institute at James Cook University.
- **Haberland, Eike. 1966:** 'Zur Ethnographie der Alfendio-Region (Südlicher Sepik-Distrikt, Neuguinea)'. In: *Jahrbuch des Museums für Völkerkunde zu Leipzig* 23. 33–67.
- **Haberland, Eike. 1987:** 'Die Neuguinea-Sammlung des Museums für Völkerkunde in Frankfurt am Main seit 1961'. In: Münzel, Mark (ed.): *Roter Faden zur Ausstellung Neuguinea Nutzung und Deutung der Umwelt* 1. 29–73.
- **Roscoe, Paul and Borut Telban. 2004:** 'The People of the Lower Arafundi. Tropical Foragers of the New Guinea Rainforest'. In: *Ethnology* 43 (2). 93–115.
- **Telban, Borut. 2001:** *Arafundi River 2001.* Unpublished Fieldwork Report. Ljubljana: Research Centre of the Slovenian Academy of Sciences and Arts.
- **Sullivan, Nancy. 2012:** 'Sago Bark Painting and the Transformation of Community Identity on the Arafundi River, East Sepik Province, Papua New Guinea'. In: *Pacific Arts* 12 (2). 5–23.
- **Sullivan, Nancy. Not dated:** *Creative Sago Fronds. Ontological Identity in an Arafundi Community.* Unpublished Draft Article.

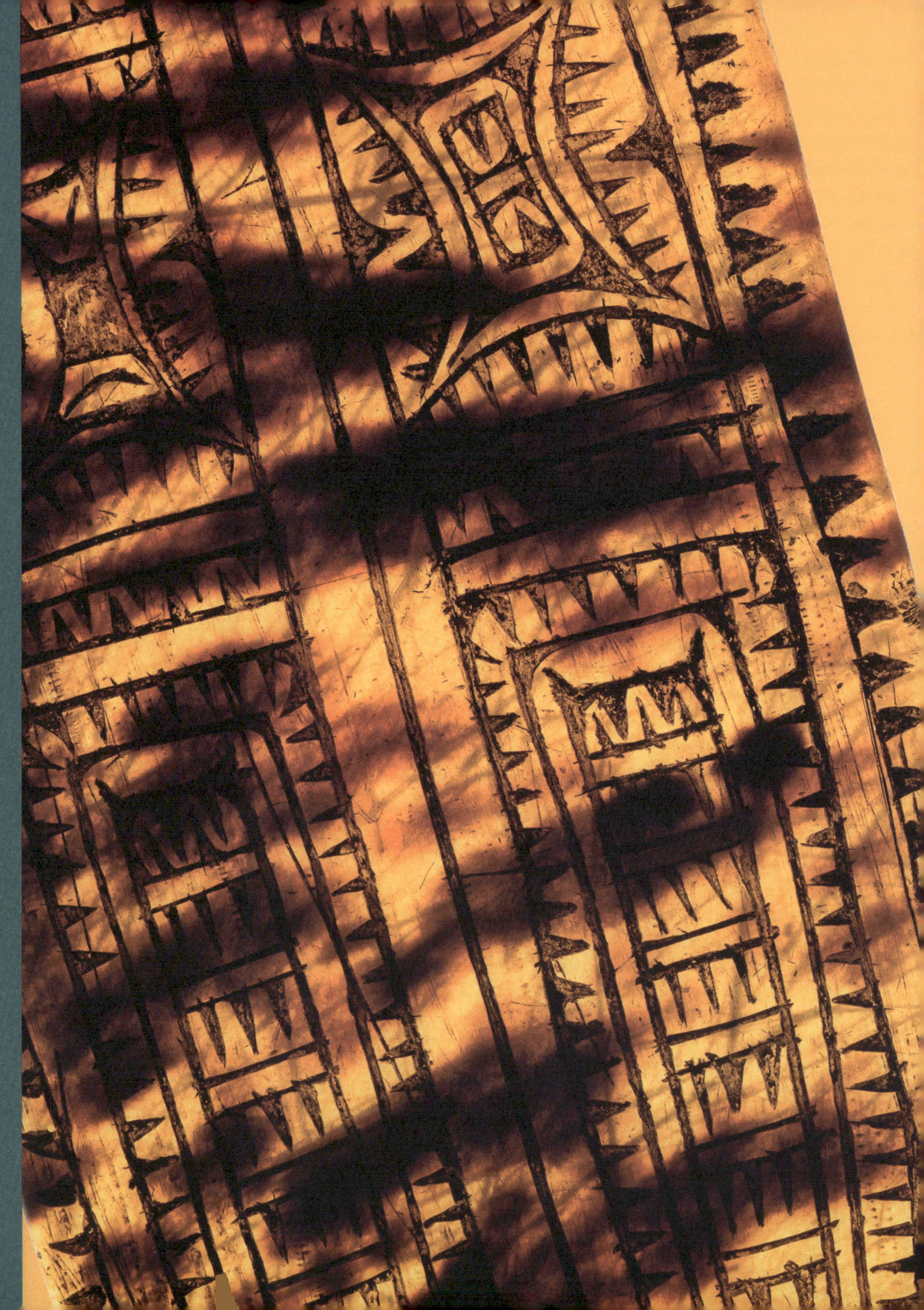

PLATES

This strip of tortoise shell with its artistically engraved patterns has a fiery glow when held up to the light. The material, obtained from the flat horn scutes of a sea turtle carapace, is heated and then bent to form a bracelet. However, if too much heat is applied the material can potentially lose its transparency and becomes dull. Southeast New Guinea, Melanesia. Collection and acquisition period unknown.

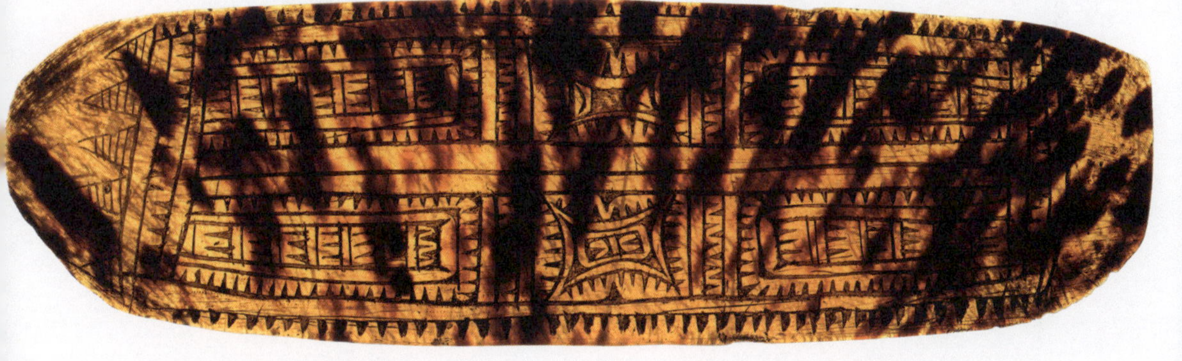

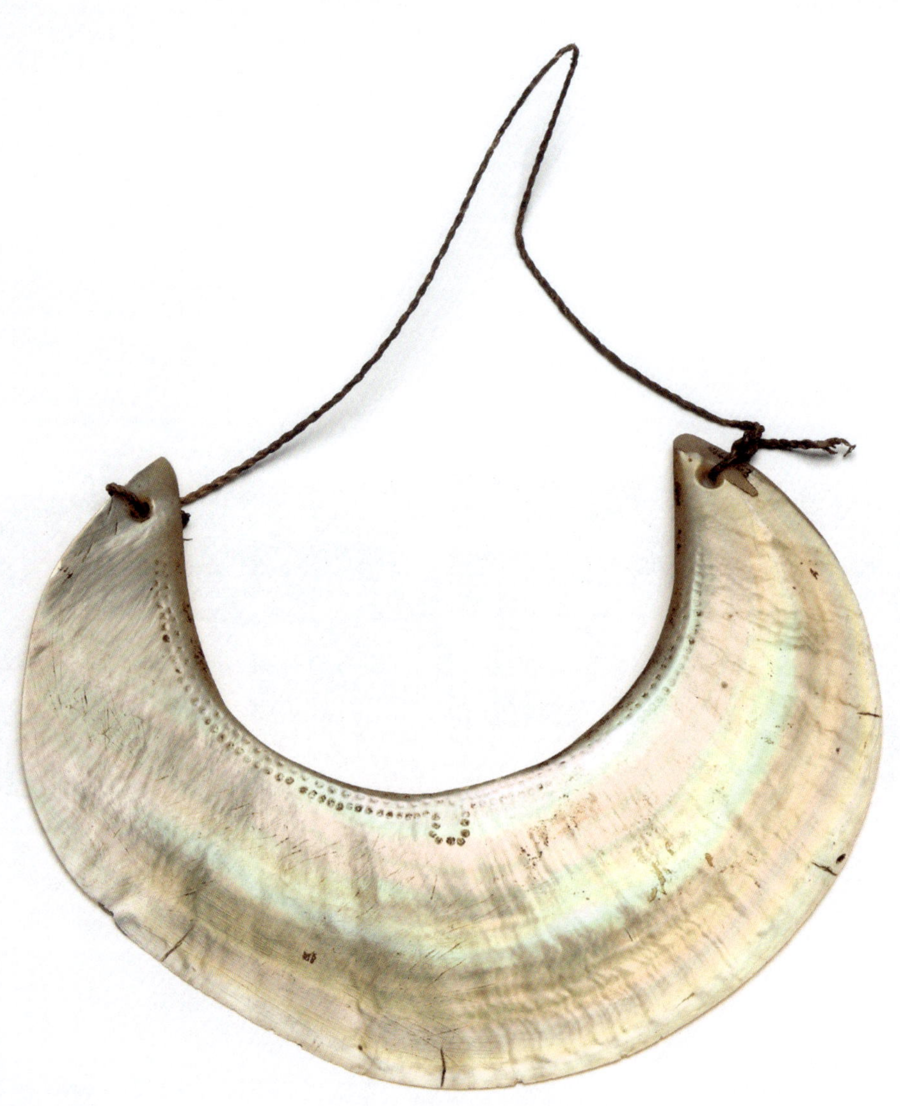

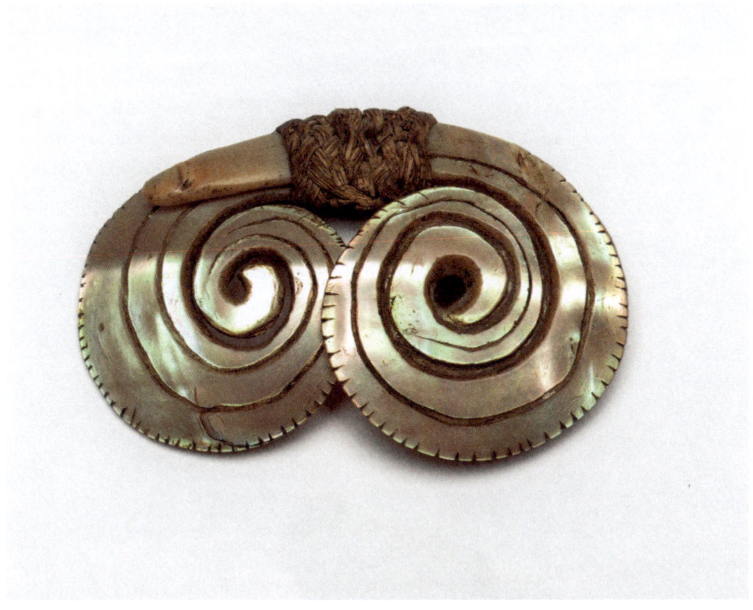

Plate 1 This sickle-shaped pectoral necklace made from the inner layer of the Gold Lipped Mussel, was also used as a standard of value. Its sheen results from the mother of pearl formed by the mussel. In addition to pretty natural interference, on closer inspection the jewellery also displays dots on its edge applied in red paint. Attributed to the Dani, Wamena, Baliem Valley, however probably from the Central Highlands, New Guinea. Collected by Richard Mehlhorn, c. 1972.

Plate 2 This nose jewellery made from mother of pearl symbolises the tusks of a boar. Pigs are prized throughout New Guinea as domestic animals, as well as embodying mythical clan ancestors. Iatmul, Mindimbo, Central Sepik, New Guinea. Collected by Eike Haberland, Sepik Expedition, 1961.

Plates 3 and 4 (detail) Obsidian blade in the form of an arrowhead. The black volcanic glass absorbs light, but also reflects a portion of it – which can be best seen at breakage points. Unknown ethnos, California, USA. Donation from Richard Mehlhorn, 2014.

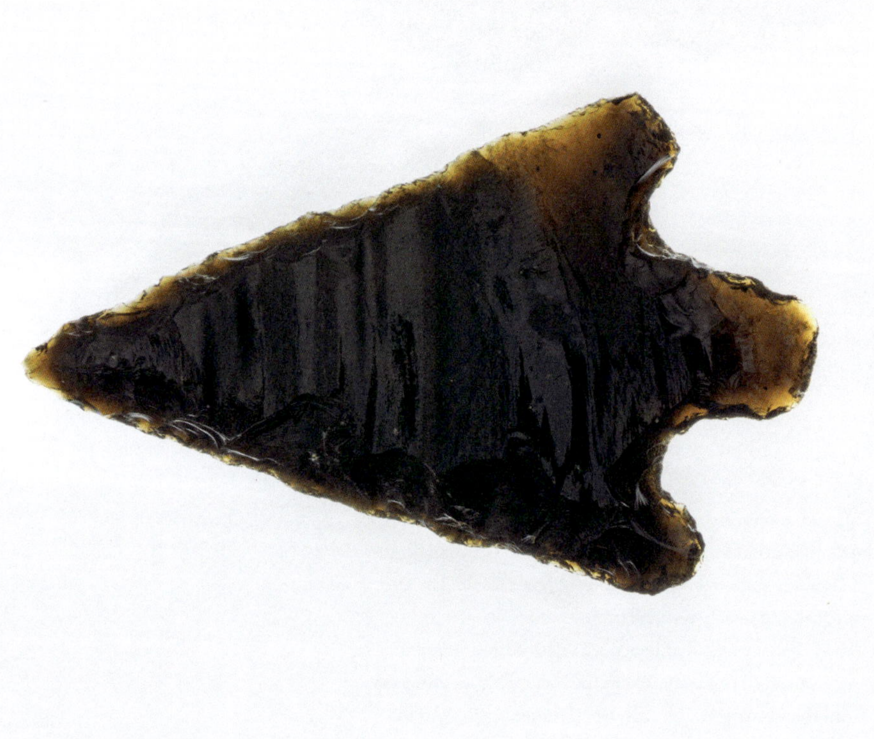

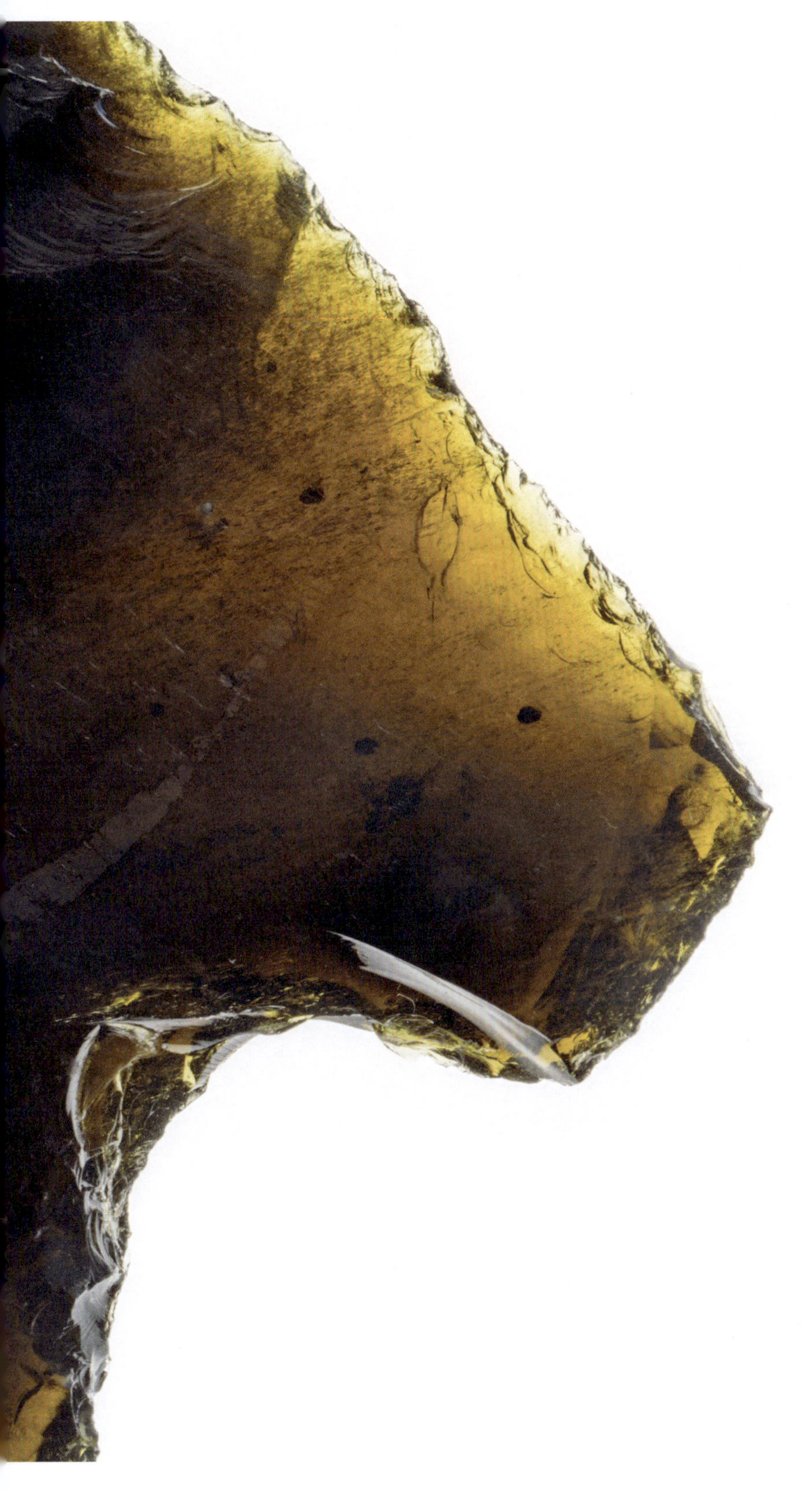

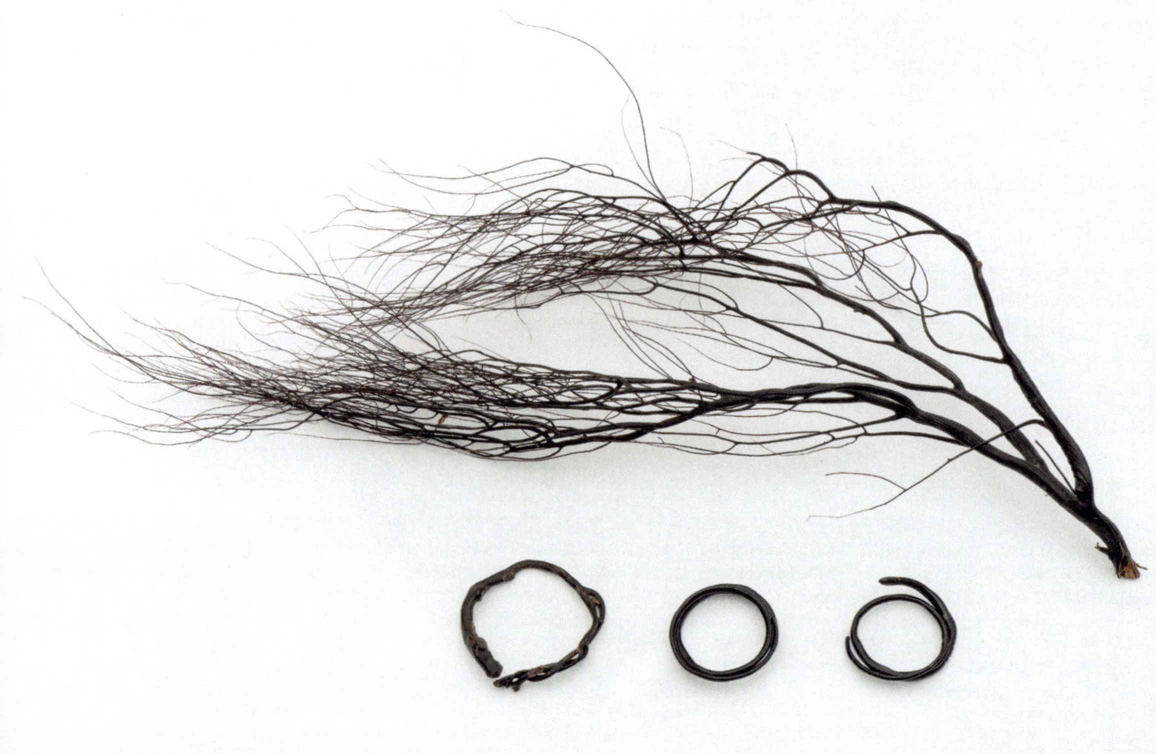

Plate 5 Bracelets made from black coral were popular on many islands of today's Indonesia, probably due to their shine. Raw material and three bracelets from Muna and Bangka, Indonesia. Collected by Johannes Elbert, 1909 and Bernhard Hagen, 1905.

Plate 6 Two clubs *(patu).* The dark grey to black basalt *(onewa),* and in particular the dark green, shimmering nephrite *(pounamu)* were highly valued for both their material and colour characteristics. In Māori the names of the respective colours are derived from the materials. *Patu onewa* and *patu pounamu.* Māori, New Zealand. Purchased from H. E. Loppé, 1908 and O. Brozukat, 1936.

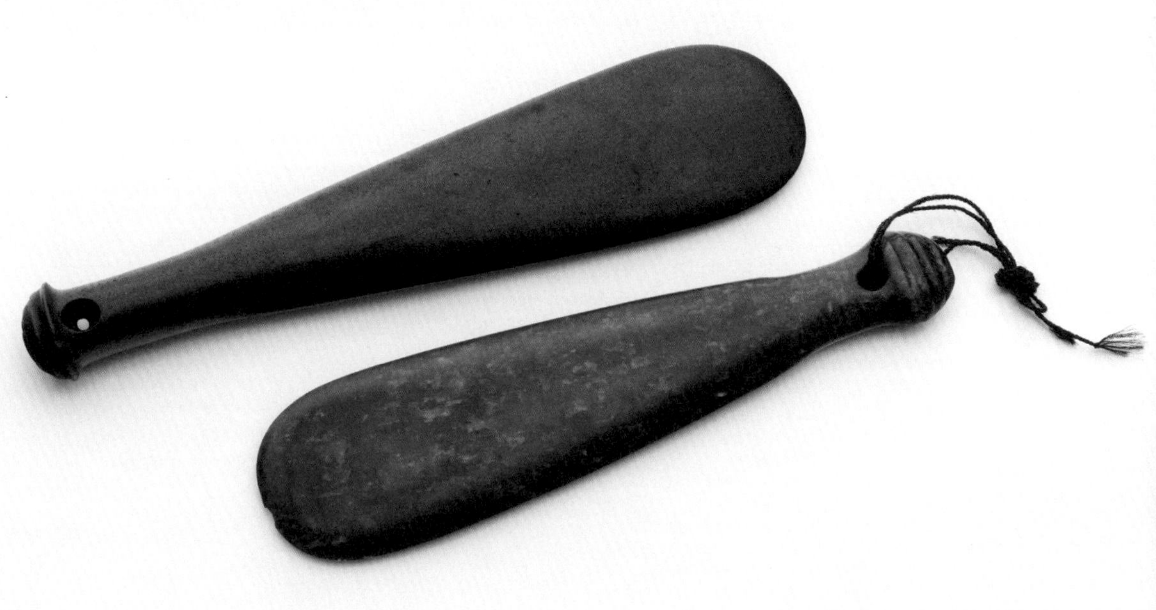

Plate 8 This necklace from threaded beetle legs shines, depending on the incidence of light, in pretty interferences from bright green, through yellow to violet. Such beetle chains were also used as currency. Mussau, St. Matthias Islands, Bismarck Archipelago, Melanesia. Purchased from Julius Konietzko, 1921.

Plate 7 Headband, made from plant material and bright green jewel beetles. Such headbands were generally worn on ceremonial occasions. Mount Hagen, New Guinea. Purchased from R. Diepen during the Sepik Expedition, 1961.

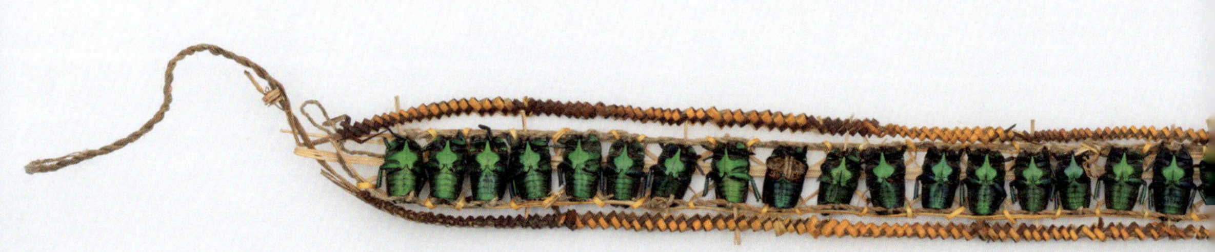

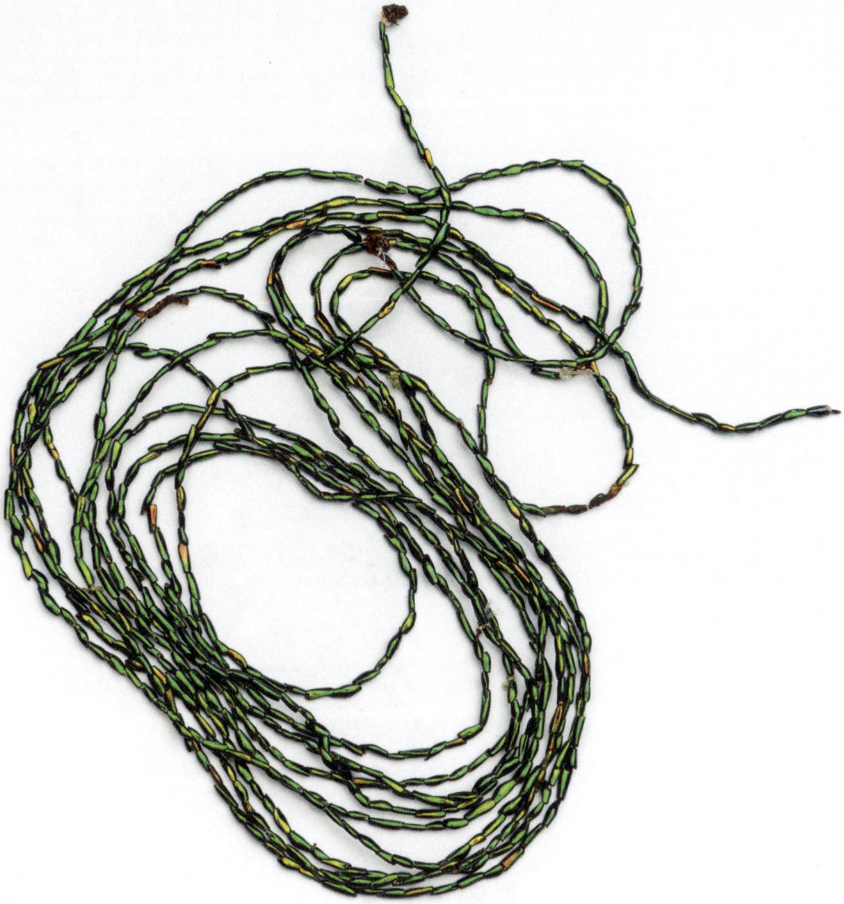

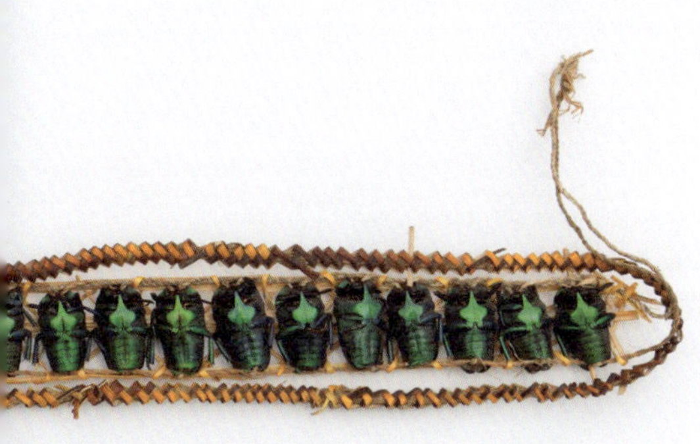

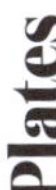
Plates

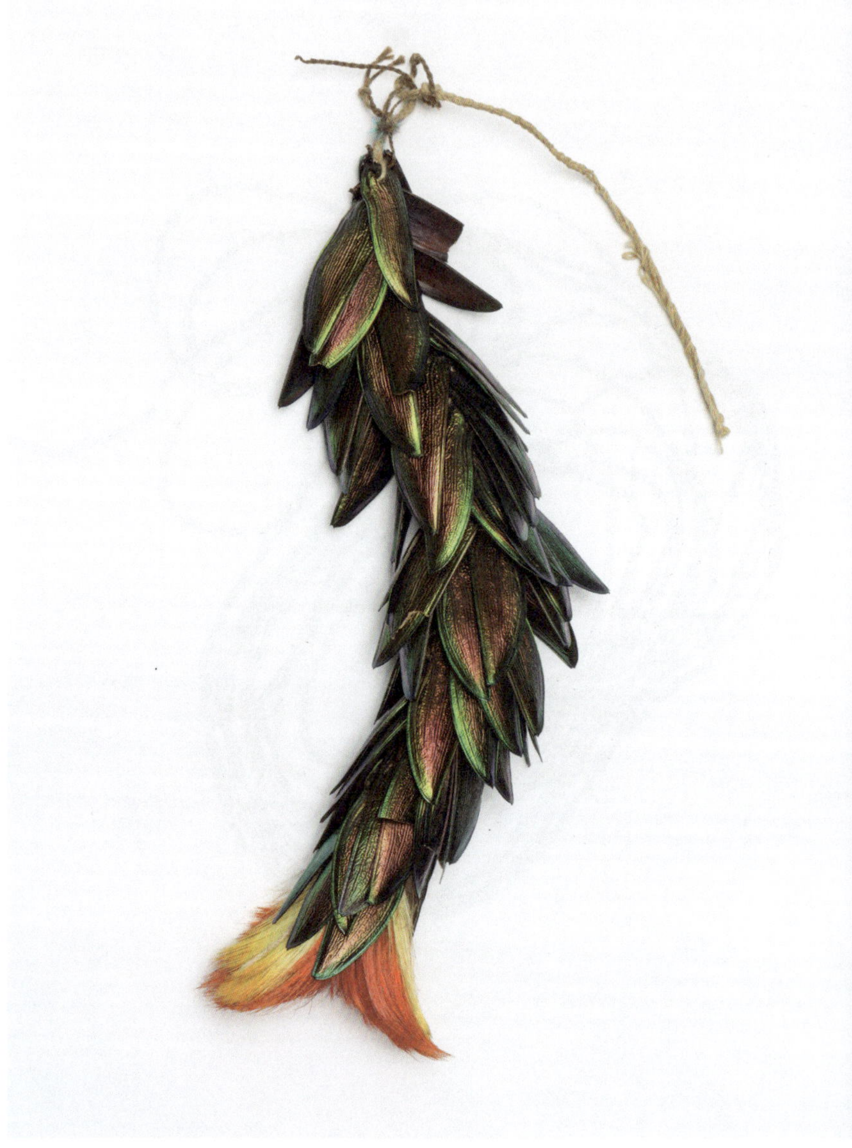

Plates 9 and 10 Ear pendants. The iridescent wings of tropical jewel beetles are excellently suited to the manufacture of jewellery. When moved in the sunlight different colour impressions are produced depending on the angle. Beetle wings, feathers. Jíbaro/Shuar, Peru. Collected by Alfred Großmann, 1925–1930.

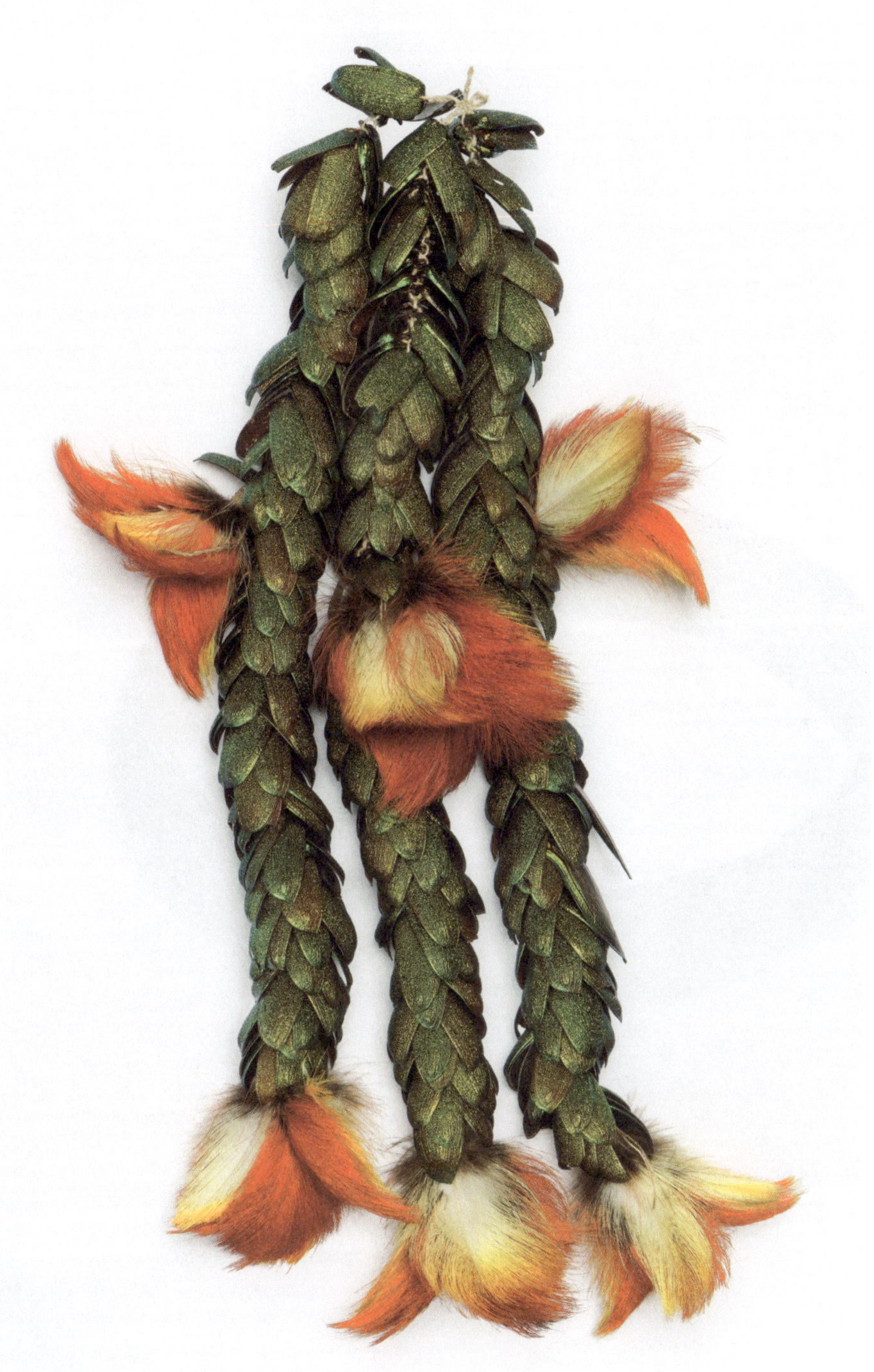

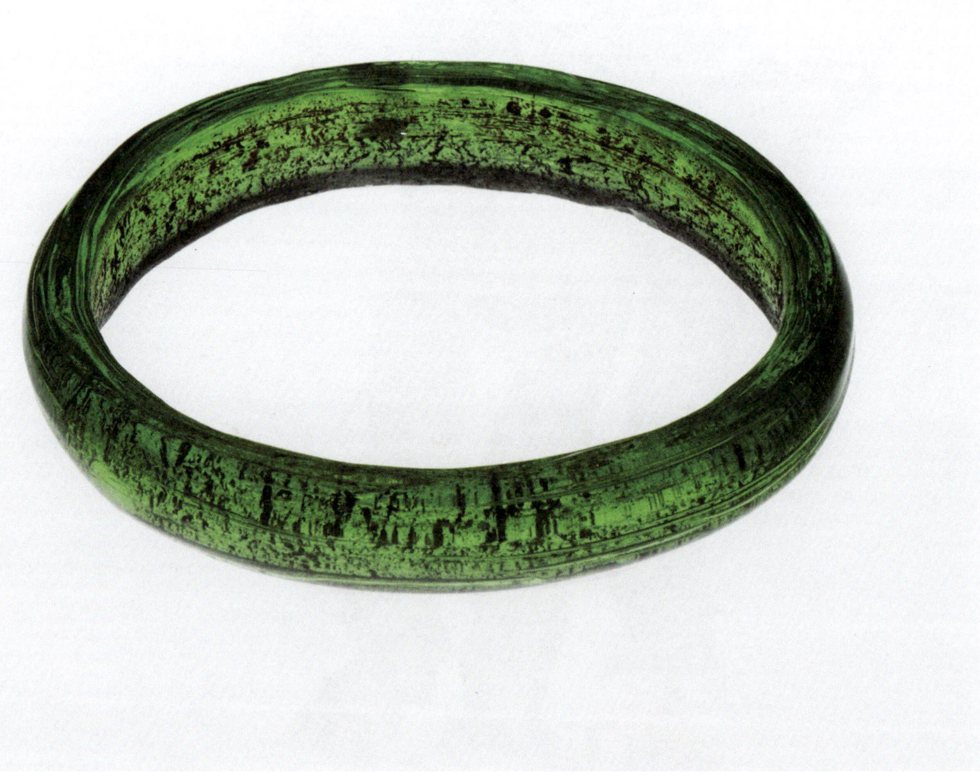

Plate 11 This bracelet from the Nupe of Nigeria was made from ground, transparent, green glass. As the majority of the Nupe are of the Muslim faith, it is possible that the colour of the bracelet is connected to green as the colour of Islam. Purchased from the Museum für Völkerkunde Berlin, c. 1908.

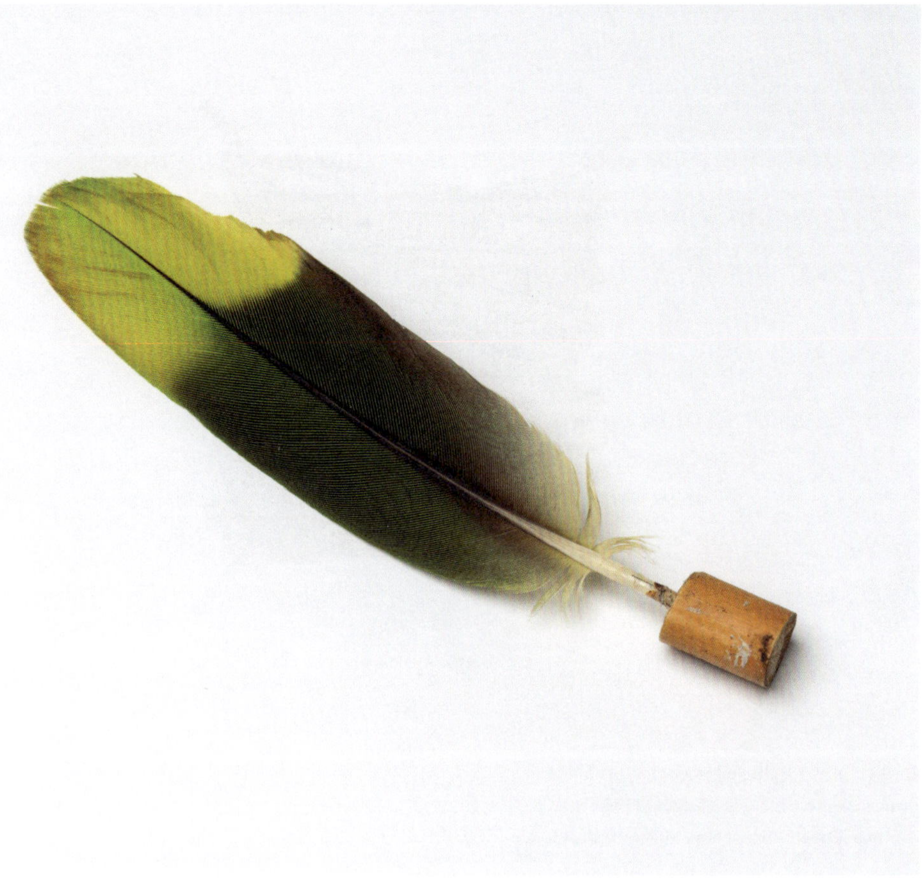

Plate 12 Ear jewellery made from a tube and a feather. Depending on the angle, one can observe interferences between yellow and green. Yanomami/Waika, Roraima, Brazil. Collected by Fritz Trupp, before 1988.

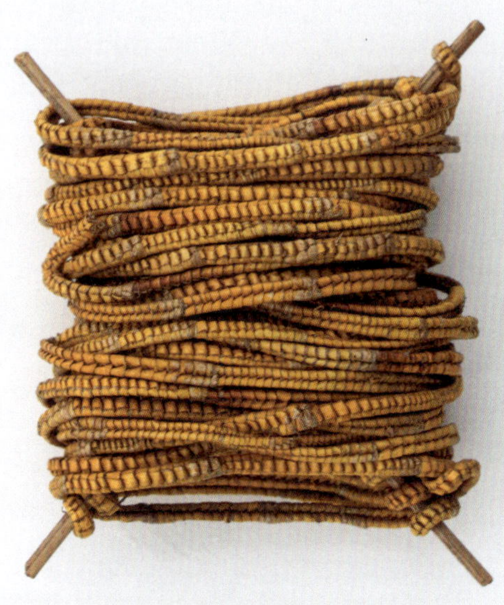

Plate 13 Thanks to their pretty light yellow colour, orchid stalks are made into decorative twine. String from orchid bast. Finschhafen, New Guinea. Collected by Hans Meier, 1904–1905.

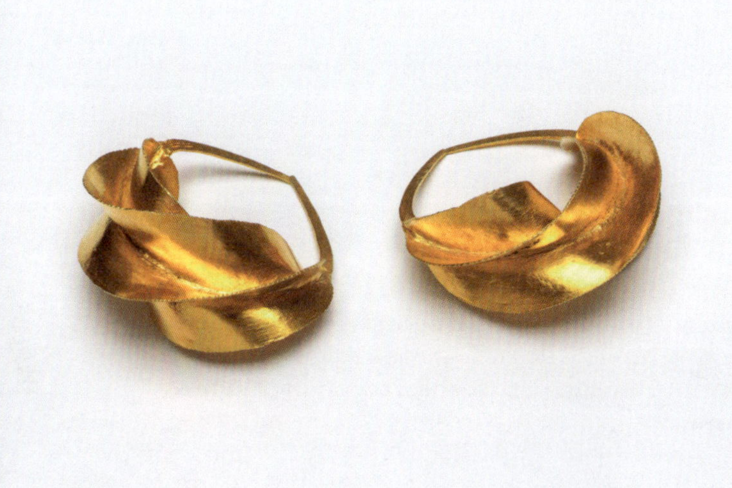

Plate 14 These gold earrings with the typical curved form are a status symbol amongst the Peulh of Mali, West Africa. They symbolise status and wealth. Girls generally receive their first earring after reaching the age of one. Purchased from Thomas Schunk, 1989.

Plate 15 Feather diadem. The feathers of the light red Ara were coloured yellow or orange on the living bird by means of tapirage. Sewed onto a ribbon of plant fibres and monkey hairs. Tukano, Uaupés Region, Northwest Amazonia. Collected by Hermann Schmidt, before 1914.

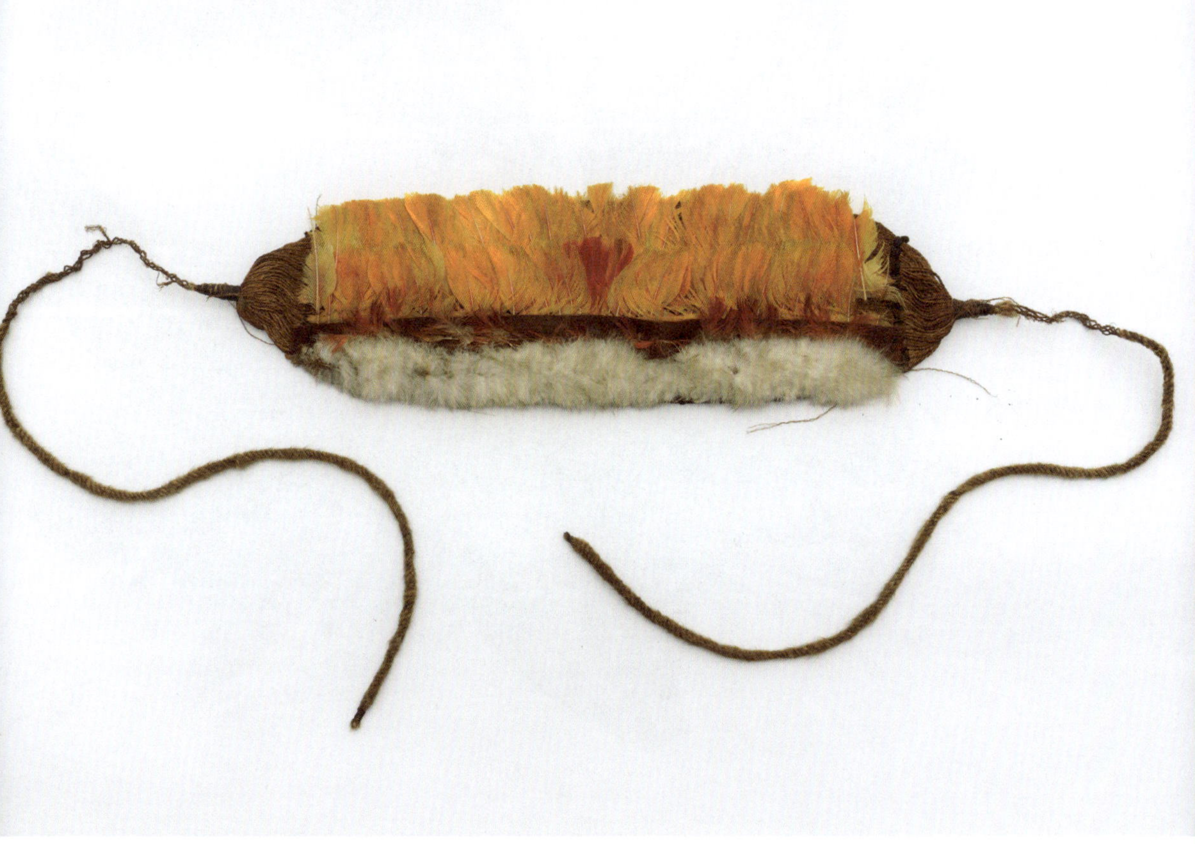

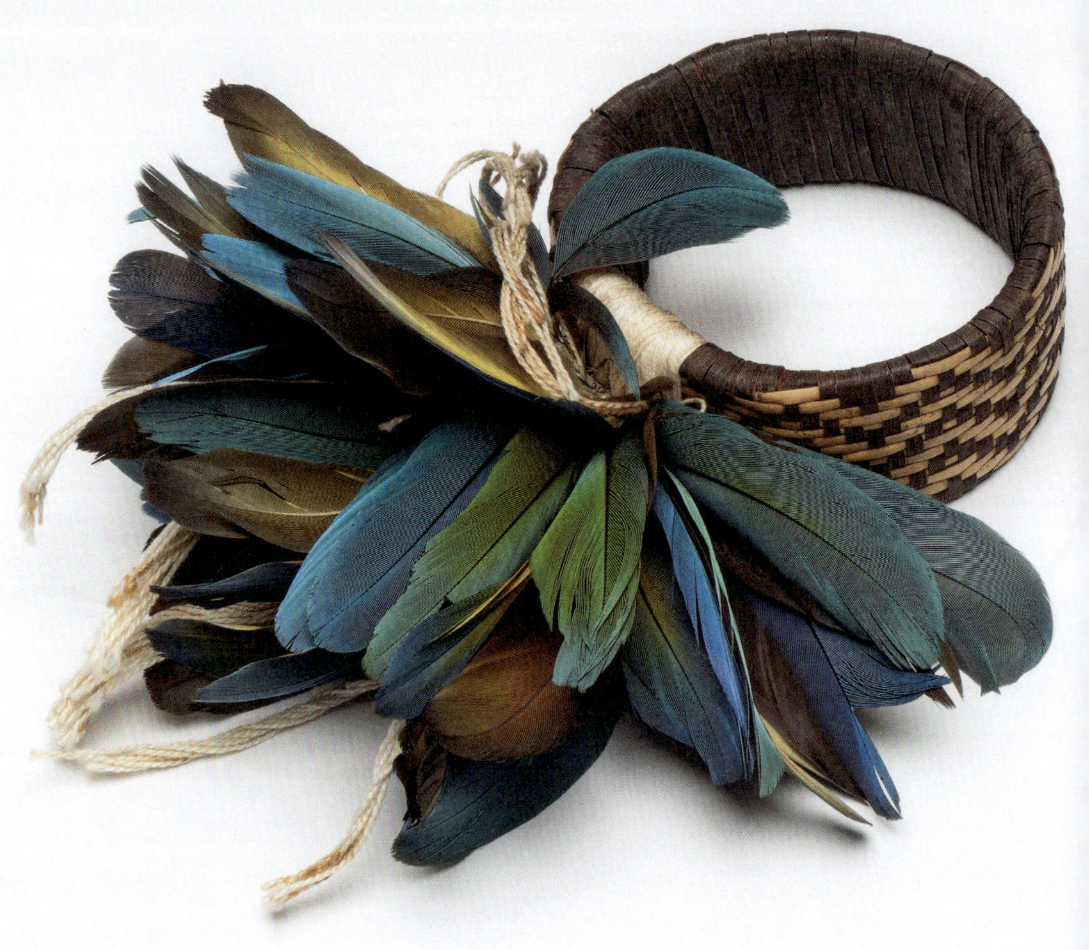

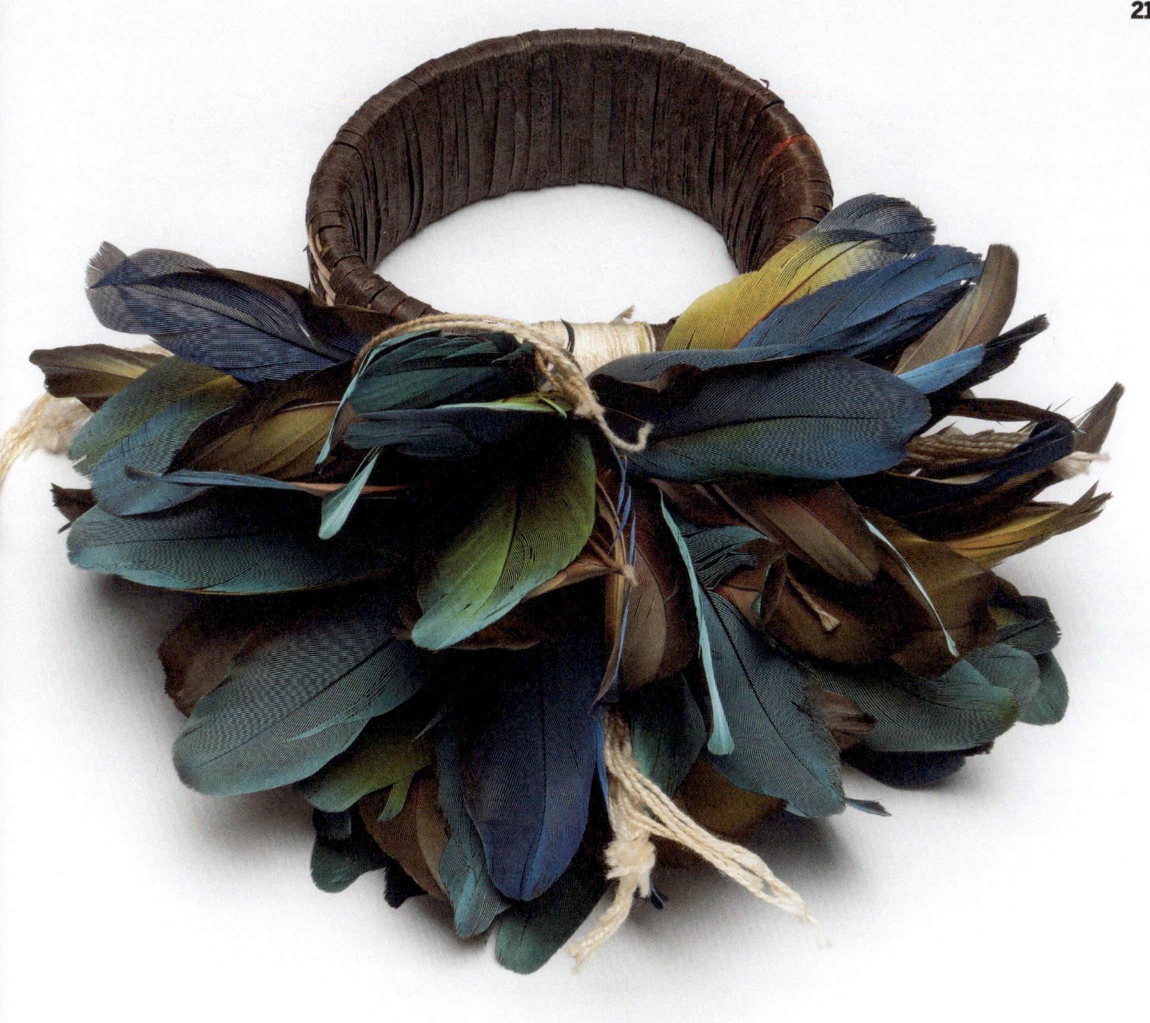

Plate 16 Wristlets. Iridescent feathers in the colours blue-yellow-green-black on a ring made from barkcloth, palm leaves and cotton. Kayapó Txukarramãe, Pará, Brazil. Collected by Luiz Boglar, 1988.

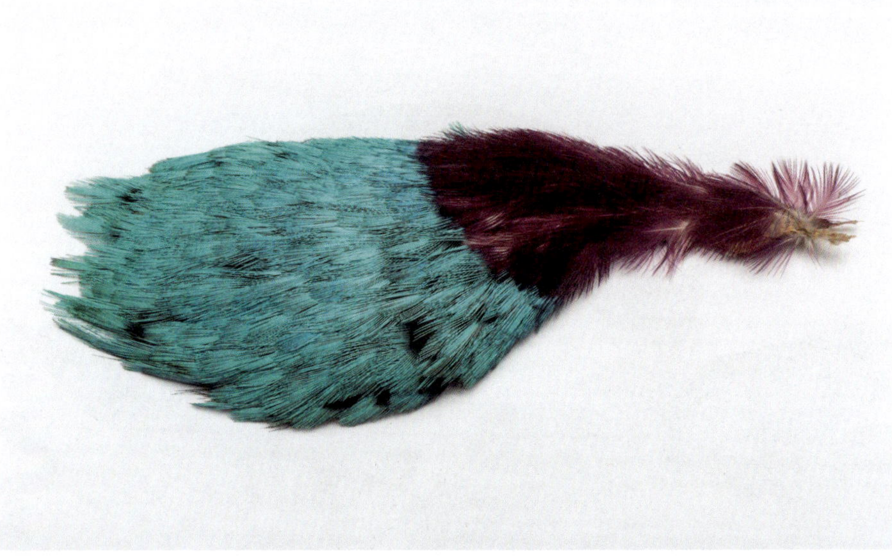

Plate 17 Ear jewellery, made from the shiny metallic, light blue to turquoise and violet plumage of the spangled cotinga *(Cotinga cayana)*. Yanomami/Waika, Roraima, Brazil. Collected by Fritz Trupp, before 1988.

Plate 18 This Yoruban helmet mask from the region around Cotonou, Dahomey in today's Republic of Benin shows a face with scarifications and blue painting on the rear of the head. The form of the plait points to the God of Thunder, Shango. The blue paint could refer to Yemayá (Yemoja), the primordial mother and deity of the sea and motherhood. Purchased from Karl-Heinz Krieg, before 1964.

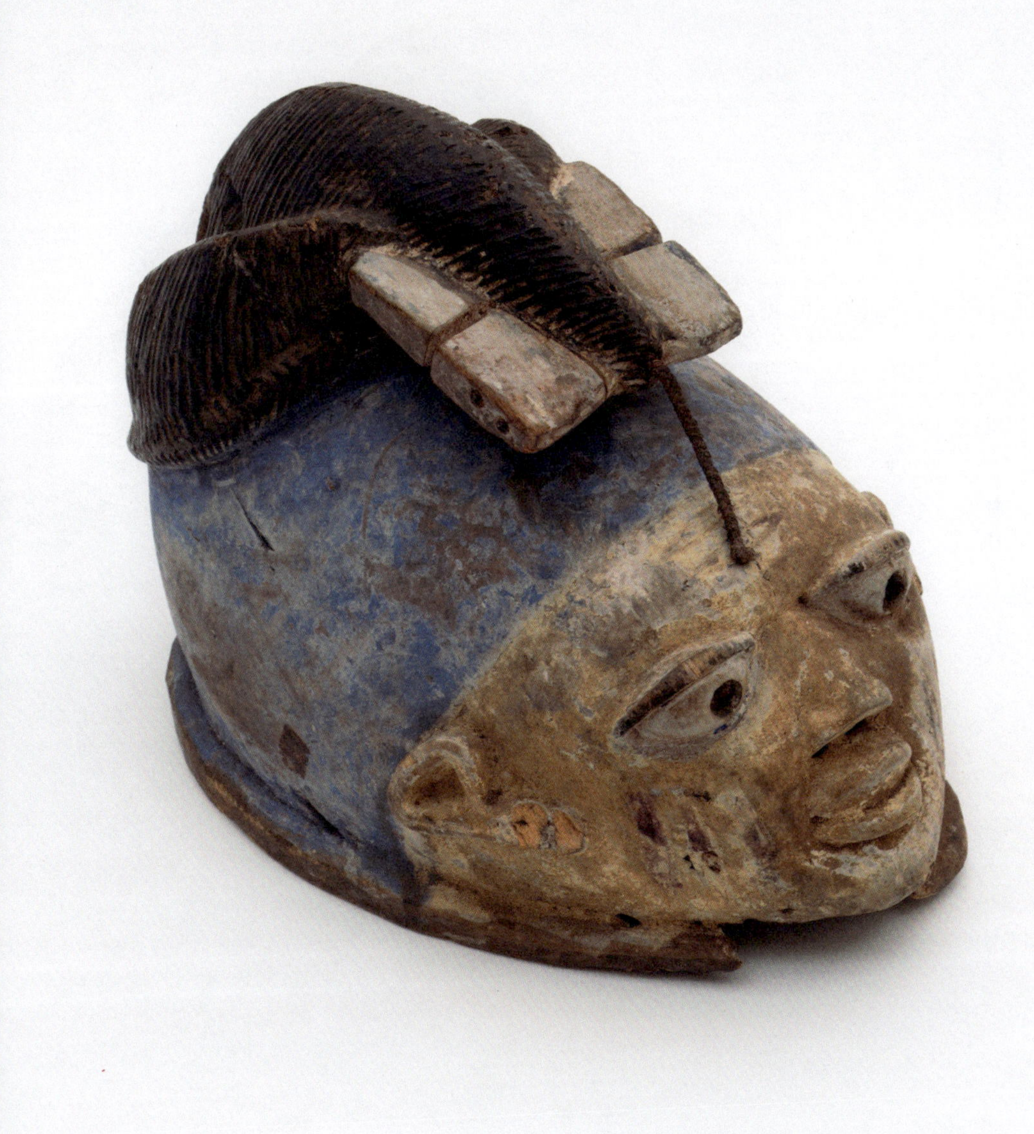

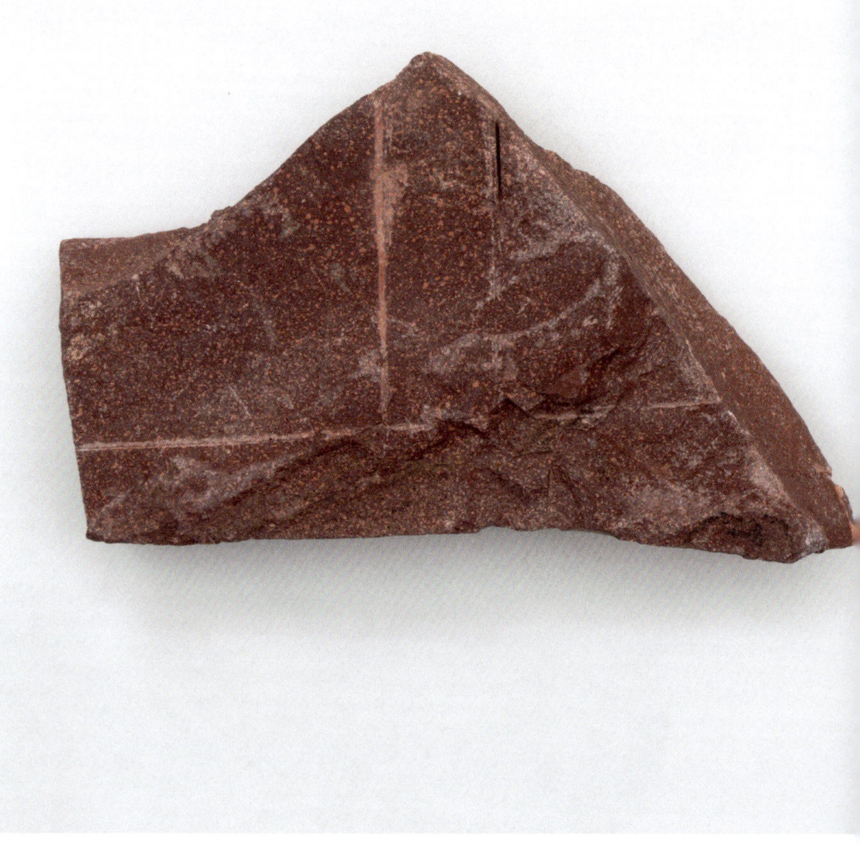

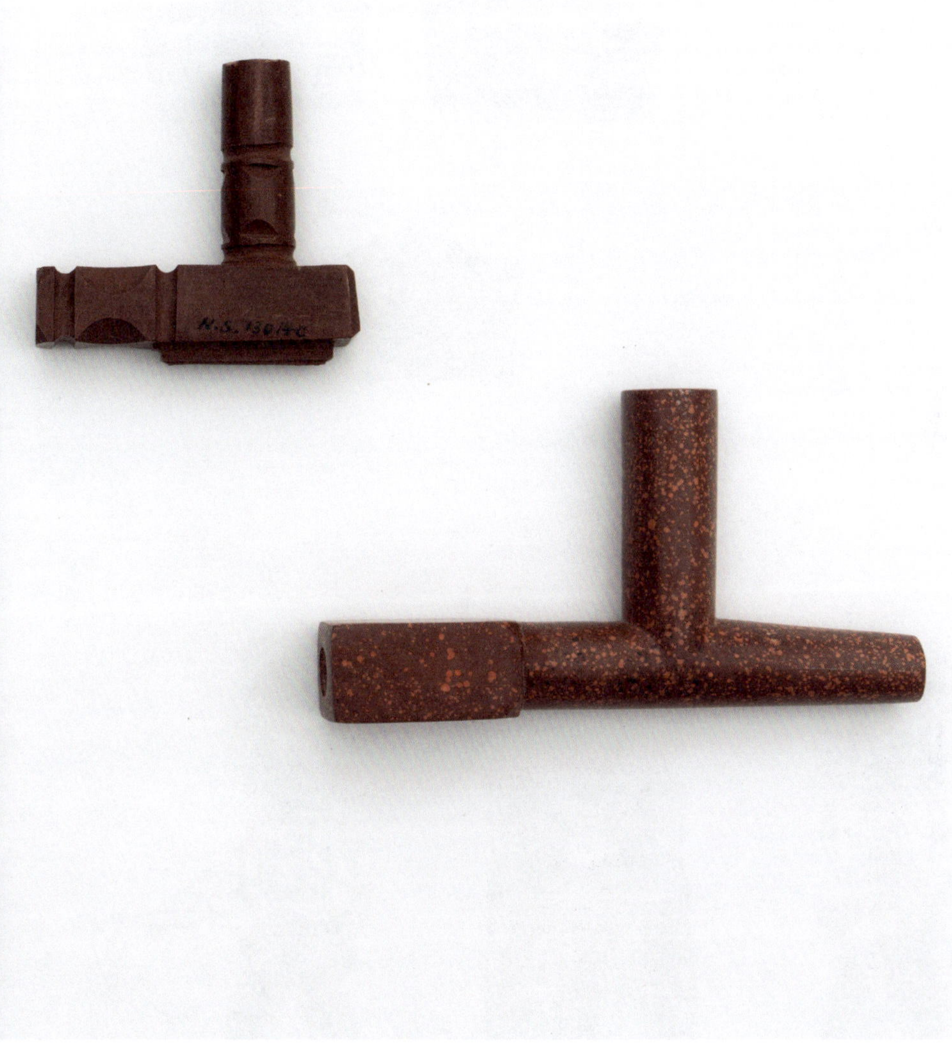

Plate 19 The red pipestone, named after the American painter George Catlin, is only found in a single quarry in Minnesota. It was already traded over great distances in Pre-Columbian times. In the myths of the indigenous peoples its red colour was associated with blood. Raw material for the manufacture of pipe bowls and two tobacco pipe bowls from catlinite. Santee Sioux. The plains and prairies of North America. Collected by Sylvia Kasprycki and Christian Feest, 2001, and purchased from Johann G. F. Umlauff, c. 1910.

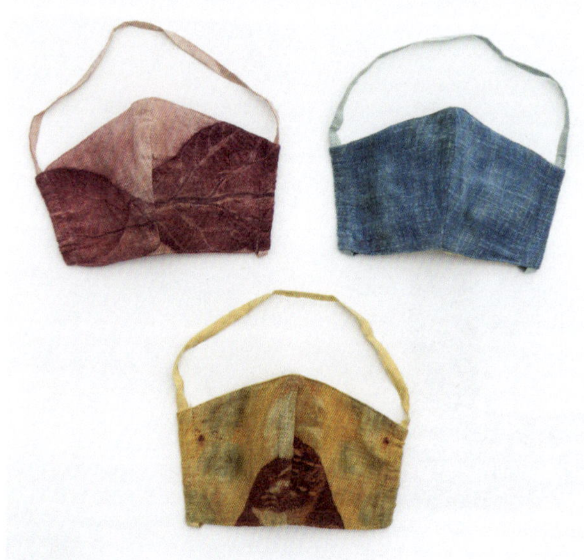

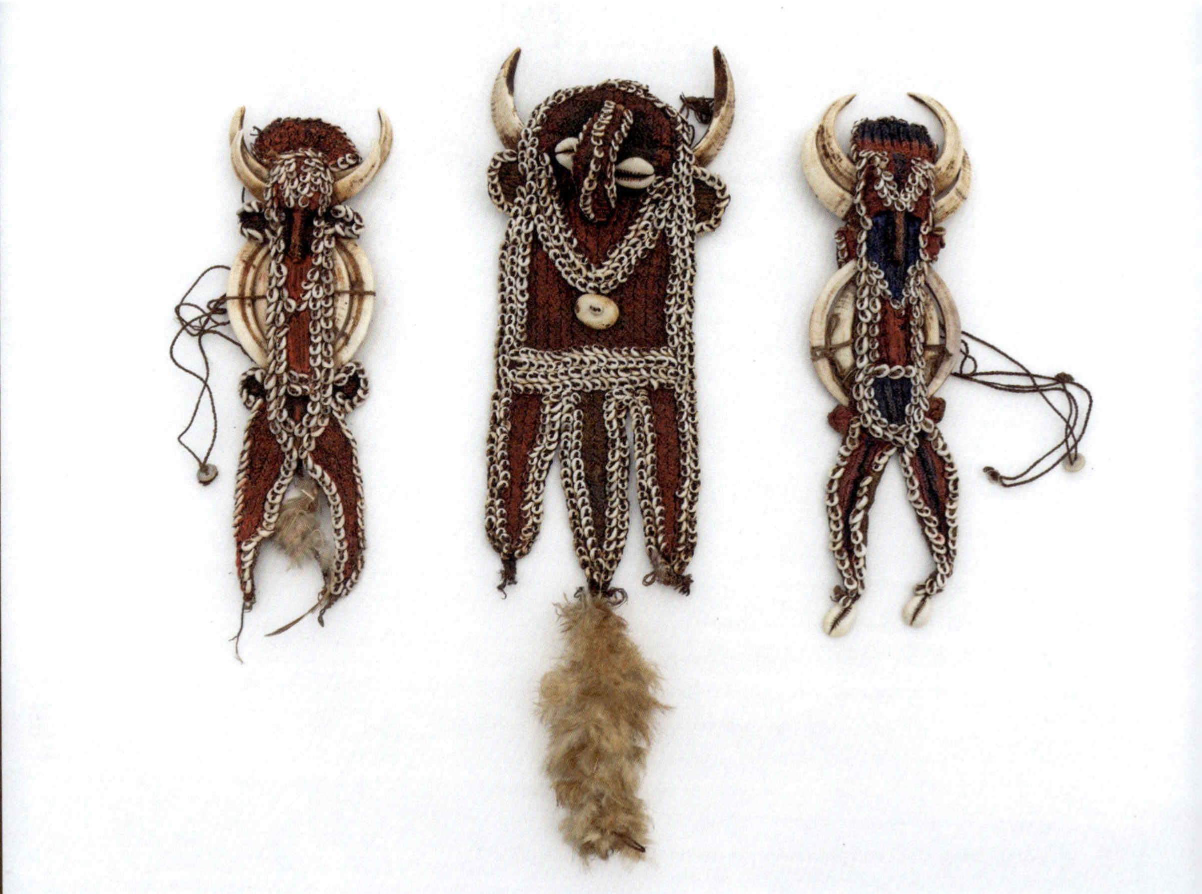

Plate 20 These cotton face masks were coloured using vegetable dyes. Sappanwood produces pink to lilac. Assam indigo produces blue. A mixture of jackfruit wood and marigolds produces yellow. Purchased from Cinta Bumi Artisans, Bali, Indonesia, 2020.

Plate 21 This boar-tusk decoration *(kara-ut)* was held between the teeth by men during battle and symbolizes the ferocious boar. It lends protection and strength; and simultaneously signals to the enemy that he will be bitten and killed. When dancing the colour's magical efficacy of adornments and body paint temporarily transforms the wearer into a supernatural being. Decoration made from boar tusks, nassa shells, knitted cloth and natural dyes. Abelam, Maprik, New Guinea. Collected by Meinhard Schuster, Sepik Expedition, 1961.

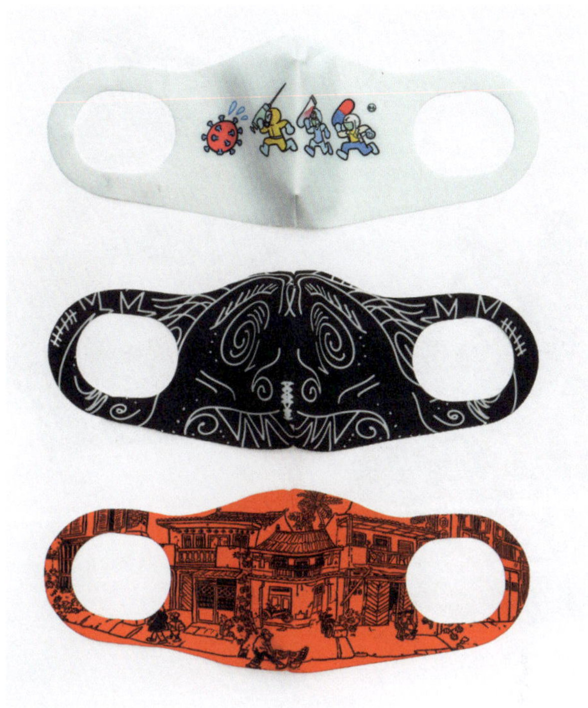

Plate 22 In Indonesia, too, the colour and patterns of the face masks are also a means of expressing one's own personality. From top to bottom The artist Komik Ga Jelas (KGJ) shows the hunting of the corona virus. Calon Pelaku Seni's design is reminiscent of traditional masks. The comic-strip artist Sheila Rooswitha Putri has depicted Glodok, the Chinese neighbourhood in Jakarta. Here against a red background – the 'colour of China.' Purchased from Tokome.id, Jakarta, Indonesia, 2020.

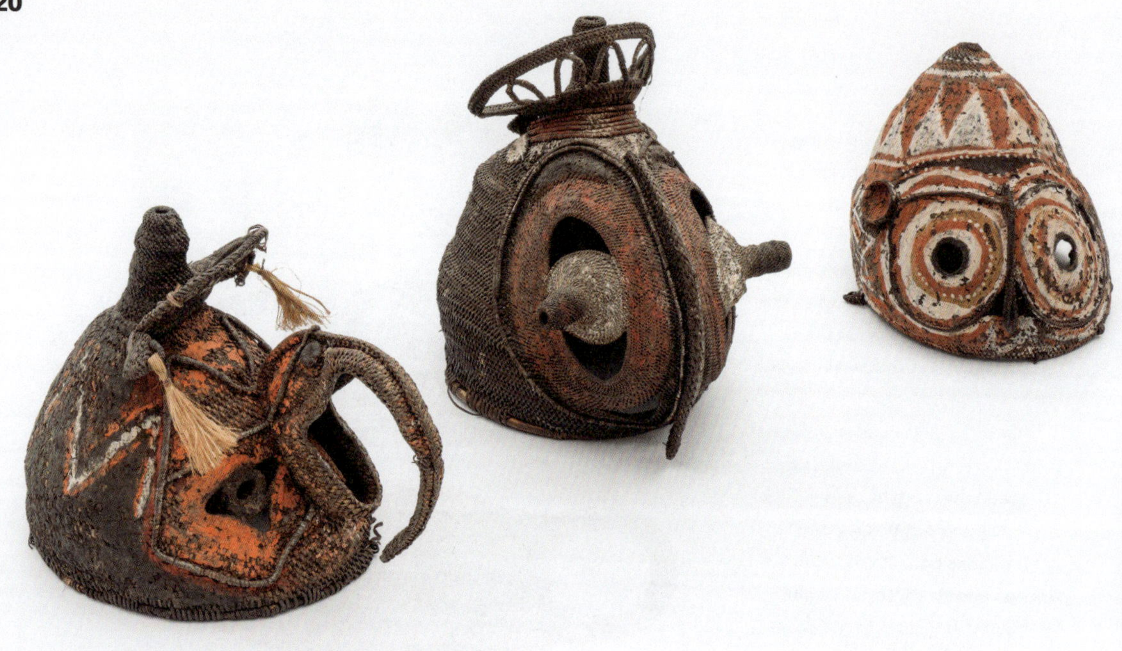

Plate 23 Colour has a ritual meaning amongst the Abelam. The painted *baba* masks represent spirit beings in the form of pigs, whose appearance in the village announce the beginning of a ritual period. Three masks from painted basketwork. Maprik, New Guinea. Purchased during the Sepik Expedition, 1961.

Plate 24 These receptacles were used for storing red wood powder and mixing the red wood paste. It was made by mixing the powder with water or palm oil and used to paint objects such as masks or for body painting. Two wooden boxes for red wood powder and two pieces of red wood. BaKuba, today's Dem. Rep. Congo and Kisi/Nyakyusa, Tanzania/Malawi.

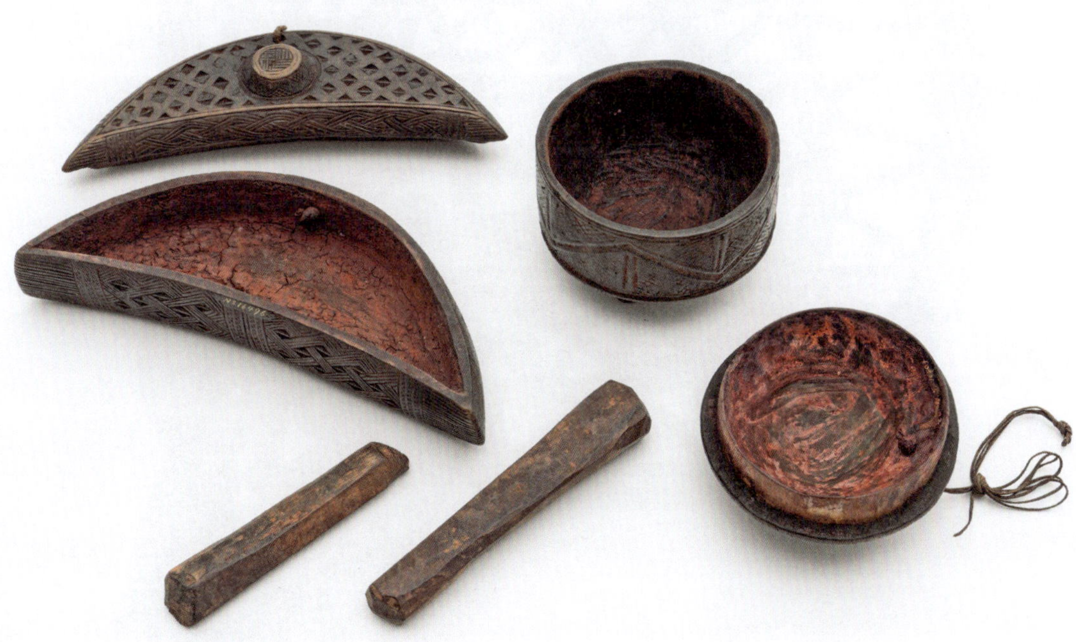

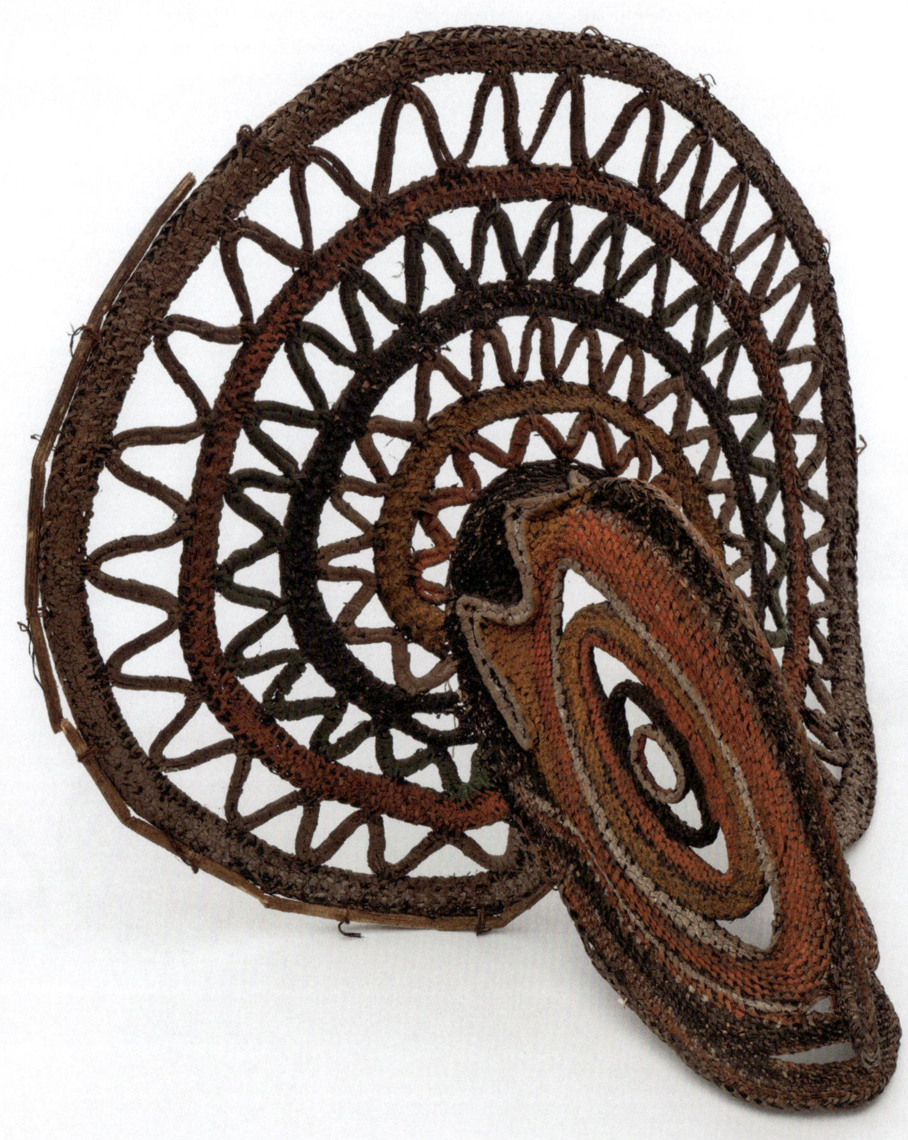

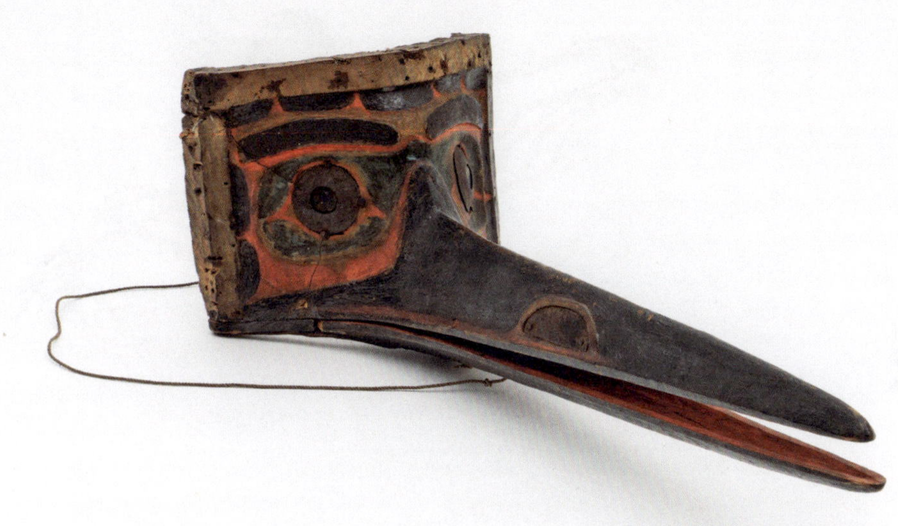

Plate 25 Yam tubers were decorated with such plaited and painted masks for their ritual presentation at festivities. The colourful rear headdress is the same as that worn by the festival dancers. Such masks identify the tubers as ensouled beings during the ritual. Mask with basketwork headdress. Abelam, Kaugia, Maprik, New Guinea. Collected during the Sepik Expedition, 1961.

Plate 26 Mask made from wood, leather and iron. The hinged beak with a string for opening and closing points to the man-eating raven Gwaxwgwakwalanuksiwe‘, while the straight form would indicate a mosquito, which the female cannibal Dzunuk'wa transformed into following her death. These masks were used during performances of the secret *brotherhood Hamats'a.* Kwakwaka'wakw, British Columbia, Canada. Collected by Fred Harvey Company, 1880–90. Purchased from the dealer Charles Ratton, 1941.

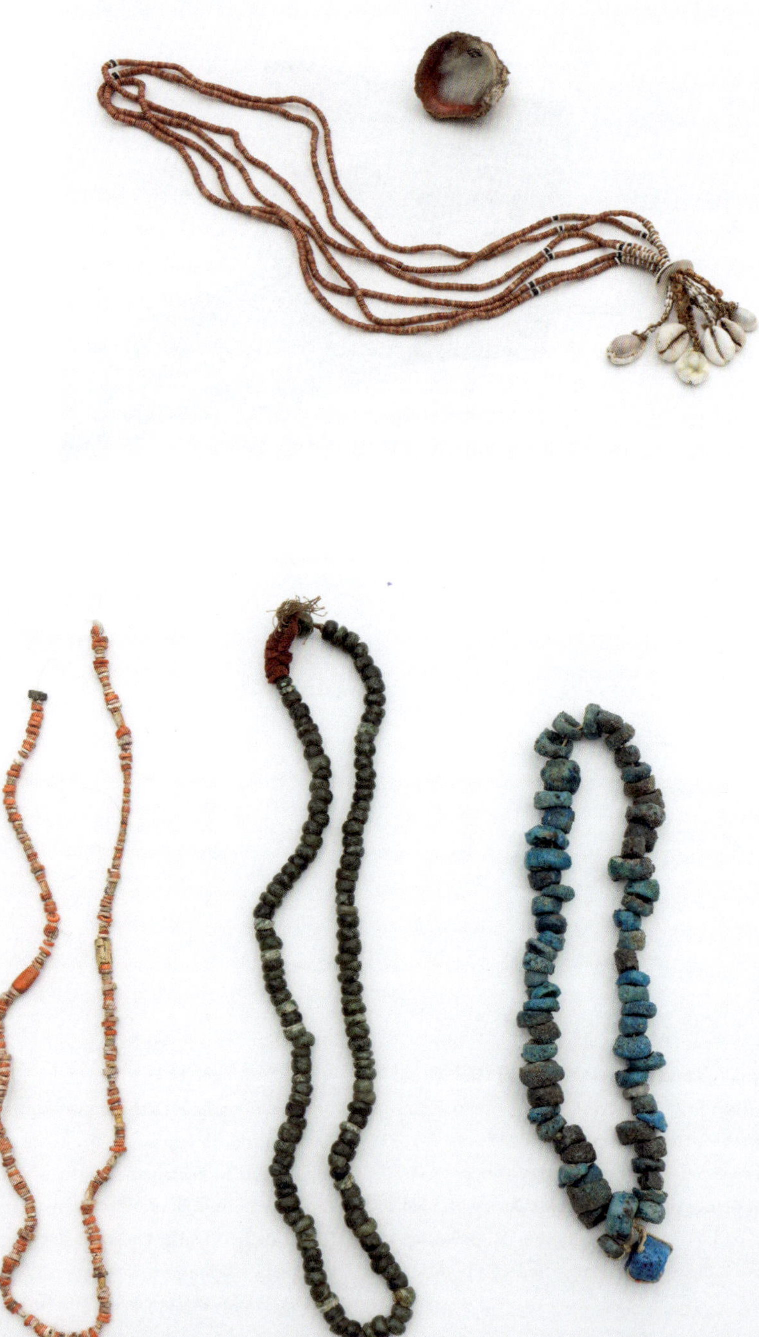

Plate 27 Necklaces made from red, black and white shell beads as well as cowrie shells primarily serve as valuables, i.e. currency, in traditional gift exchange. The value of a necklace is determined by the length and the red colour of the beads. This traditional valuables made from conches were sometimes used in parallel with the official monetary currency. Necklace. Solomon Islands, Melanesia. Collected by Volker Schneider, 1988; spondylus shell. Lavongai, Bismarck Archipelago, Melanesia. Collected by Karl Friedrich Wandres, c. 1907.

Plate 28 Different coloured necklaces from various materials. From left to right: Necklace from white-reddish spondylus shell discs from Ecuador, necklace from green nephrite from New Caledonia and necklace of blue faience beads made from quartz ceramic, Egypt.

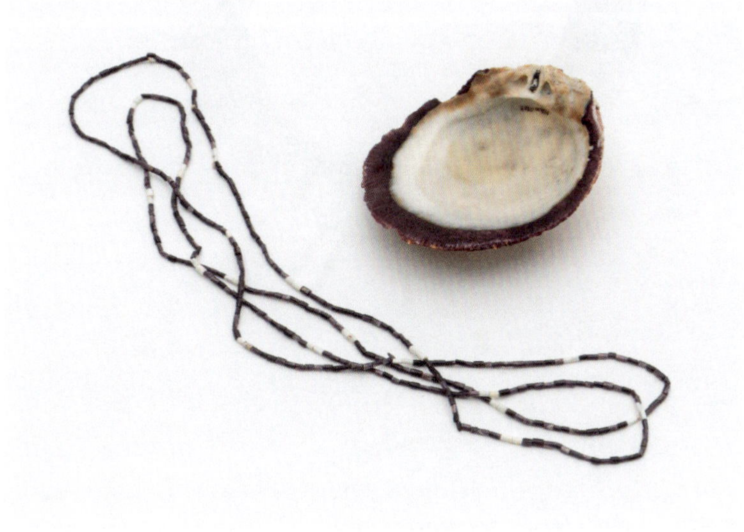

Plate 29 Both the violet edge as well as the white interior of the wampum shell were fashioned into beads. For a long time wampum beads served as a currency east of the Rocky Mountains. Belts made from the beads were used to document contracts. Wampum chain. Penobscot, Maine, USA. Collected by Emil W. Lenders, before 1915.

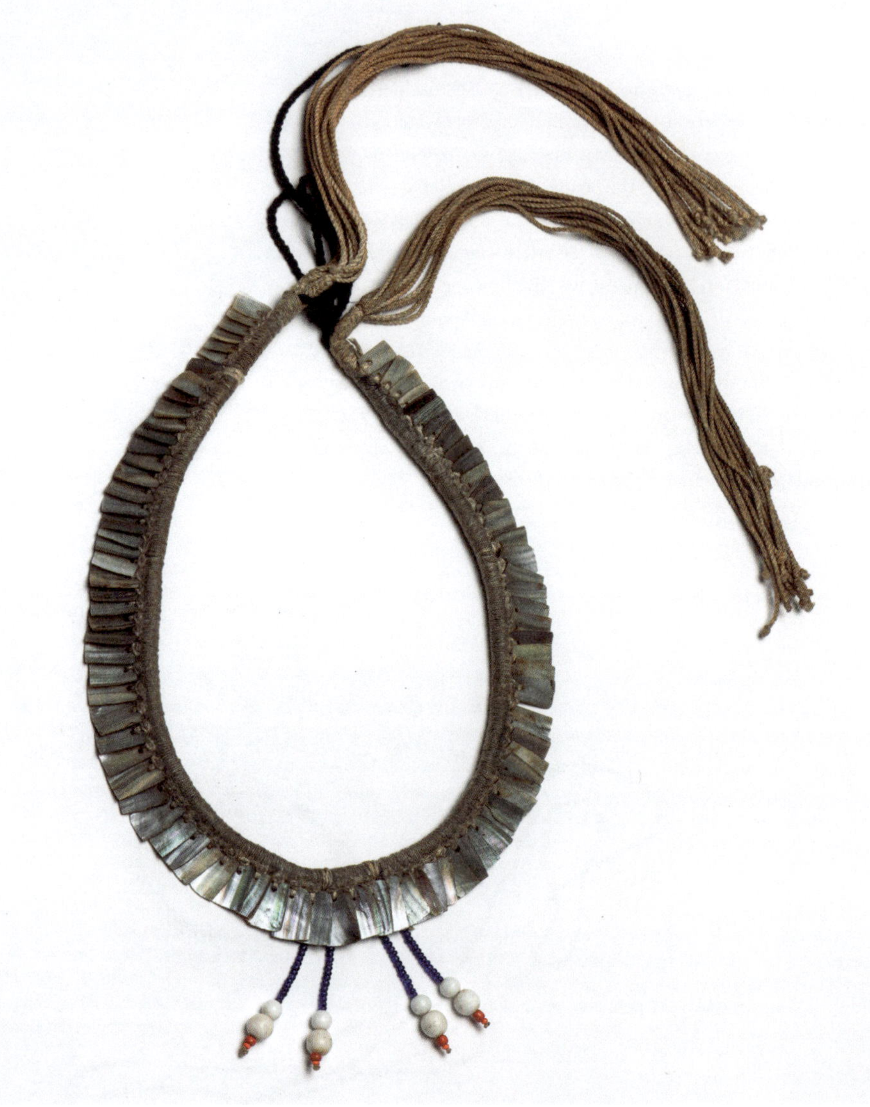

Plate 30 Necklace *Ngap-o-kre-dje* made from polished river mussel shells, cotton thread and glass beads. This dazzling piece of jewellery is used exclusively by the Kayapó and is highly valued. Kayapó Mekrãgnoti, Pará, Brazil. Collected by Luiz Boglar, 1988.

Plate 31 This neck ring from the Massai of Kenya points to a change in the use of materials. The brightly coloured glass beads were first employed in the manufacture of such items of jewellery in the 20th century as a result of trade. Prior to this metal beads were generally used. At the same time the arrangement of the beads provides an indication of the wearer's origin, social status, or family. Purchased from William Ockelford Oldman, 1911.

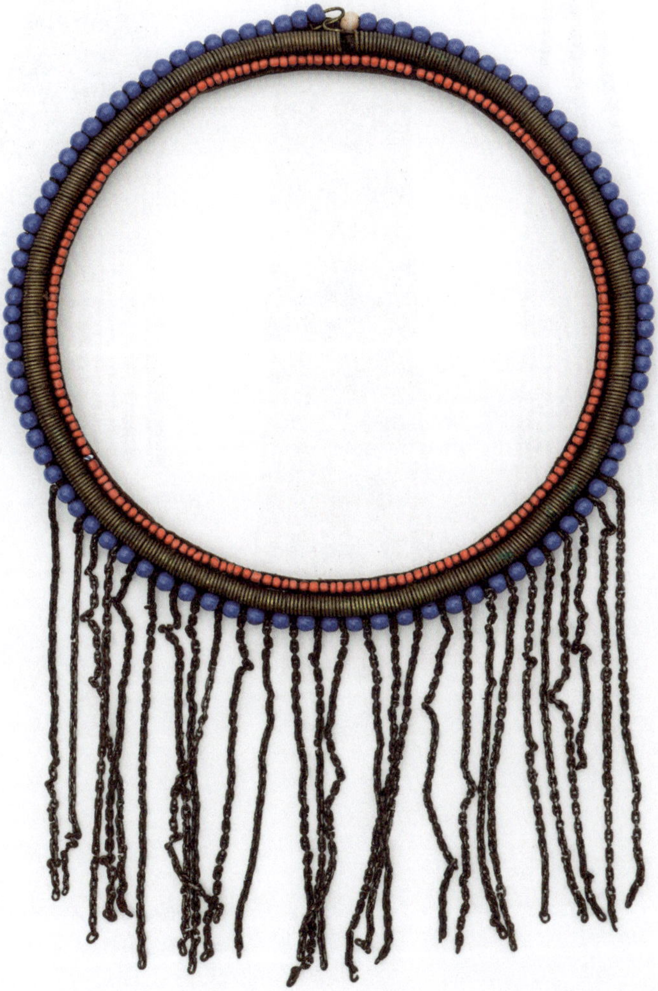

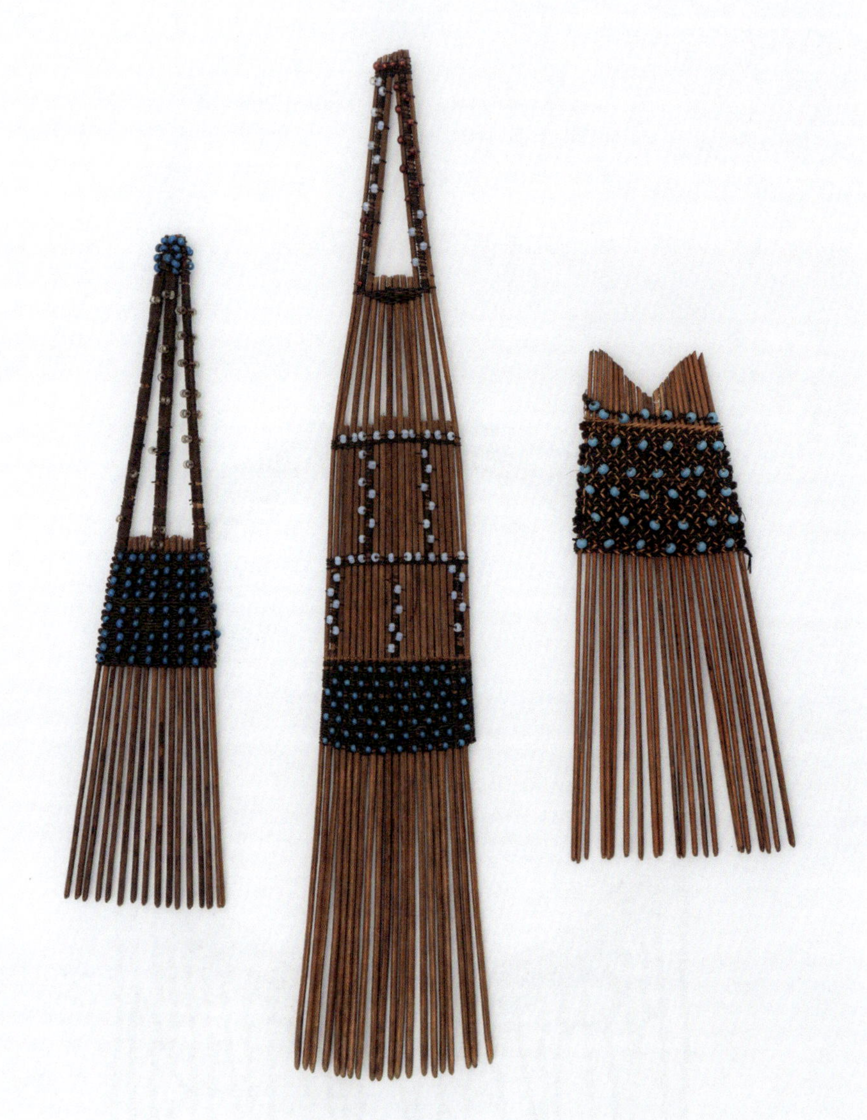

Plate 32 In the 19th century blue glass beads were highly valued as curiosities due to their colour which was unusual in Samoa. For a period they found their way into the indigenous culture as status symbols. Decorative combs, *selu toga*. Coconut leaf mid-ribs, glass beads. Samoan Islands, Polynesia. Collected by tax commissioner Krause, 1882; donation from the Gramlich family, 1933; collected by Fritz Hauck, 1902–1905.

Plate 33 Thanks to the different cut of these Indian agates, the stones glow in different nuances. Collected by Leo Frobenius, not dated.

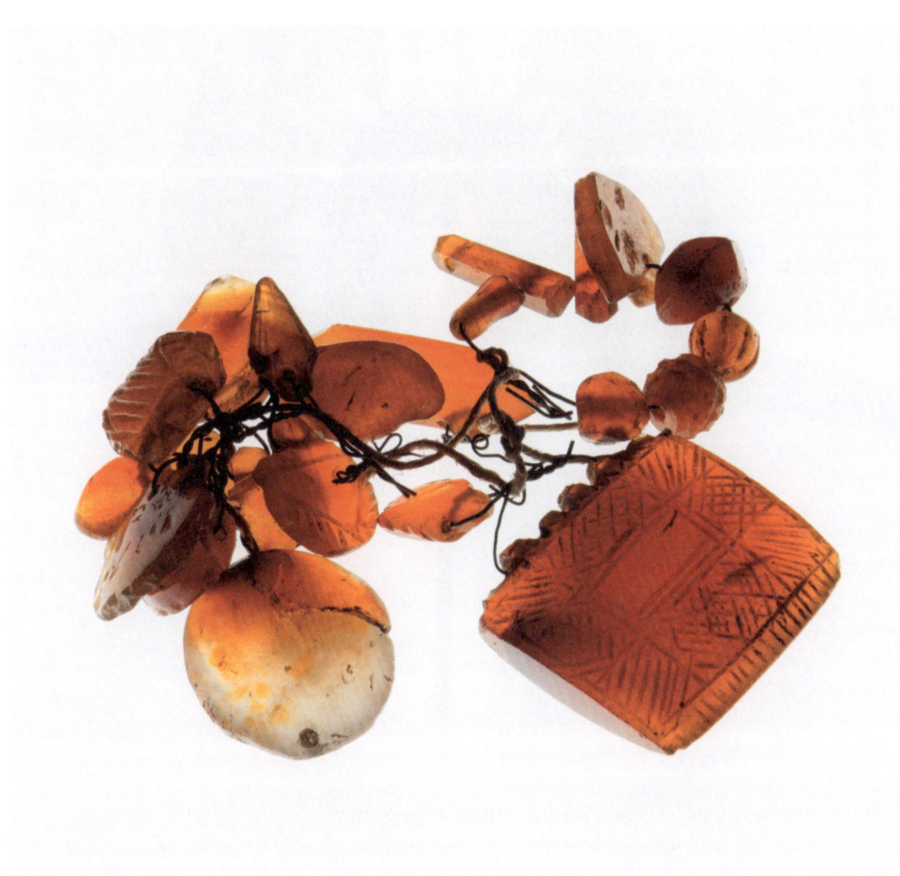

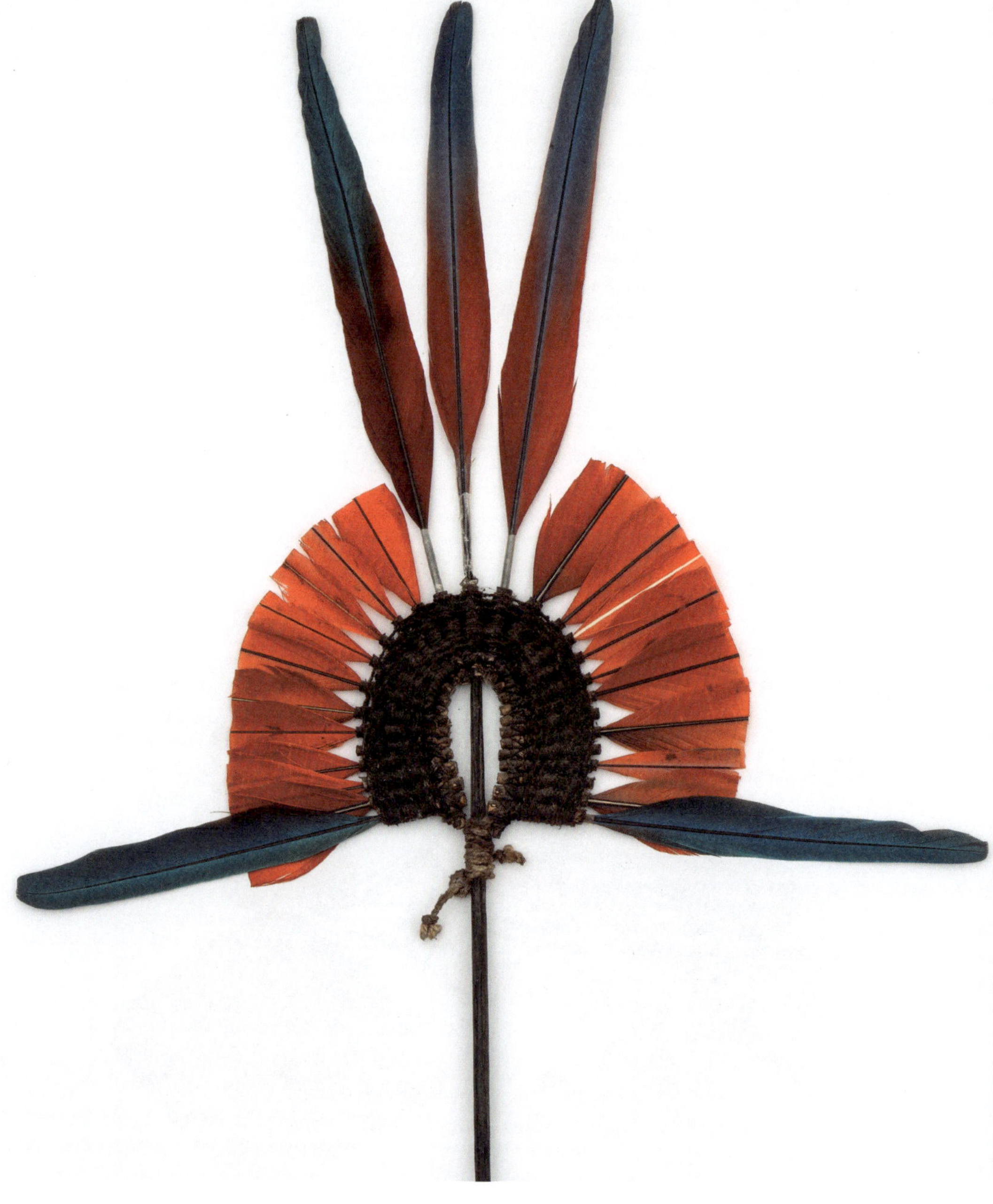

Plate 34 The headdress *Àkkàpa'ri* is stuck into a 'hat' made from painted beeswax which is glued into the hair. This headdress is made and worn exclusively by men. The colour of the feathers used is dependent on personal privileges. Feathers, cotton and wood. Kayapó Mekrãgnoti, Pará, Brazil. Collected by Gustaaf Verswijver, 1992.

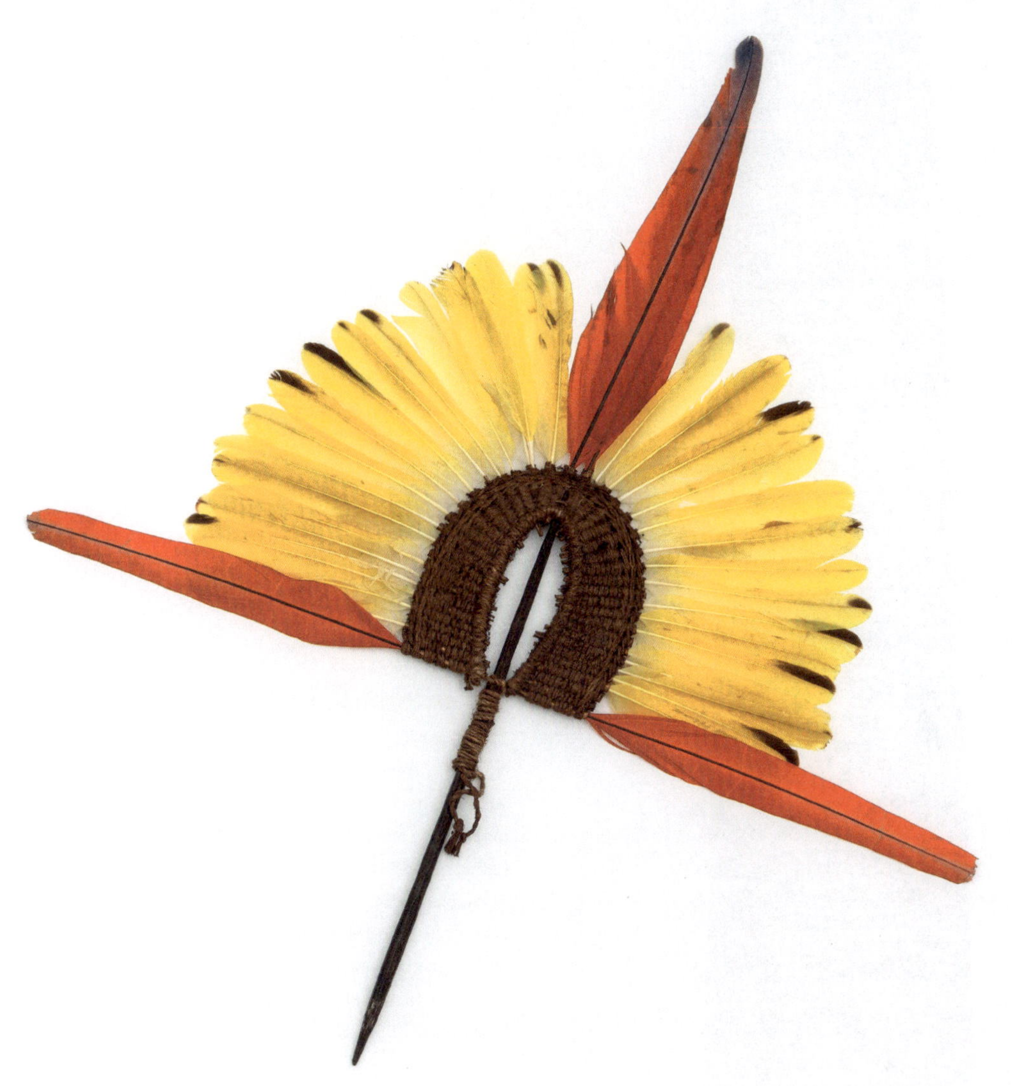

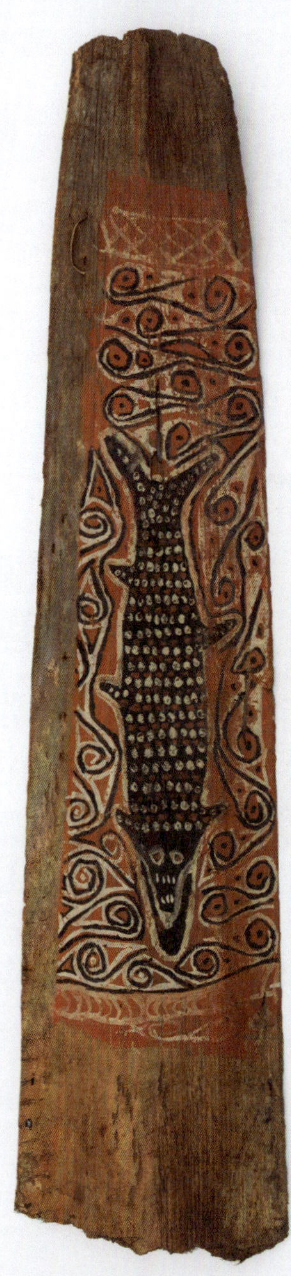

Plate 35 This painting is part of the wall cladding of a men's house. The motif *Kinin Kumnya* ('Mother of Fish') was painted onto a sago palm sheath in red, black and white paint. It refers to a myth about the origin of all fish. Avim, Upper Karawari, New Guinea. Collected by Eike Haberland, Sepik Expedition, 1961.

Plate 36 This triptych, painted on three sago palm sheaths joined together, also originates from the interior lining of the men's house from Avim. It shows the motif *Tokopai* ('Creation Pot'). In the myth the culture hero Api fills it with his penile blood, from out of which people and spirits arise. During the male initiation, i.e. circumcision, the blood is collected in a bowl, mixed with sago and eaten. Avim, Upper Karawari, New Guinea. Collected by Eike Haberland, Sepik Expedition, 1961.

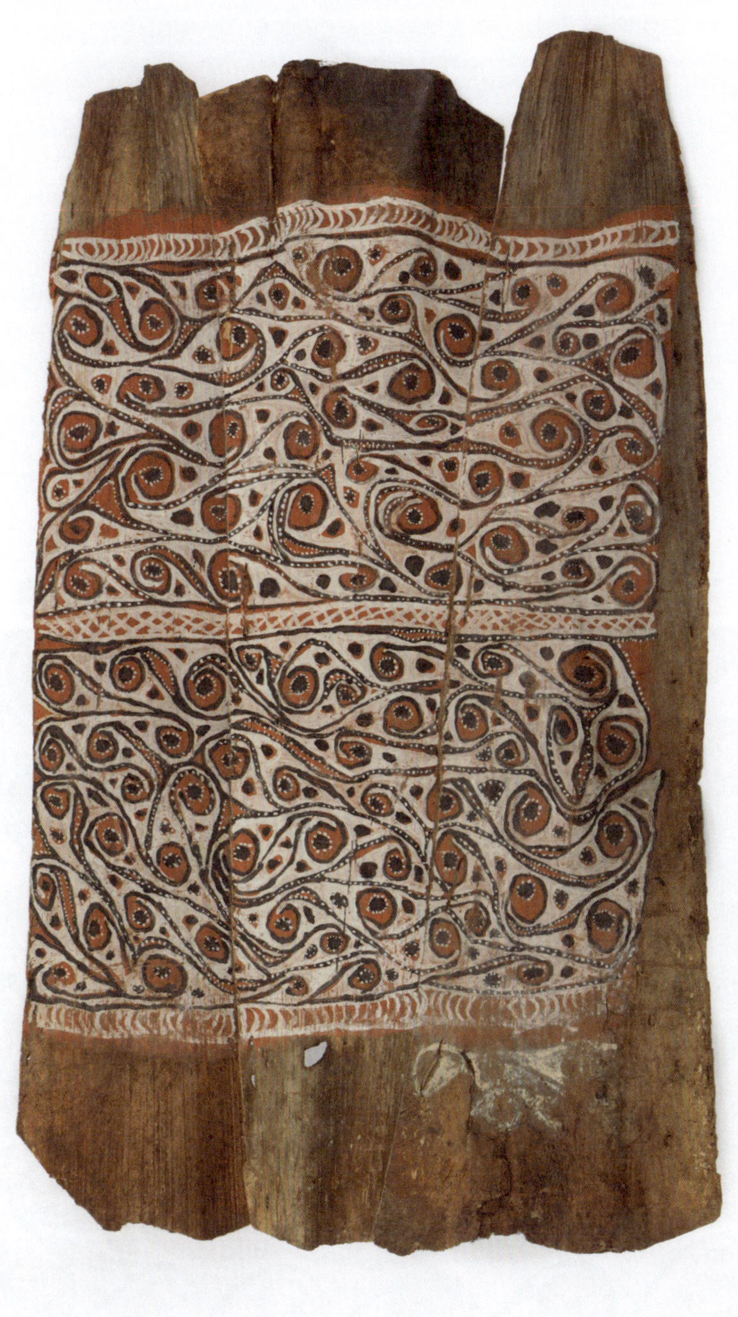

Plate 37 This contemporary painting from Nelson Apap shows *Memanja,* the spirit of the dead, who lives in the underworld, which transpires to be an exact copy of the upper world, together with water spirits. The acrylic painting continues the traditional sequence of colours in Avim painting, first applying red, then white, then finally black. Nelson Apap, 2019: *Memanja.* Acrylic on paper. Avim, Upper Karawari, New Guinea. Collected by Tomi Bartole, 2019.

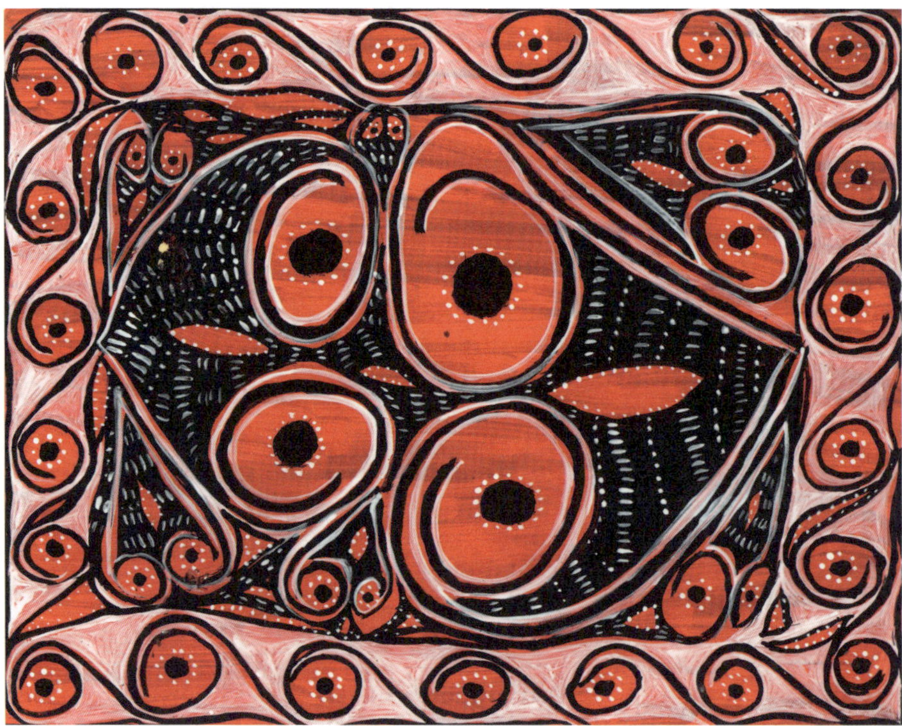

Plate 38 The contemporary painting from Andrias Aimo depicts *Etoka Enunga,* a spirit that lives in both weapons and slit drums. If this motif is applied to arrows, then they should fly further and have greater penetration power. If it is painted onto slit drums then they can be heard over long distances and are effective during hunting. Andrias Aimo, 2019: *Etoka Enunga.* Acrylic on paper. Avim, Upper Karawari, New Guinea. Collected by Tomi Bartole, 2019.

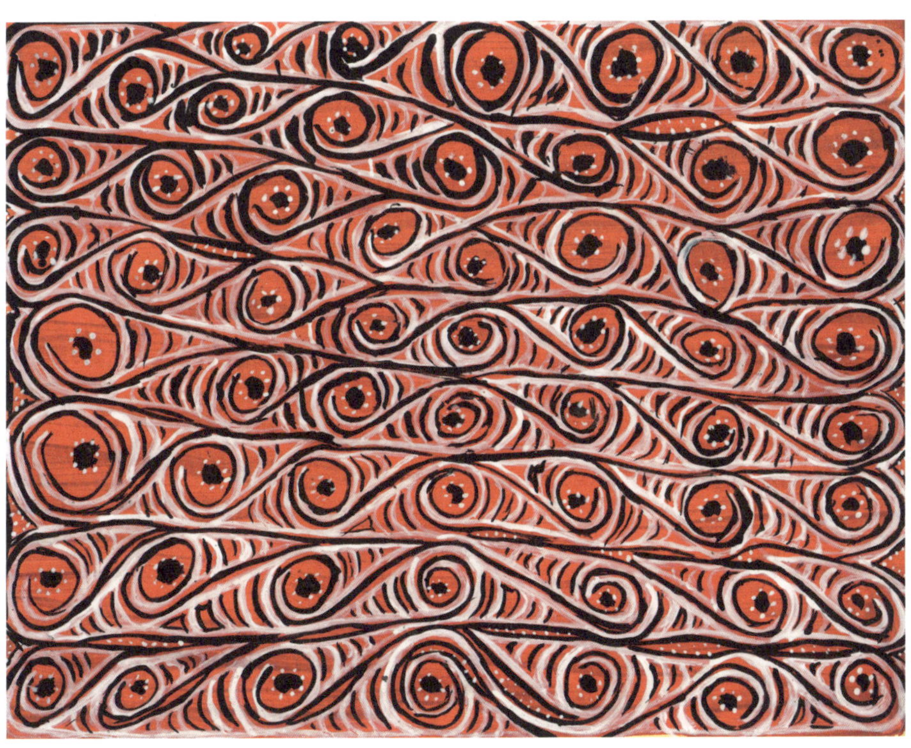

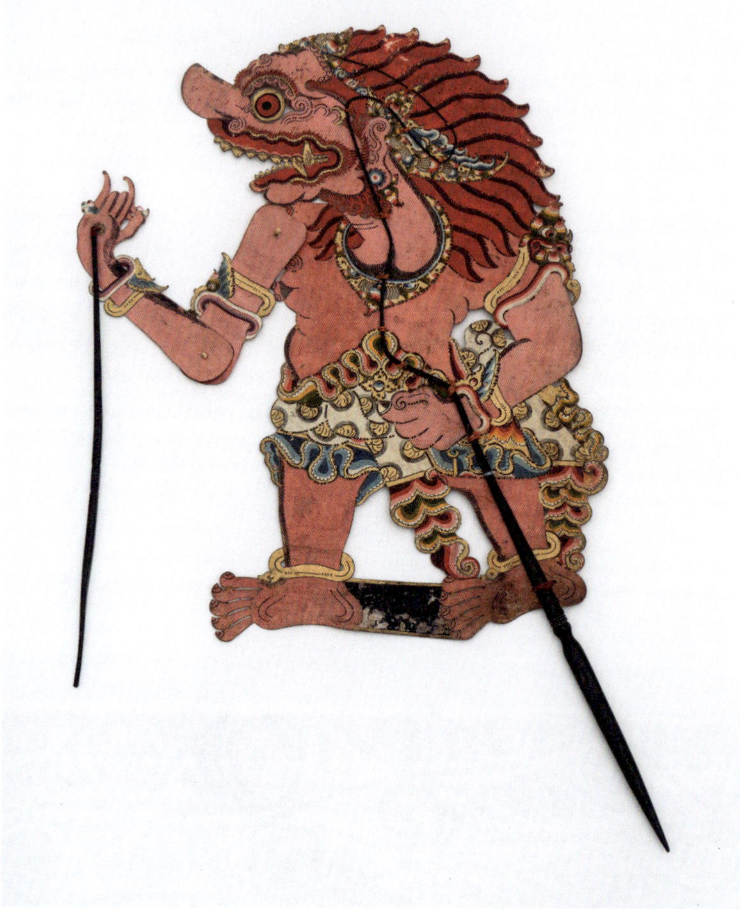

Plate 39 In the Javanese shadow play *wayang kulit* the colour red, as in the case of this giant, stands for energy, rage and an untamed temperament. Shadow puppet Buta Rambut Geni. Java, Indonesia. Painted parchment, horn. Purchased from August Flick, 1989.

Plate 40 In the shadow play the colour red also has positive connotations, for example courage and strength in battle, as in the case of the young Baladewa (left). In the case of the fire god Batara Brahma (right) the red colouration indicates his assigned element. Shadow puppets. Java, Indonesia. Painted parchment, horn. Purchased from August Flick, 1989.

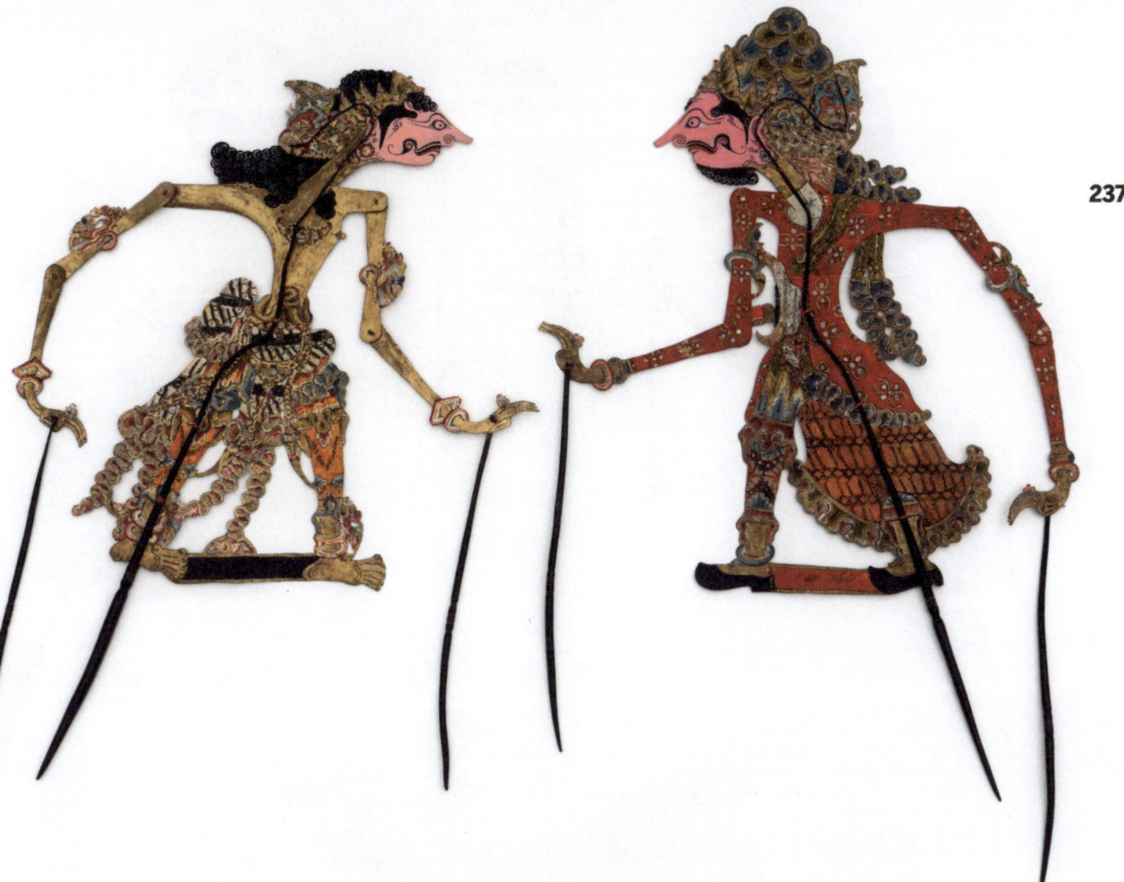

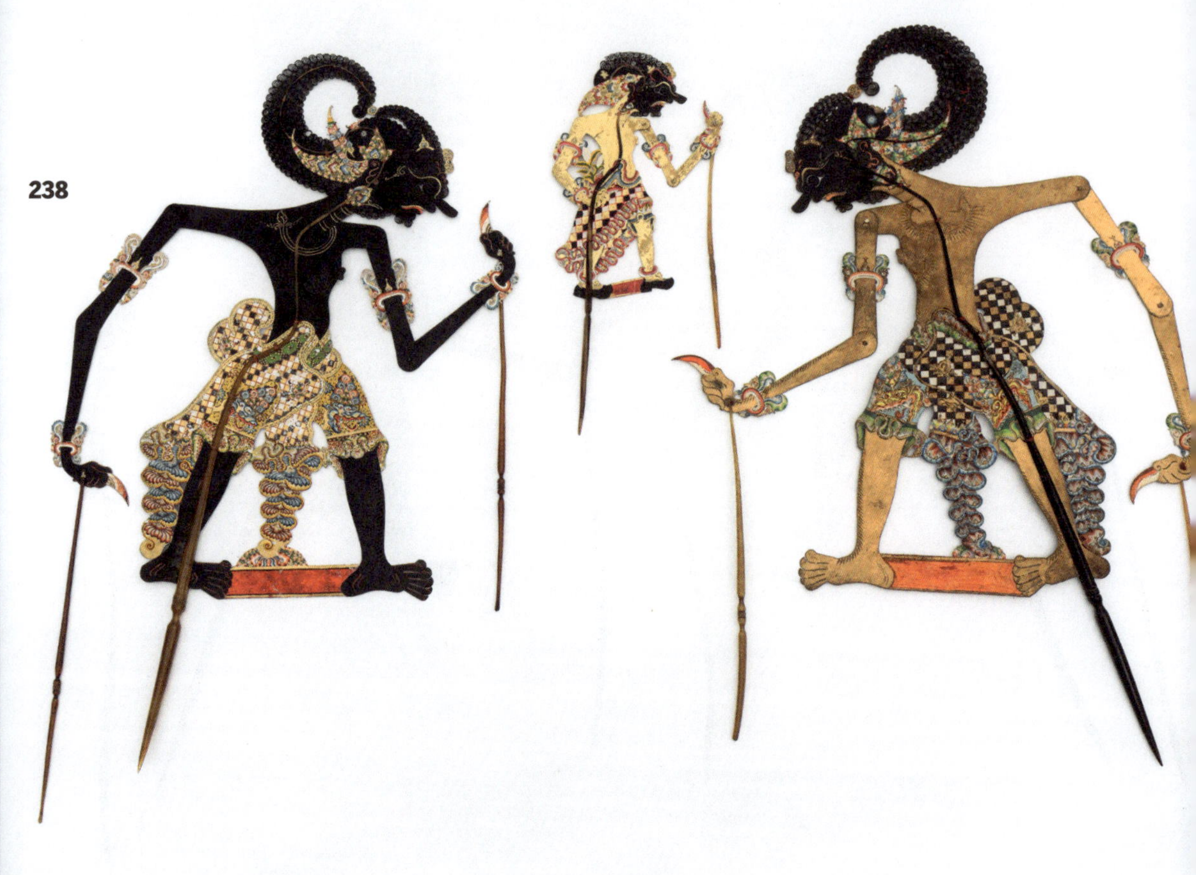

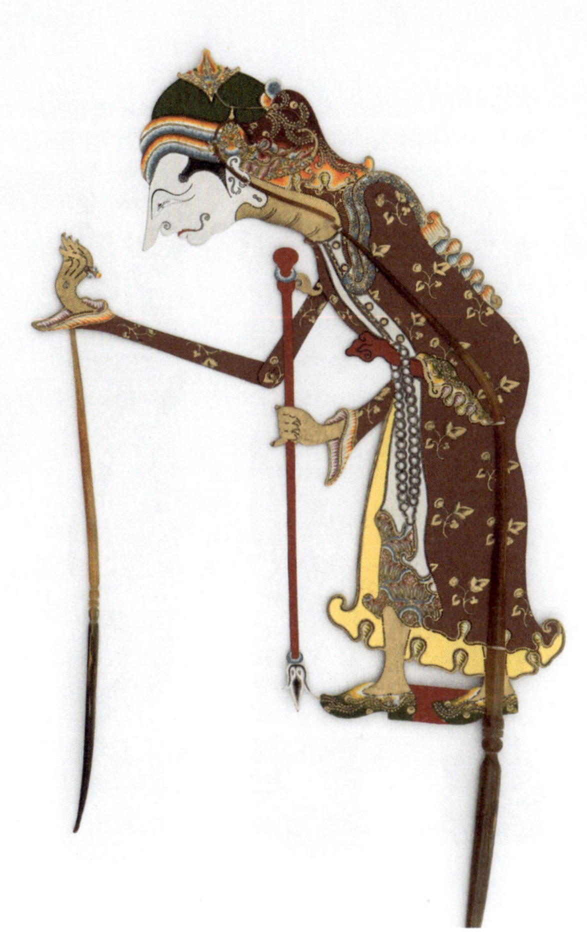

Plate 41 The Pandawa hero Bima appears in eight variations. If he is shown completely in black, then this indicates his full maturity. From left to right: Bima as king, Bima's 'soul' and Bima Wrekodara. Shadow puppet. Java, Indonesia. Painted parchment and horn. Collected by Annegret Haake, 1970–2000 and purchased from August Flick, 1989.

Plate 42 In *wayang kulit* the colour white stands for purity, spirituality and wisdom. That is why many hermits have a white face. The shadow puppet Abiyasa or Resi Kanawa. Java, Indonesia. Painted parchment and horn. Collected by Annegret Haake, 1970–2000.

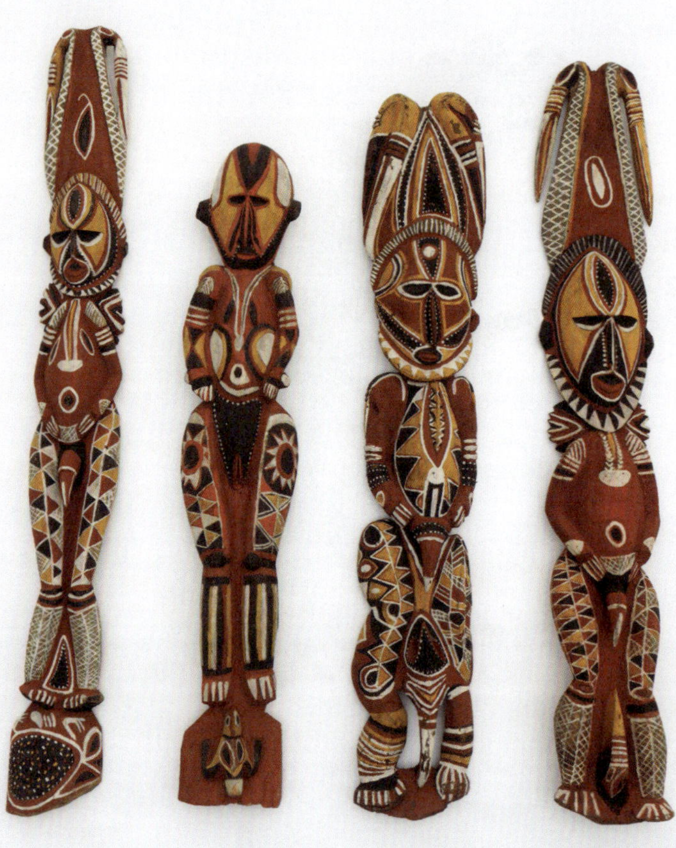

Plate 43 Amongst the Abelam of the Maprik region of New Guinea the colour itself is considered a magic substance. It is only by being painted in the colours black, white, red and yellow that the anthropomorphic figures are transformed from a lifeless piece of wood into mystical and powerful beings. Wood painted with earth pigments. Maprik, New Guinea. Collected by Meinhard Schuster and Eike Haberland, Sepik Expedition, 1961.

Plate 44 The over six meter high gable painting of a spirit house is painted onto numerous sago palm sheaths sewn together. The colour itself is considered a powerful substance which establishes contact to the spirit world. The three face images in the bottom third represent the spirits of ancestors who – with their hypnotic looking eyes formed from concentric circles – establish eye contact with the living from the afterworld. Abelam. Ulupu, Maprik, New Guinea. Collected by Meinhard Schuster and Eike Haberland, Sepik Expedition, 1961.

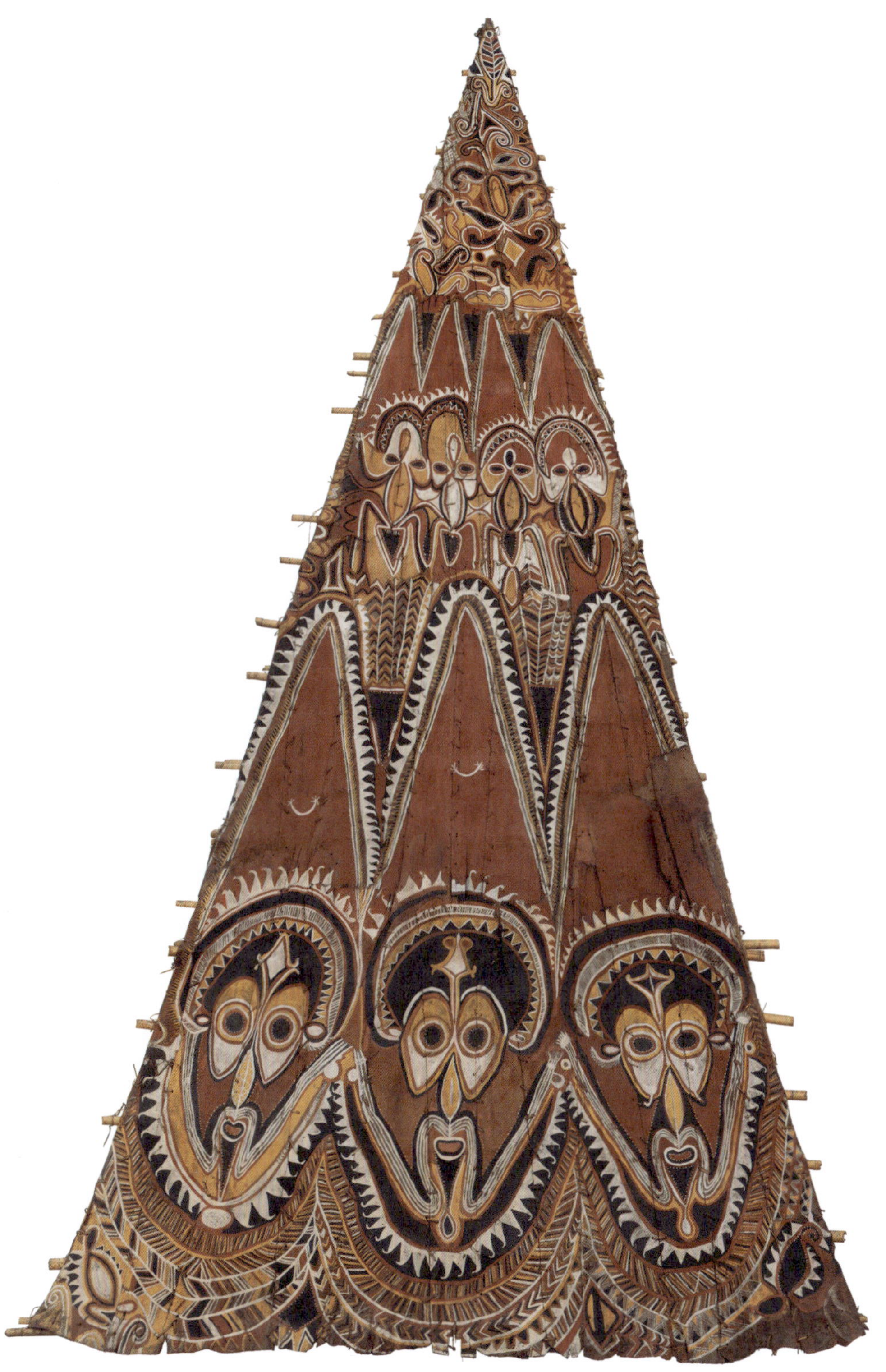

Plate 45 The skull holder from a men's house of the Sawos shows a *wakin,* a clan ancestor and guardian spirit. The painting of the face with the boldly accentuated eyes can also be found in other depictions of ancestors, as well as the skulls of the dead overmodelled with clay which are stored on such holders. It indicates the clan affiliation. Painted sago palm sheaths on a bamboo stand. Collected by Meinhard Schuster during the Sepik Expedition, 1961.

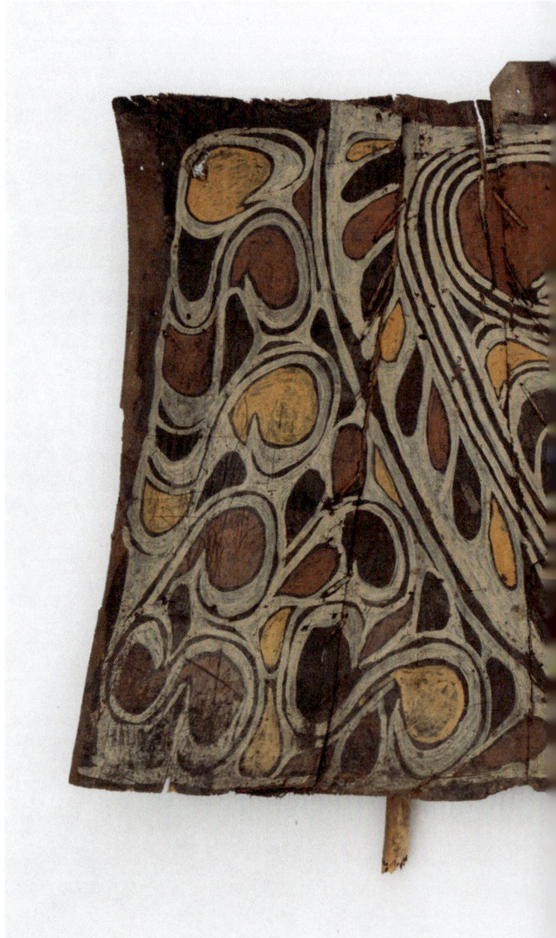

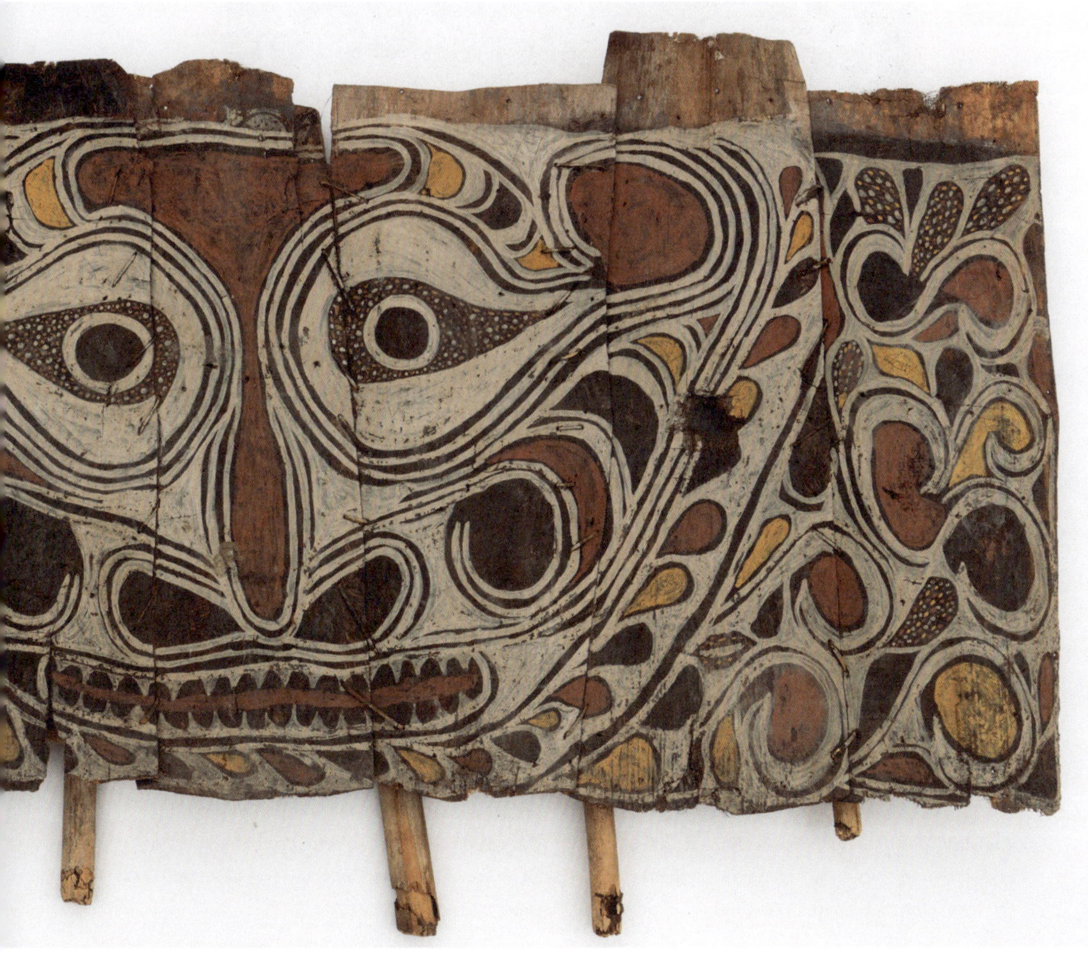

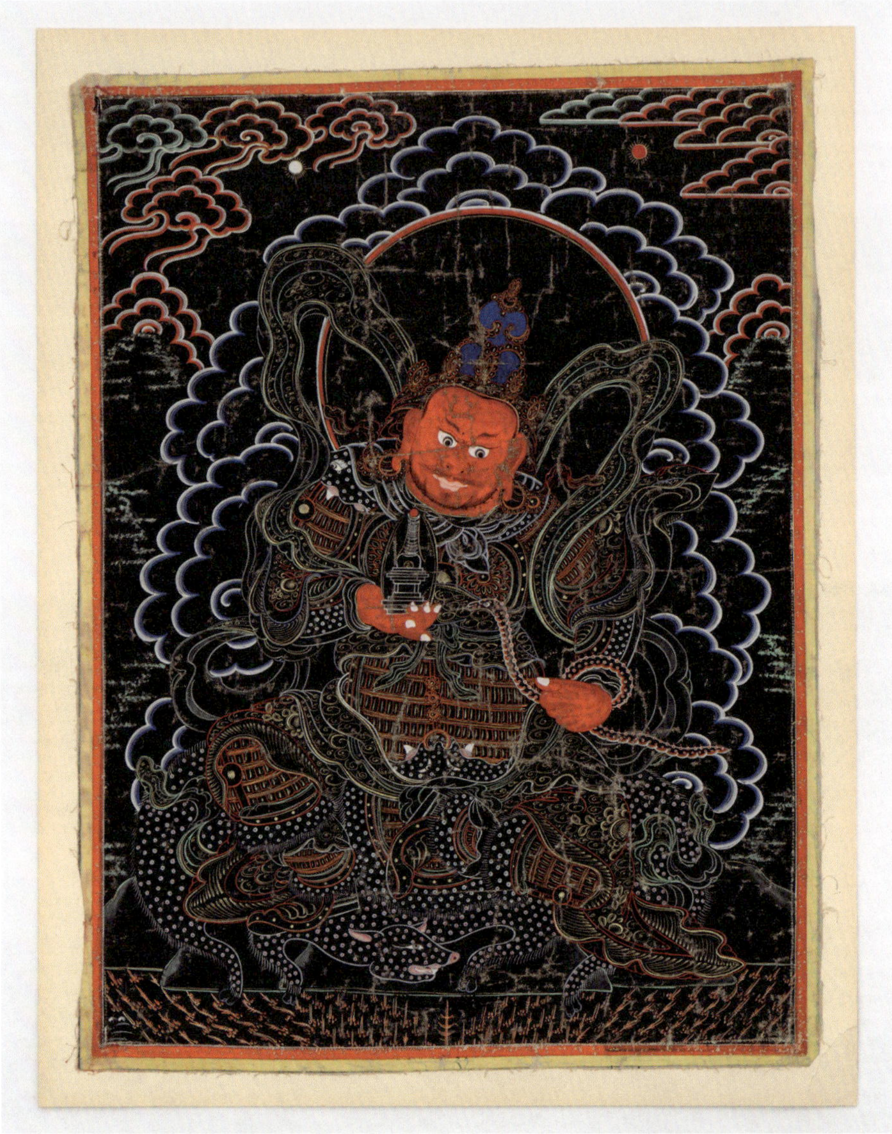

Plate 46 This painting of Virūpākṣa with its red face underlines his power, while the dark background points to the terrifying nature of the guardian of the western hemisphere. Scroll painting *(thangka)*. Tibet. Oil on canvas. Collected by Horst Günther Klein, 1979–1980.

Plate 47 This *thangka* depicts the wheel of life. In this tantric colour scheme the sun (male) and the moon (female) are depicted as a couple in white and red. Scroll painting *(thangka)*. Tibet. Oil on canvas. Tibet. Collected by Horst Günther Klein, 1979–1980.

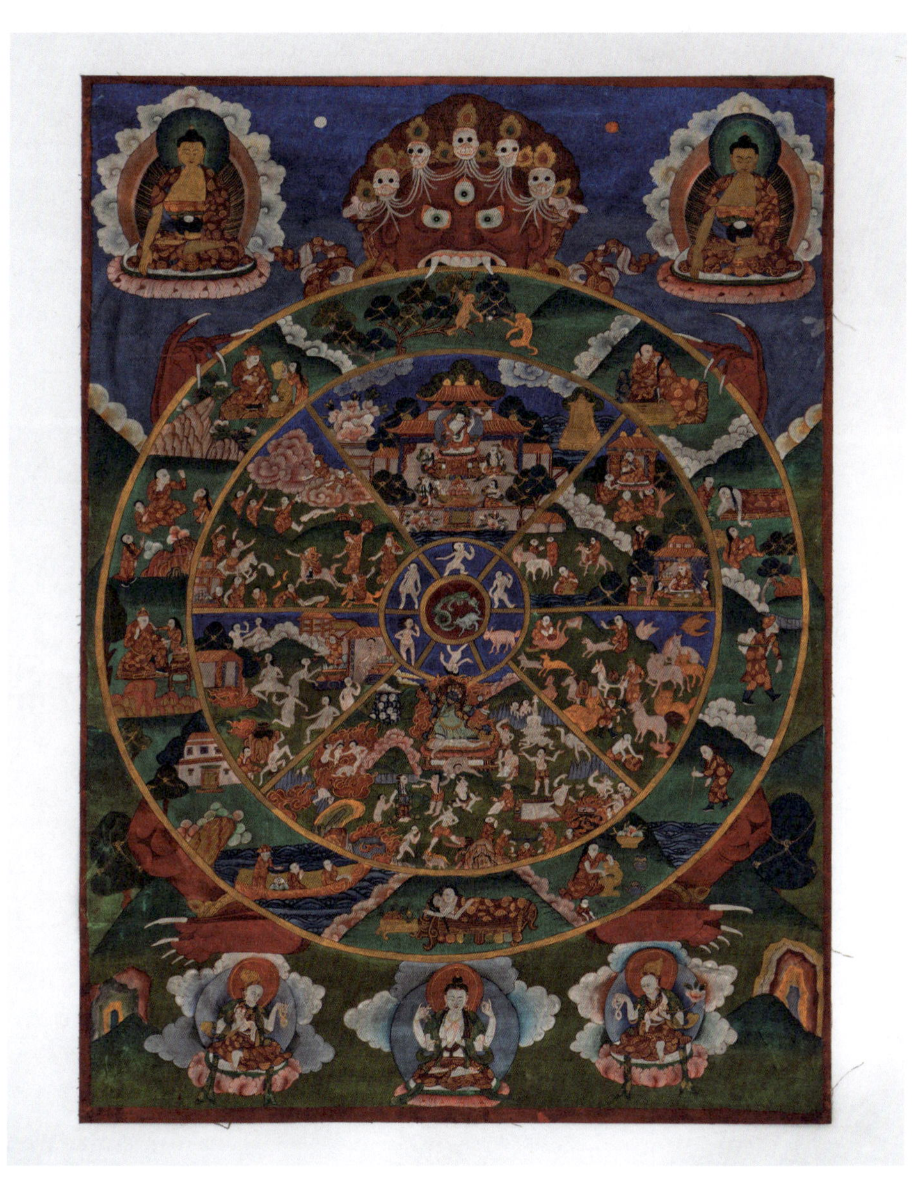

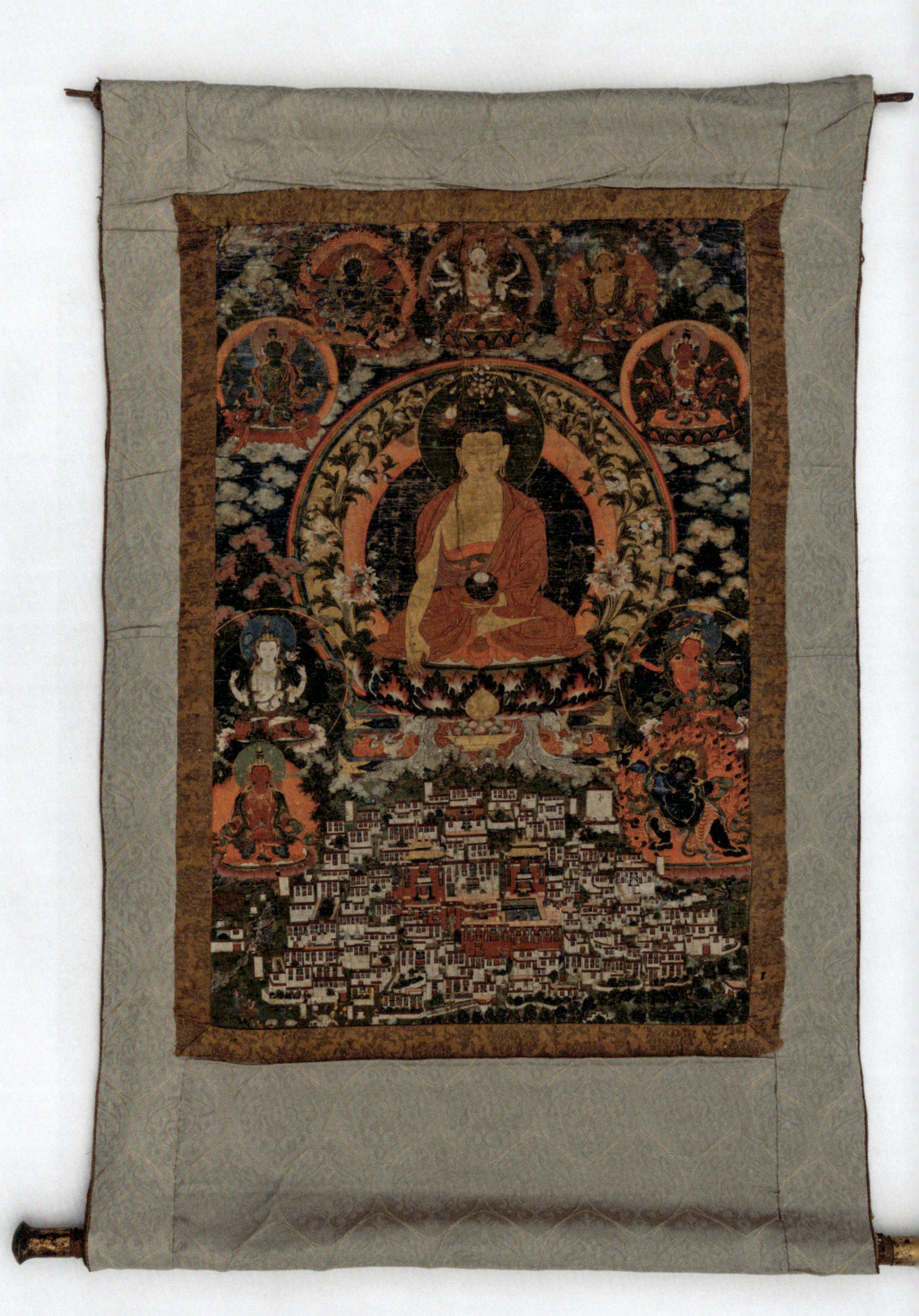

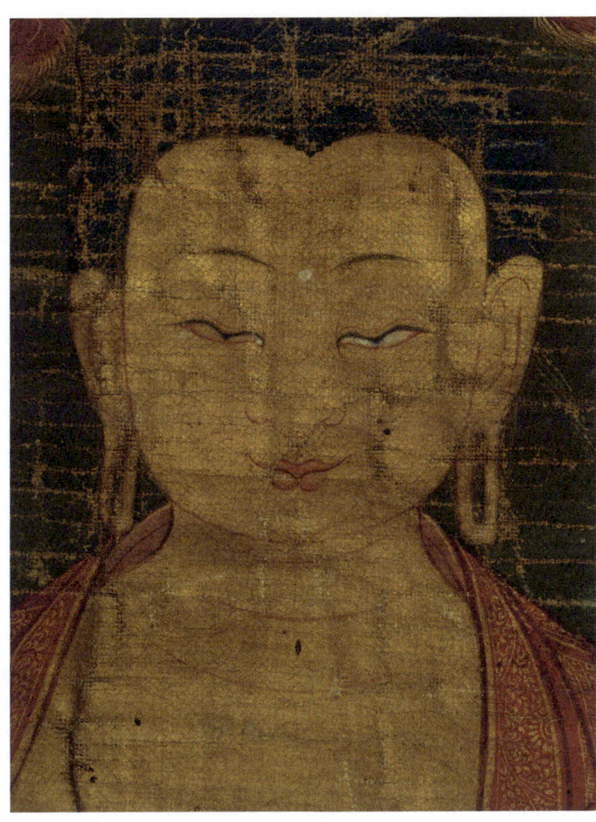

Plates 48 and 49 (detail) The Buddha Śākyamuni (also called Siddhārtha or Gautama) is frequently painted in gold pigments in order to symbolize his uniqueness. Here he is sitting under a rainbow nimbus, whose radiant colours are also designed to underline the Buddha's singularity. Scroll painting *(thangka)*. Tibet. Brocade and canvas, painted. Collected by Hermann Niggemeyer during the Frobenius Expedition to India, 1955–1956.

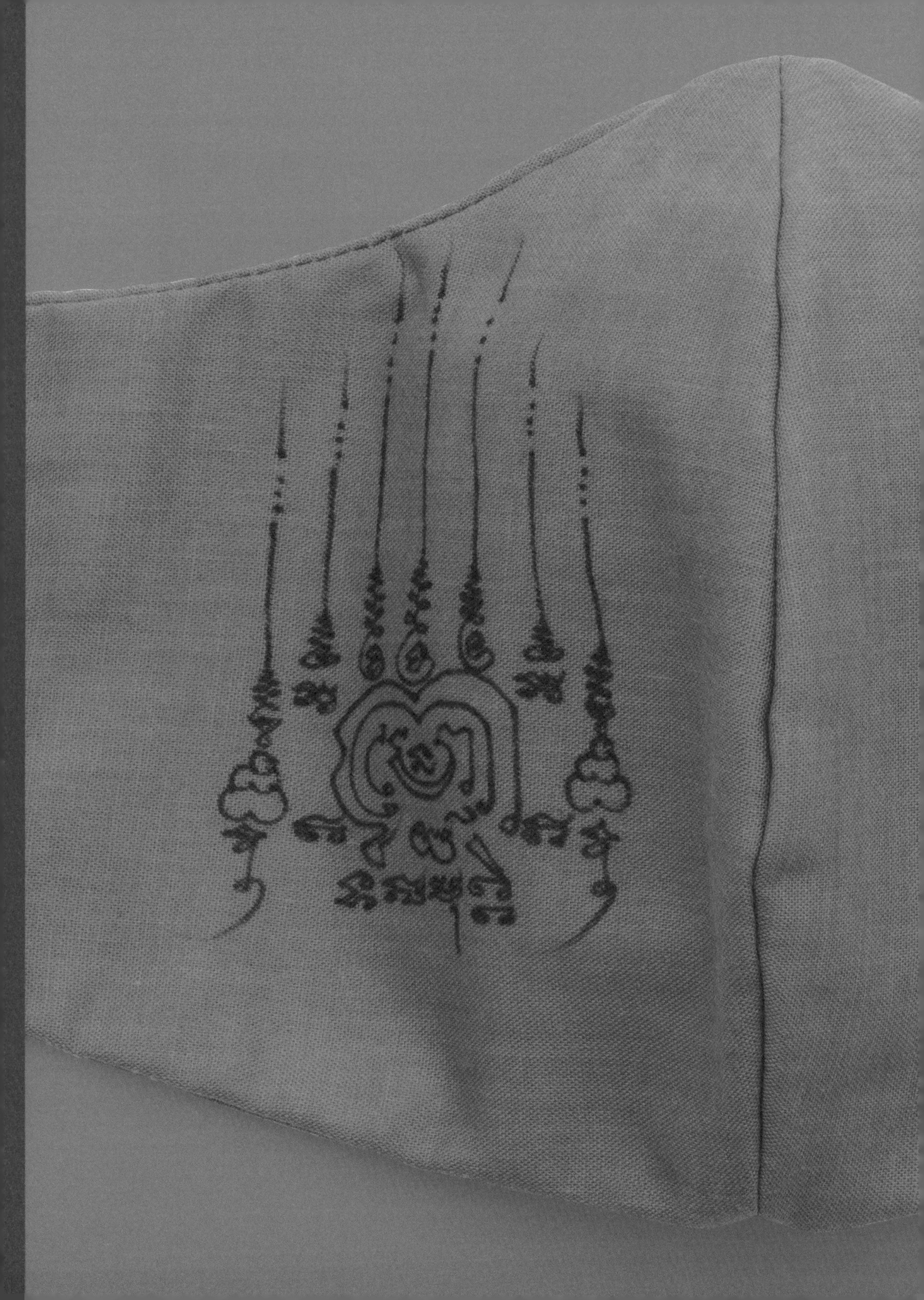

"... cannot dispense with light."

Adapted from Johann Wolfgang von Goethe.
1810: *Zur Farbenlehre (Theory of Colours)*. §694.

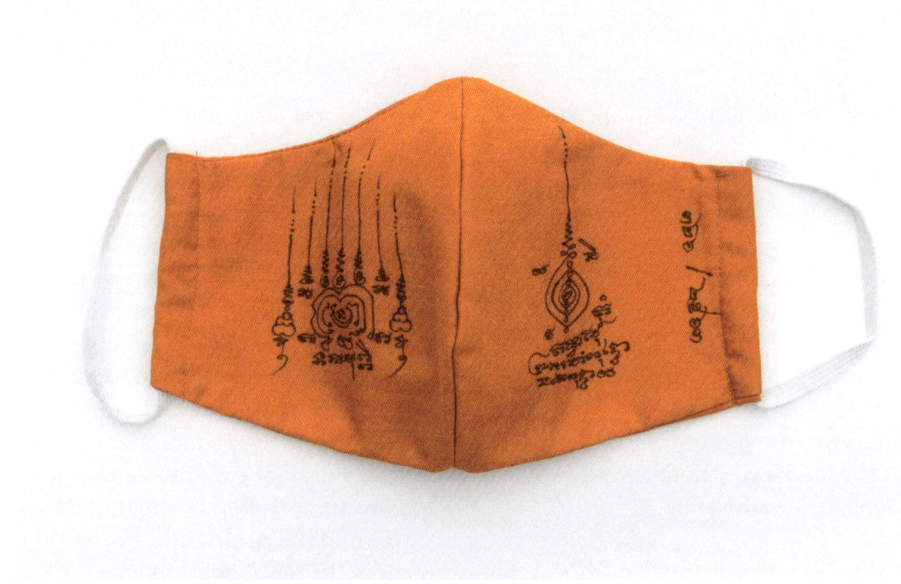

In Buddhism orange is the colour of the highest enlightenment, wisdom, devotion and asceticism. The mantra on the face mask states “Recognising the problem is the path to the end of the suffering.” Fibres from recycled plastic bottles. Purchased from Wat Chak Daeng temple, Thailand, 2020.

AUTHORS

Tomi Bartole is an anthropologist at the Research Centre of the Slovenian Academy of Sciences and Arts. He has conducted fieldwork among the Avim people of Papua New Guinea, studying their rituals, religion and politics.

Chantal Courtois is assistant curator for the Americas collections and in charge of the photographic collection at the Musée d'Ethnographie (MEG), Geneva, Switzerland.

Eystein Dahl is a visiting professor at the *Institut für Empirische Sprachwissenschaft,* Johann Wolfgang Goethe-Universität, Frankfurt am Main.

Roger Erb is a professor at the *Institut für Didaktik der Physik,* Johann Wolfgang Goethe-Universität, Frankfurt am Main. His main areas of interest are experimentation in physics lessons and improving learning processes in physics teaching, as well as improving lessons in optics.

René Fuerst is an ethnologist and indigenist who conducted research and produced photographic work among indigenous groups in Amazonia between 1955 and 1975. He has made extensive contributions to the collections of several European museums. From 1983 to 1998 he was a curator at the Musée d'Ethnographie (MEG) in Geneva, Switzerland.
In addition, he was a member of fact-finding missions on Amazonian Indians undertaken by the Red Cross (1970) and the Aborigines Protection Society (1972), and is a former president of the IWGIA.

Frauke Gathof is a research assistant for the Africa collection at the Weltkulturen Museum, Frankfurt am Main.

Vanessa J. von Gliszczynski is an ethnomusicologist and curator of the South-East Asia collection at the Weltkulturen Museum, Frankfurt am Main.

Brigitta Hauser-Schäublin has been Professor of Anthropology at the University of Göttingen since 1992 (emerita since 2016). She has conducted field research in Papua New Guinea, Indonesia (primarily in Bali) and Cambodia (from 1972 to 2012). Her areas of special interest are cult houses in New Guinea, material culture, the ritual and political organisation of space, and cultural politics.

Matthias Claudius Hofmann is curator of the Oceania collection at the Weltkulturen Museum, Frankfurt am Main.

Arno R. Holl is an ethnologist specialising in Indigenous Amazonia and Afro-Brazil. He is a project assistant at the Weltkulturen Museum, Frankfurt am Main. Since early 2021 he has been working as a locally hired member of staff at the Goethe-Institut in Luanda, Angola.

Eric Huntington studies relationships between visual culture, ritual and philosophy in the Buddhist traditions of southern and central Asia. He is currently a Gragg postdoctoral fellow in the Chao Center for Asian Studies at Rice University.

Olaf L. Müller studied mathematics and philosophy in Göttingen. After completing his post-doctoral research (Habilitation) he took up a post in 2003 at the Humboldt-Universität Berlin, teaching philosophy with a special focus on the philosophy of science. One of his core interests is the dispute about colour between Goethe and Newton (farbenstreit.de).

Eva Ch. Raabe has been director of the Weltkulturen Museums, Frankfurt am Main, since October 2019. She was previously curator of the Oceania collection for around 30 years.

Gustaaf Verswijver is an ethnologist. Since 1974 he has conducted extensive fieldwork among the Kayapó in Brazil. His research has focused on ethnohistory, warfare and material culture. From 1990 to 2012 he was a curator at the Royal Museum for Central Africa, Tervuren, Belgium. Between 2003 and 2005 he was the first coordinator of the *Instituto Raoni,* a Kayapó cultural institute.

CREDITS

Exhibition

Green Sky, Blue Grass.
Colour Coding Worlds
1 April 2021 – 30 January 2022
Weltkulturen Museum
Schaumainkai 29–37
60594 Frankfurt am Main
Tel. +49 (0) 69 212 45115
www.weltkulturenmuseum.de

Exhibition curator
Matthias Claudius Hofmann

Co-curators
Tomi Bartole, Roger Erb, Vanessa von Gliszczynski, Arno Holl

Project management
Vanessa von Gliszczynski

Project assistance
Oliver Hahn, Arno Holl

Exhibition design
Graphics: U9 Visuelle Allianz, Offenbach am Main
Framing and construction: Bernd Vossmerbäumer

Exhibition technology
Jakob Nebel, Sascha Svoboda, Thomas Weiser

Conservation
Mareike Mehlis, Sarah Reyer, Kristina Werner
Trainees: Annika Franz, Mirjam Heins

Library and archive
Renate Lindner, Maria Reith-Deigert

Education
Julia Albrecht, Stephanie Endter

Press and public relations
Andrea Löser, Julia Rajkovic-Kamara, Christine Sturm

Events
Margit Zimmler

Administration
Susanne Becker, Claudia Bodens, Heide Schott

Publication

This publication accompanies the exhibition:
Green Sky, Blue Grass.
Colour Coding Worlds
1 April 2021 – 30 January 2022
Weltkulturen Museum

Editor
Matthias Claudius Hofmann

Editorial team
Vanessa J. von Gliszczynski, Oliver Hahn, Matthias Claudius Hofmann, Arno Holl

Design
U9 Visuelle Allianz, Offenbach am Main

Copy-editing
Vanessa von Gliszczynski, Oliver Hahn, Arno Holl, Matthias Claudius Hofmann, Renate Lindner, Nicola Morris, Maria Reith-Deigert

Translation
Herwig Engelmann, Martin Hager, Nicola Morris, Colin Shepherd

Photography
Unless otherwise specified, all objects depicted in this publication are part of the collection of the Weltkulturen Museum and were photographed by Wolfgang Günzel.

Our thanks to the publishers, institutions and individuals who kindly gave permission for the reproduction of photos and texts from their publications.

The images used were either made available by the lenders and copyright holders specified in the captions or come from our archives. In cases where it was not possible to identify the copyright holder correctly, legitimate claims are subject to compensation in accordance with the standard agreements.

Printed and published by
Kerber Verlag
Windelsbleicher Str. 166–170
33659 Bielefeld
Germany
+49 521 950 08 10
+49 521 950 08 88 (F)

Kerber publications are distributed worldwide:

ACC Art Books
Sandy Lane
Old Martlesham
Woodbridge, IP12 4SD
UK
+44 1394 38 99 50
+44 1394 38 99 99 (F)
accartbooks.com
uksales@accartbooks.com

Artbook | D.A.P.
75 Broad Street, Suite 630
New York, NY 10004
USA
+1 212 627 19 99
+1 212 627 94 84 (F)
artbook.com
orders@dapinc.com

AVA Verlagsauslieferung AG
Centralweg 16
8910 Affoltern am Albis
Switzerland
+41 44 762 42 50
+41 44 762 42 10 (F)
avainfo@ava.ch

Zeitfracht GmbH
Verlagsauslieferung
kerber-verlag@knv-zeitfracht.de

The Deutsche National-bibliothek lists this publication in the Deutsche National-bibliografie: dnb.de

ISBN 978-3-7356-0750-8
Grüner Himmel, blaues Gras. Farben ordnen Welten
(German)

ISBN 978-3-7356-0751-5
Green Sky, Blue Grass. Colour Coding Worlds
(English)

kerberverlag.com

Printed in Germany

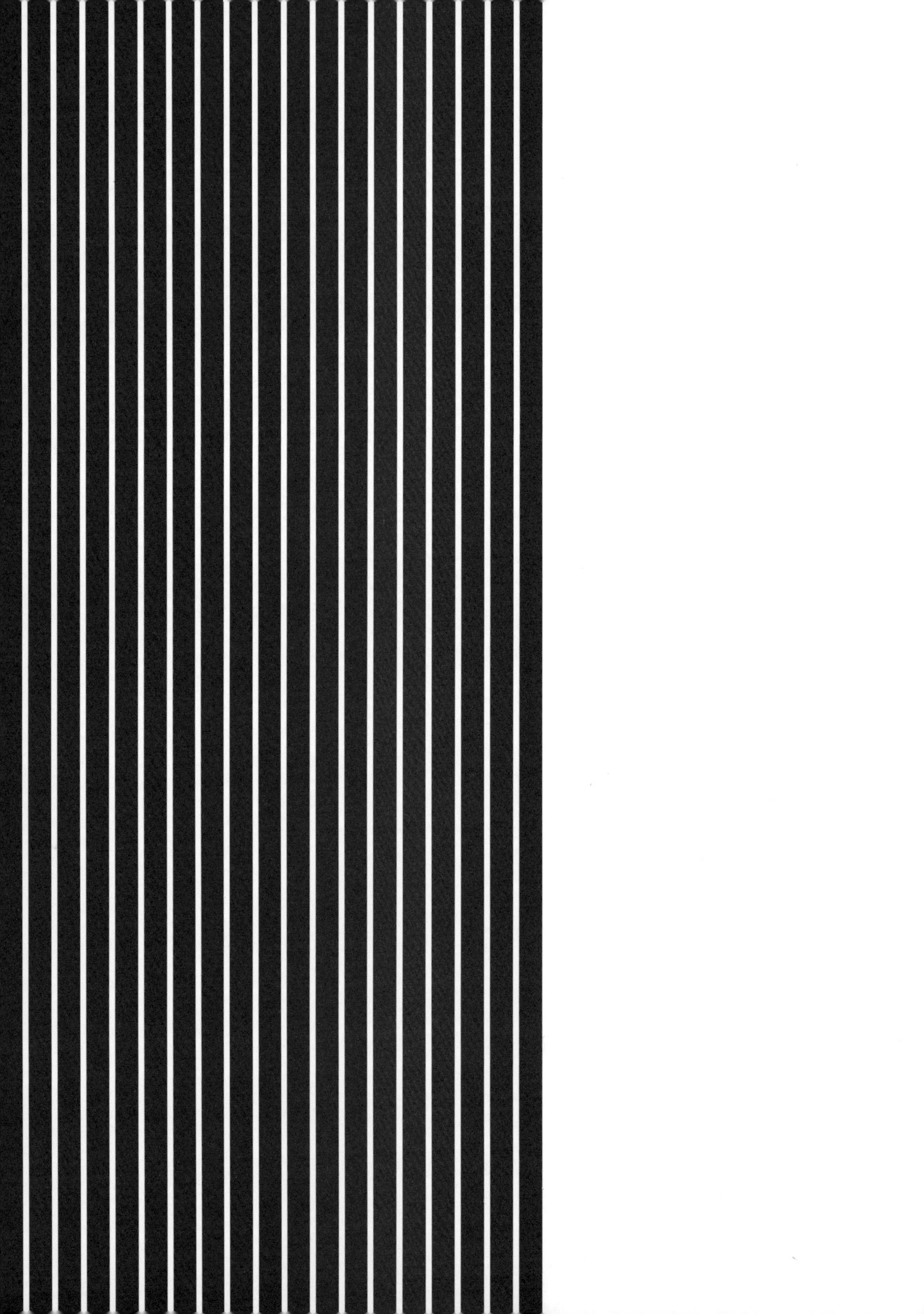